Top Federal Tax Issues for 2022 | CPE Course

Bradley Burnett, J.D., LL.M.

Greg White, CPA

Jennifer Kowal, J.D.

Jim Buttonow, CPA, CITP

Klaralee Charlton, J.D., LL.M.

Robert K. Minniti DBA, CPA, CFE, Cr.FA, CVA, MAFF, CFF, CGMA, PI

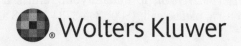
Wolters Kluwer

Contributors

Contributing Editors . . . . Bradley Burnett, J.D., LL.M.

Greg White, CPA

Jennifer Kowal, J.D.

Jim Buttonow, CPA, CITP

Klaralee Charlton, J.D., LL.M.

Robert K. Minniti DBA, CPA, CFE, Cr.FA, CVA, MAFF, CFF, CGMA, PI

Production Coordinator . . . . Mariela de la Torre; Jennifer Schencker;

Gokiladevi Sashikumar

Production . . . . Sharon Sofinski; Anbarasu Anbumani

ISBN: 978-0-8080-5696-6

SUSTAINABLE FORESTRY INITIATIVE

Certified Sourcing
www.sfiprogram.org
SFI-01681

Do not send returns to the above address. If for any reason you are not satisfied with your book purchase, it can easily be returned within 30 days of shipment. Please go to *support.cch.com/returns* to initiate your return. If you require further assistance with your return, please call: (800) 344-3734 M-F, 8 a.m. – 6 p.m. CT.

Printed in the United States of America

Introduction

Each year, a handful of tax issues typically require special attention by tax practitioners. The reasons vary, from tax legislation, a particularly complicated new provision in the Internal Revenue Code, to a planning technique opened up by a new regulation or ruling, or the availability of a significant tax benefit with a short window of opportunity. Sometimes a developing business need creates a new set of tax problems, or pressure exerted by Congress or the Administration puts more heat on some taxpayers while giving others more slack. All these share in creating a unique mix that in turn creates special opportunities and pitfalls in the coming year and beyond. The past year has seen more than its share of these developing issues.

Top Federal Tax Issues for 2022 CPE Course identifies those recent events that have developed into the current "hot" issues of the day. These tax issues have been selected as particularly relevant to tax practice in 2022. They have been selected not only because of their impact on return preparation during the 2022 tax season but also because of the important role they play in developing effective tax strategies for 2022 and beyond.

This course is designed to help reassure the tax practitioner that he or she is not missing out on advising clients about a hot, new tax opportunity; or that a brewing controversy does not blindside their practice. In addition to issue identification, this course provides the basic information needed for the tax practitioner to implement a plan that addresses the particular opportunities and pitfalls presented by any one of those issues. Among the topics examined in the *Top Federal Tax Issues for 2022 CPE Course* are:

- The IRS Interest in Small Businesses
- Unreported Income
- Business versus Hobby
- S Corporation Reasonable Compensation
- Losses in Excess of Basis
- Construction Industry
- Worker Status
- E-Commerce
- Related Returns and Multiple Years
- Form 1099 Noncompliance
- Penalties
- Other small Business Audit Issues
- Final Tips
- Failure to Deposit Penalty
- Payroll Tax Returns
- Covid-19 Relief: Many Roads Lead to Payroll Tax Returns
- Employee Retention Credit
- Aggregation Rules
- Payroll Tax Return Mechanics
- Loss Limitation Hurdles

- Excess Business Losses
- Net Operating Losses
- Qualified Business Income Deduction (QBID)
- Code Sec. 163(j) Business Interest Expense Limit
- Code Sec. 163(j): Partnerships and Partners
- Code Sec. 168(k) Qualified Improvement Property (QIP)
- Expanded Unemployment Benefits
- Business Tax Provisions
- Individual Tax Issues
- Loans Available for Businesses
- Employer filing Deadline Deferrals and Credits
- Miscellaneous Provisions
- Aid to Particular Industries
- What is Virtual Currency?
- Virtual Currency Frauds
- Virtual Currency Wallets
- Virtual Currencies and Taxes
- Common Questions about Cryptocurrency
- Legislative Developments
- Case Law Opinions
- Treasury Releases
- Client Planning Opportunities
- Administrative Releases and Case Law
- Consolidated Appropriations Act (CAA)
- American Rescue Plan Act
- 2021 Employee Retention Credit (ERC)
- Relationship Between PPP Forgiveness and ERC
- IRS Practice and Procedure
- American Families Plan Proposed Legislation
- Proposed Legislation for C Corporations
- Likely Procedural Process for Proposed Tax Reform: Budget Reconciliation
- Senate Infrastructure Investment and Jobs Act (HR 3684)
- Increased LLC Audits
- Recovering EIPs from Deceased Taxpayers

Study Questions. Throughout the course you will find Study Questions to help you test your knowledge, and comments that are vital to understanding a particular strategy or idea. Answers to the Study Questions with feedback on both correct and incorrect responses are provided in a special section beginning at ¶ 10,100.

Final Exam. This course is divided into three Modules. Take your time and review all course Modules. When you feel confident that you thoroughly understand the material, turn to the Final Exam. Complete one, or all, Module Final Exams for continuing professional education credit.

Go to **cchcpelink.com/printcpe** to complete your Final Exam online for immediate results. My Dashboard provides convenient storage for your CPE course Certificates. Further information is provided in the CPE Final Exam instructions at ¶ 10,300. **Please note, manual grading is no longer available for Top Federal Tax Issues. All answer sheets must be submitted online for grading and processing.**

Note: The material contained in this publication was current at the time it went to print.

October 2021

PLEDGE TO QUALITY

Thank you for choosing this CCH® CPE Link product. We will continue to produce high quality products that challenge your intellect and give you the best option for your Continuing Education requirements. Should you have a concern about this or any other Wolters Kluwer product, please call our Customer Service Department at 1-800-344-3734.

COURSE OBJECTIVES

This course was prepared to provide the participant with an overview of specific tax issues that impact 2021 tax return preparation and tax planning in 2022. Each impacts a significant number of taxpayers in significant ways.

Upon course completion, you will be able to:

- Describe the reasons for the IRS compliance focus on small businesses
- Recognize the top 10 IRS audit focus areas for small businesses
- Describe how to evaluate a client's records and identify the critical records in every IRS small business audit
- Identify the steps to prepare for a small business audit
- Recognize how coronavirus pandemic relief programs affect payroll tax
- Identify employee retention credit (ERC) and Families First Coronavirus Response Act (FFCRA) credits, and Paycheck Protection Program (PPP) forgiveness wage absorption
- Recognize the complexity in the Code Sec. 461(l) and net operating loss (NOL) rules
- Identify loss limitation hurdles post–Tax Cuts and Jobs Act
- Describe non–C corporation excess business losses
- Describe the changes to the tax treatment of NOLs as a result of the Tax Cuts and Jobs Act
- Explain the provisions of Code Sec. 461(l)
- Describe the qualified business income deduction
- Recognize which entities are ineligible for the qualified business income deduction
- Describe the key features of the American Rescue Plan Act of 2021 that apply to businesses and individual taxpayers
- Explain how provisions of these acts apply in common factual scenarios

- Identify how to determine whether taxpayers are eligible for provided benefits under the new legislation
- Recognize how the American Rescue Plan Act stimulus package applies
- Identify the interest rate on Paycheck Protection Program loans per year
- Describe cryptocurrency
- Identify the tax implications of using cryptocurrency
- Recognize characteristics of blockchain technology
- Recognize which federal agencies want to regulate initial coin offerings
- Differentiate which type of virtual currency wallet is the safest from online hacking
- Recognize how the IRS requires virtual currencies to be reported
- Summarize legislative developments affecting clients' estate and financial planning goals
- Recognize and analyze the potential tax impacts related to revenue rulings and case law decisions affecting estate tax and fiduciary income tax
- Recommend estate and financial planning ideas for clients looking to reduce tax liability while achieving estate planning goals
- Identify employers who qualify for the employee retention credit (ERC)
- Recognize how to utilize strategies for maximizing Paycheck Protection Program (PPP) loan forgiveness
- Identify and apply tax rules from the Consolidated Appropriations Act (CAA) and the American Rescue Plan Act (ARPA)

Additional copies of this course may be downloaded from **cchcpelink.com/printcpe**. Printed copies of the course are available for $6.50 by calling 1-800-344-3734 (ask for product 10024491-0009).

Contents

MODULE 1: BUSINESS—Chapter 1: How to Handle the Top 10 Issues in an IRS Small Business Audit

¶ 101 WELCOME

This chapter identifies which businesses the IRS primarily targets in small business audits. The discussion covers the scope of IRS small business audits and the most common issues the IRS targets in these examinations. The chapter also outlines the IRS's audit steps in examining income and which records it expects in an examination.

¶ 102 LEARNING OBJECTIVES

Upon completion of this chapter, you will be able to:

- Describe the reasons for the IRS compliance focus on small businesses
- Recognize the top 10 IRS audit focus areas for small businesses
- Describe how to evaluate a client's records and identify the critical records in every IRS small business audit
- Identify the steps to prepare for a small business audit

¶ 103 INTRODUCTION

According to IRS tax gap studies, individuals make up 81 percent of the tax gap, and small businesses account for the largest segment of the approximately $630 billion annual loss in tax revenue to the U.S. Treasury, largely due to the underreporting of income and overstating of credits and deductions. As a result, the IRS field audit resources focus much of their audit activity on small businesses. Not only is small business the largest noncompliant segment, but it is the costliest for the IRS to audit. This chapter outlines the steps in the audit and offers critical insight on preparing a client's records for an audit.

¶ 104 THE IRS INTEREST IN SMALL BUSINESSES

According to recent statistics, approximately 27 million tax returns are filed by Schedule C sole proprietors. These are small businesses; 90 percent have gross revenue of less than $100,000. There are also approximately 5.1 million S corporations, the majority of which have only one shareholder, and their assets and gross receipts are also very low. The IRS is focusing on these small business employers, which constitute 6 million of the 7.6 million employers in business today.

Audit rates are down for all taxpayers compared to where they were in 2010. As a result of the COVID-19 pandemic, the audit rates are about half of what they were for 2019. However, the audit rates for small businesses are almost double the audit rate of other taxpayers.

Common Business Audits

Business audits are generally audits of Schedule C, Form 1120S, Form 1120, and Form 1065 taxpayers. These audits are primarily conducted in the field; that means the IRS revenue agent (an IRS field auditor) visits the taxpayer and/or the taxpayer's representative, typically at the taxpayer's place of business. However, in some cases, these audits are done by mail. IRS letters, forms, and notices associated with these audits include the following:

- Letter 2205: This letter notifies the taxpayer that the tax return is being audited and requests that the taxpayer make an audit appointment. (Note: There can be other letters similar to the Letter 2205 that trigger the small business audit.)
- Form 4564: Formal Information Document Request (IDR) from the IRS.
- Form 4549/886: Revenue Agent Report (RAR) that is sent toward the end of the audit to notify the taxpayer about income tax adjustments.
- Letter 950: Used for unagreed, straight deficiency, straight overassessment, or mixed deficiency and overassessment cases.
- Letter 525: 30-day letter; notifies the taxpayer of proposed adjustments to the tax return and allows the taxpayer to appeal within 30 days.
- Letter 915: Explains the adjustments to the taxpayer and offers instructions about appealing the determination to the IRS Independent Office of Appeals if the taxpayer does not agree with the adjustments.
- Letter 3219: 90-day letter; allows the taxpayer to appeal changes to their tax return to the Tax Court.
- Notice CP22E: Final audit assessment, in which the amount is assessed to the taxpayer's tax year.

Audit Process/Representation

There are four main stages of a field audit: the audit appointment, audit preparation, issue development, and the appeal/finalization.

During the audit appointment, the tax professional files a power of attorney for the client and begins interacting with the auditor to determine the scope of the examination. The tax professional will review the IDRs and start the analysis. The next stage is preparing for the audit. This entails evaluating the client's records and systems, preparing responses, and other pre-audit steps.

The longest stage of an audit is the issue development phase. This is where the tax professional responds to the IDRs from the IRS, reviews and analyzes any issues presented by the IRS agent (i.e., adjustments to the return), and negotiates agreements on the issues presented by the IRS. In the final stage, the tax professional receives the RAR and consults with the taxpayer to decide whether to agree with the report findings or appeal. Approximately 6 percent of field audits are appealed. The tax professional then works through to the closure of the audit process.

The current trend is for many Schedule C expense audits to be done by mail. For these audits, it is critical that the tax professional respond on time, with one complete response. Because a large number of records may be involved, practitioners should index them and provide explanations of receipts. (If there are no written records, in some cases the IRS will accept reconstruction or explanation by oral testimony.) If the records have not yet been sent and it is within a week of the deadline for submitting the documents, they should be sent by fax, with a follow-up by phone to the Practitioner Priority Service (PPS) line (option 6 for the IRS Correspondence Examination Unit) for a status update. Practitioners should always request an appeal in all mail audit responses to protect their client's appeal rights if the IRS disagrees with the response.

It is important to be aware of the unique characteristics of small business audits:

- There is little accountability through information statements
- Facts and circumstances apply
- These audits are more intrusive and comprehensive
- Field auditors (revenue agents) are used
- It takes the IRS approximately 46 hours, on average, to conduct an audit of each tax year

Many clients rely on tax professionals to help them with small business audits. Tax professionals prepare 55 percent of all tax returns and more than three-quarters of small business returns. They also prepare more than 9 out of 10 corporation and flow-through entity returns.

The following sections of this chapter will examine the top 10 audit issues/targets in small business audits:

- Unreported income
- Business versus hobby
- S corporation reasonable compensation
- Losses in excess of basis
- Construction industry
- Worker status
- E-commerce
- Related returns and multiple years
- Form 1099 noncompliance
- Penalties

¶ 105 UNREPORTED INCOME

Unreported income is always the first issue in a small business audit. Internal Revenue Manual (IRM) 4.10.4.3 states that the IRS examiner, in an audit, *must always consider whether income is accurately reported.* Therefore, the purpose of auditing income is to determine whether taxable income was accurately reported on the tax return.

The depth of an audit depends on the type of return filed—individual/nonbusiness, individual/business, or corporation/partnership. For nonbusiness returns, there are essentially four required audit techniques:

- Information statement (i.e., Forms W-2, 1099, etc.) reconciliation and specific items omitted
- Taxpayer interview
- Financial status analysis, which entails reviewing how much the taxpayer reported versus how much they spent to see if there is a discrepancy (called the "Cash-T")
- Bank deposit analysis if the initial Cash-T has a gross imbalance (gross imbalance is defined as $10,000 or more of unexplained expenses in excess of income/incoming proceeds) or there is an unreported Form 1099-MISC or Form 1099-K

When it comes to business returns, there are many more steps. The many audit requirements for individual and closely held businesses are outlined in the following chart:

Minimum Field Audit Requirements		
Nonbusiness Returns	**Individual "Business" Returns**	**Corporation/Partnership**
• Information statement reconciliation and specific items omitted • Taxpayer interview • Financial status analysis (Cash-T) • Bank deposit analysis if initial Cash-T has a gross imbalance or there is an unreported 1099-MISC or 1099-K	• Financial status analysis (Cash-T) • Taxpayer interview • Tour of business • Internal control review • Income reconciliation to books • Information statement reconciliation • Gross receipts test to books • Bank analysis • Ratio analysis • E-commerce activity	**Additional audit steps:** • Balance sheet analysis • M-1 and M-2 reconciliation • Shareholder/partner tax return evaluation
Sources: IRM 4.10.4.3 (8/9/2011); IRM 4.10.4.4 (5/27/2011).		

As shown in the chart, if a corporation or partnership is involved, additional requirements include a balance sheet analysis, Schedule M-1 and M-2 reconciliation, and a shareholder/partner tax return. For these returns, the tax professional should review IRM 4.10.3.7 prior to the audit and follow the procedures in this IRM section in preparing for the audit.

A breakdown of the minimum income probes for individual "business" returns is as follows:

- **Financial status analysis.** Prepare a financial status analysis to estimate whether reported income is sufficient to support the taxpayer's financial activities. See IRM 4.10.4.3.3.1.

- **Interview.** Conduct an interview with the taxpayer (or representative) to gain an understanding of the taxpayer's financial history, identify sources of nontaxable funds, and establish the amount of currency the taxpayer has on hand. Consider possible bartering income as part of the minimum income probes. See IRM 4.10.4.3.3.2.

- **Tour of business.** Tour the business site and review the taxpayer's website to gain familiarity with the taxpayer's operations and internal controls and to identify potential sources of unreported income. Note that a tour of the physical business site is not required for office audit cases but may be conducted if appropriate and with manager approval. See IRM 4.10.4.3.3.3.

- **Internal control.** Evaluate internal controls to determine the reliability of the books and records (including electronic books and records), identify high-risk issues, and determine the depth of the examination of income. See IRM 4.10.4.3.3.4.

- **Reconciliation of income.** Reconcile the income reported on the tax return to the taxpayer's books and records. An analysis of the Information Returns Processing (IRP) information in the file should also be completed to ensure all business and/or investment activities reflected on the IRP document are properly accounted for on the tax return. See IRM 4.10.4.3.3.5.

- **Testing gross receipts.** Test the gross receipts by tying the original source documents to the books. See IRM 4.10.4.3.3.6.

- **Bank analysis.** Prepare an analysis of the taxpayer's personal and business bank and financial accounts (including investment accounts) to evaluate the accuracy of gross receipts reported on the tax return. See IRM 4.10.4.3.3.7.

- **Business ratios.** Prepare an analysis of business ratios to evaluate the reasonableness of the taxpayer's business operations and identify issues needing a more thorough examination. See IRM 4.10.4.3.3.8.
- **E-commerce and/or Internet use.** Determine if there is Internet use and e-commerce income activity. See IRM 4.10.4.3.7.1.

Verifications the IRS conducts routinely at the start of a small business audit include return to trial balance, information statements amounts/sources to records and return, income reported to the IRS (under Social Security number [SSN] and/or employer identification number [EIN]), Cash-T, bank deposit analysis, and digital cash to records.

Common issues that arise in information return matching are Form 1099-K reconciliation, Form 1099-MISC/NEC reconciliation, and SSN and EIN income information matching from the IRS. To find the information returns filed under a client's EIN, practitioners can request an Information Returns Processing Transcript Request (IRPTR) from the IRS. Practitioners can call the IRS PPS hotline (option 3 for business accounts) and request the IRS to provide this document (the IRS will redact it and fax it to the tax practitioner).

When the IRS uses indirect methods, it reconstructs the taxpayer's finances through circumstantial evidence. For example, the agent can show unreported income through increases in unexplained net worth, increases in unexplained bank deposits, and increases in unexplained wealth from more than the taxpayer's reported income. Indirect methods allow the IRS to support an inference of unreported income through this circumstantial evidence.

Although there are several methods the IRS can use to reconstruct income, it is most comfortable with the bank deposit analysis and cash transaction methods. In the cash transaction, or "cash T" or "T-account," method, the agent calculates the amount of cash coming in and the amount going out—reconciling the differences against cash at the beginning and the end of the year and to all other sources. This is compared to the income reported on the return. If there is a discrepancy that concludes the taxpayer should have more income than reported, the agent has a basis for an income adjustment. If there is an unexplained discrepancy, the agent will not have to show the source; the circumstances become the basis for an income adjustment.

Tax Court cases illustrate the use of these methods. In *Porch v. Commissioner*, TC Summary Opinion 2012-25 (March 21, 2012), the taxpayer owned a carpet sales and installation business. It was audited for 2005 and 2006. The taxpayer reported $75,000 per year in gross sales and provided documentation to prove $75,000 in income at the initial interview. The IRS auditor initially determined a Cash-T imbalance of $49,000 in 2005. Few records were provided in the audit, bank records were summonsed and examined, and cash deposits were found. The taxpayer stated these amounts were used to pay cash expenses.

The taxpayer agreed to additional business income of $84,712 for two years but wanted additional cash expenses and no fraud penalty. The IRS was upheld for tax and penalties. The Tax Court did not like that the taxpayer and counsel were not cooperative with the agent. The IRS Cash-T and bank deposits method prevailed and rendered the taxpayer's records and testimony implausible. Consequently, the taxpayer was liable for the fraud penalty.

The case of *Azimzadeh v. Commissioner*, TC Memo 2013-169 (July 23, 2013), involved the owner of a used car business in California who did not keep good records. Its bank deposits exceeded its income by $179,209. The IRS bank deposits analysis was upheld by the court in this case. The Tax Court held that unexplained bank deposits are prima facie evidence of income when a taxpayer fails to maintain adequate records, and that it is the taxpayer's burden to show the deposits were not income. The taxpayer in this case did not meet that burden.

> **PRACTICE POINTER:** To prevent such issues, tax professionals should conduct heightened due diligence at the preparation stage:
> - Follow three IRS audit litmus tests:
>   — Cash-T and "ask the second question" if there is an imbalance.
>   — Match bank deposits to client records.
>   — Match income against IRS income records.
> - Look past the trial balance.
> - Trace several transactions to the source.
> - Are the ratios reasonable?
>   — Three-year review: Are there significant variances?
>   — Do the financials align to industry averages?
> - Check information statements against client records.
>   — Do the client's records reconcile to the Form 1099-MISC received from a customer?
> - Correct the business/personal "commingler."
> - Your tax workpapers are critical.

Audit due diligence is very important in this area. In representing a client, the tax practitioner should do the agent's analysis prior to the on-site examination:

- Reconcile the books to the return and be prepared to explain discrepancies.
- Provide a chart of account mapping the workpapers to the return.
- Do an income audit and be prepared to explain discrepancies.
- Follow the three litmus tests and test gross receipts against source documents, including digital cash.
- Analyze the business ratios against industry norms.
- Review the client's website for questioned income sources.
- Be prepared for related-entity audits: File a Form 2848 or 8821 for these entities to receive information directly from the agent.

¶106 BUSINESS VERSUS HOBBY

A common issue is whether a taxpayer's activity is a business or a hobby. This has become more important since the passage of the Tax Cuts and Jobs Act of 2017 (TCJA), which does not allow miscellaneous deductions. The taxpayer has a burden of proof that their activity is engaged in for profit under the presumption rule under Code Sec. 183(d). Under that rule, if the taxpayer shows a profit from the activity in three of the last five years, the burden of proof shifts to the IRS.

Code Sec. 183 targets businesses including the following:

- Multilevel marketing businesses
- Entertainers
- Farming
- Writers
- Personal pleasure businesses

— Horse and dog breeding
— Yacht and airplane charters
— Fishing
— Auto racing
— Gamblers
— Photography
— Bowling
— Stamp collecting
— Craft sales

There are many court cases on the business versus hobby issue. If the taxpayer meets the presumption rule, the IRS can still argue that the activity is not engaged in for profit; however, the burden of proving that the activity is not engaged in for profit shifts to the IRS. In addition, examiners cannot use Code Sec. 183(d) as the sole basis for disallowing losses under that section even if it is shown that the taxpayer has not met the presumption rule. If an activity is deemed a hobby, its income is reported as other income on line 21 of Form 1040, *U.S. Individual Income Tax Return*, and the related expenses are not allowed under the TCJA.

Presumption That Activity Is Engaged in for Profit

As mentioned earlier, Code Sec. 183(d) provides a presumption that an activity is engaged in for profit if the activity is profitable for three years of a consecutive five-year period (or two years of a consecutive seven-year period for activities that consist of breeding, showing, training, or racing horses). If the taxpayer meets the presumption rule, the IRS can still argue that the activity is not engaged in for profit; however, the burden of proving that the activity is not engaged in for profit shifts to the IRS. In addition, examiners cannot use Code Sec. 183(d) as the sole basis for disallowing losses under Code Sec. 183 even if it is shown that the taxpayer has not met the presumption rule.

Examiners should be alert for situations where the taxpayer may have manipulated income and or expenses to meet the presumption rule determination. Questions to consider include:

• What is the true intent of the taxpayer?
• Do the facts objectively support the intent to make a profit?

Treas. Reg. § 1.183-2(b) focuses on nine nonexclusive factors in determining whether an activity is a business or a hobby:

• Manner in which the taxpayer carries on the activity
• Expertise of the taxpayer and advisors
• Time and effort expended on the activity
• Expectations that the assets will increase in value
• Success of the taxpayer in carrying on other activities
• History of income/loss for the activity
• Amount of occasional earned profits, if any
• Financial status of the taxpayer (tax savings benefit motive)
• Elements of personal pleasure

In *Campbell v. Commissioner*, TC Memo 2011-42 (February 17, 2011), the Code Sec. 183 limits were sustained. The taxpayer in this case, a multilevel marketing business with losses, was audited for 1998–2001. The taxpayer had other businesses in real estate and construction. It sold business opportunities for downstream pyramid revenue and sold products directly. The taxpayer did not develop its own business plan and purchased products for itself. The business had no budgets and was not aware whether it was making a profit until the tax returns were filed. Losses were reported for every year between 1995 and 2001. The taxpayer maintained separate records and bank accounts for the business and spent an extensive amount of time on the business. The business had significant gross receipts ($103,266) that were boosted by product sales to itself and its construction business.

The Tax Court found the following, and the Code Sec. 183 limits were sustained:

- The taxpayer received significant tax benefits from the losses.
- It never used records to analyze its profitability and adjust operations.
- Little effort was made to change its operations in seven years, despite the loss of $20,000 annually.
- The taxpayer made purchases that were withdrawn for personal consumption. The IRS agent had to reconstruct the proper cost of sales to eliminate personal items.
- The taxpayer did not seek independent advice on the business; instead, it was persuaded by other "upline" marketers. (Its stockbroker actually advised the taxpayer not to become involved in the activity.)
- The taxpayer's continued activity, despite its losses, underscored the fact that the activity was for personal pleasure.

PRACTICE POINTER: Practitioners should ask their clients the following six litmus test questions to determine whether their activity is a hobby or a business:

- Are losses from the activity offsetting other income on the tax return, resulting in a significant tax benefit?
- Is the activity a personal pleasure activity?
- Are there separate books and records?
- Are there large expenses and little or no current (anticipated) income?
- Does the history of the activity show that it is generating any profit in any years?
- Does the client have "business-like" documents?

Documentation That Helps in Code Sec. 183 Arguments
• Formal books and records
• Separate financial accounts
• Realistic, formal business plan (the IRS will not initially ask for this) and annual budgets
• Evidence that the business plan has been followed
• Business licenses, insurance, and permits
• Use of experts, their credentials, and how advice was utilized
• Advertising, signage, websites
• Evidence of time spent on activity
• Appraisals of asset appreciation
• Documentation of where taxpayer, in the past, abandoned unprofitable ventures
• Outside, independent investors

What to Do in an Audit

Tax practitioners should prepare such audits using the IRS's Code Sec. 183 Audit Technique Guide (ATG), *IRC § 183, Activities Not Engaged in for Profit* (https://

www.irs.gov/pub/irs-utl/irc183activitiesnotengagedinforprofit.pdf). In audits where the IRS is pursing the hobby issue and the 5-year presumptive period is not completed and conclusive, the tax practitioner should consider invoking the presumption test using Form 5213, *Election to Postpone Determination as to Whether the Presumption Applies That an Activity is Engaged in for Profit* (Code Sec. 183(e)). This will postpone the hobby loss determination until after the presumptive period is concluded. Practitioners must be able to answer all the questions for the client to prevent the IRS from insisting on interviewing the client directly. The ATG is comprehensive; it includes IDRs and all the questions for the nine factors. The ATG has not been updated since 2009, but most of it still applies to hobby loss situations.

Election to Postpone Determination

Under Code Sec. 183(e), a taxpayer may elect to postpone a determination of whether the presumption applies until the close of the fourth taxable year (or the sixth year for qualifying horse activities) following the *first* taxable year in which the taxpayer engages in the activity. An electing taxpayer may file returns in the interim on the assumption that the activity is conducted for profit.

If an activity that is generating losses has not yet been carried on for the full profit presumption period, the taxpayer may elect to postpone a determination of whether an activity is engaged in for profit. The examiner should first determine whether the activity is engaged in for profit from all available facts without regard to the presumption test or the possible election to postpone determination under Code Sec. 183(e). This determination should take into account the nine relevant factors listed in Treas. Reg. § 1.183-2(b) as well as the pertinent facts. Upon the filing of all or a sufficient number of the returns of the presumption period, the case file will be returned to the examiner for a determination of whether the activity is presumed to be an activity engaged in for profit.

Form 5213 is used when taxpayers wish to postpone an IRS determination as to whether the presumption applies that they are engaged in an activity for profit. An election made by a partnership or an S corporation is binding on all persons who were partners or shareholders at any time during the presumption period. The election to postpone determination generally can be filed anytime within three years after the due date of the return (determined without regard to extensions) for the first year of the activity but not later than 60 days after the taxpayer receives written notice from the IRS proposing to disallow deductions attributable to the activity.

> **NOTE:** Form 5213 is rarely used by the taxpayer until an examiner proposes to disallow the activity as not engaged in for profit.

The IRS auditor will determine if the taxpayer wants to, and is eligible to, elect to postpone the determination under Code Sec. 183(e). If the taxpayer makes the decision to make the election, the IRS agent will explain all legal and procedural implications. If the taxpayer is eligible to make the election but does not wish to, the auditor will normally obtain a written statement from the taxpayer or his representative stating that the taxpayer does not wish to elect the provisions of Code Sec. 183(e).

¶ 107 S CORPORATION REASONABLE COMPENSATION

Two out of three S corporations have only one shareholder. Thirteen percent of S corporations examined in 2003 and 2004 paid inadequate compensation to shareholders. Therefore, the issue is whether the officer/shareholder compensation is unreasonable, resulting in FICA and Medicare tax avoidance. The IRS looks for the following red flags in this area:

- The S corporation has distributions and/or repayments to the officer or shareholder.
- There is little or no officer compensation, and the S corporation has ordinary income.

There are many cases involving this issue. One is *Glass Blocks Unlimited v. Commissioner*, TC Memo 2013-180 (August 7, 2013), involving a sole shareholder S corporation that was a distributor of glass blocks used in construction. The taxpayer worked full-time and had no salary; the taxpayer's Form 1040 only had $10,000 in ordinary income from the S corporation. It had a repayment of a loan to the shareholder of $62,000, but little evidence of loan transactions. The Tax Court found that the loans were not bona fide—rather, they were contribution of capital to the S corporation. The repayments were wages. The IRS asserted failure to file and failure to deposit penalties, in addition to FICA/Medicare taxes, on the taxpayer.

In *McAlary, Ltd. v. Commissioner*, TC Summary Opinion 2013-62 (August 12, 2013), the taxpayer was a sole shareholder S corporation real estate broker. The taxpayer worked full-time. When the corporation was set up, a salary of $24,000, plus commissions, was established for the taxpayer. However, no salary was paid. The taxpayer's Form 1040 showed $231,454 in ordinary income from the S corporation. The taxpayer received distributions of $240,000 but argued that his compensation should be $24,000. The IRS used a valuation expert and proposed compensation of $100,755 based on the median wages for the area.

The Tax Court disregarded the compensation agreement that had been established because the salary was not paid. It also stated that the compensation was not at arm's length, but rather was "adopted as mere window dressing." The IRS had a flawed valuation, according to the Court, and the Court stated the taxpayer's wages were $83,200. The IRS asserted failure to file and failure to deposit penalties on the taxpayer, in addition to FICA/Medicare taxes.

> **PRACTICE POINTER:** Tax professionals can help their S corporation clients determine the correct compensation by considering the following points:
>
> - What services is the client performing?
> - Salary comparisons should be based on job title, duties, and skills.
> - The taxpayer should carefully document the compensation arrangement before payment is made and record it in the minutes.
> - Taxpayers should follow the compensation agreement and file payroll returns.
> - Taxpayers should beware of distributions that are bonus compensation.
> - If the taxpayer does not make a salary payment in a quarter, it should file a -0- Form 941 to avoid any potential failure to file penalty if the compensation is challenged.

STUDY QUESTIONS

1. What is the longest phase of a field audit?
   - **a.** Audit appointment
   - **b.** Audit preparation
   - **c.** Issue development
   - **d.** Appeal/finalization

2. Which type of income contributes the largest to the tax gap?

    a. Income subject to little or no information reporting

    b. Income subject to information reporting and withholding

    c. Income subject to information reporting

    d. Income subject to some information reporting

3. Which of the following is the annual tax return filed for an S corporation?

    a. Form 1040

    b. Form 1120

    c. Form 1065

    d. Form 1120S

¶ 108 LOSSES IN EXCESS OF BASIS

As discussed, despite low audit rates in the past, S corporations are under increased focus in IRS audits. The IRS has studied S corporation compliance and has found one major area of concern: deducting losses in excess of basis.

Shareholders generally can only claim losses and deductions up to the amount of basis that the shareholder has in the S corporation's stock and debt. The calculations are often complicated and sometimes not completed before deducting the loss. The IRS also states that an added barrier to compliance is that S corporations generally do not report any basis calculations to shareholders. It is at the Form 1040 level that taxpayers determine basis and the ability to deduct S corporation losses.

How much of an issue is S corporation loss deductions? In 2011, the U.S. Government Accountability Office (GAO) testified to the Senate Finance Committee on the prevalence of misreporting losses that exceeded basis limitations. The GAO found that there is an average of $21,600 in misreported losses per return.

The only mechanism the IRS has to effectively address this issue is audits. The IRS has active audit projects related to this issue. The IRS is also looking for preparers to help in this area. In particular, it is looking at tax professionals' responsibilities for determining correct basis for their clients. When the IRS determines there are deductions in excess of basis, the IRS may pursue accuracy penalties for taxpayers *and* preparer penalties, if it deems negligence by the preparer.

IRS data shows that in audits of Forms 1040 with pass-through losses from Form 1120S between 2006 and 2008, 71 percent of S corporation returns completed by paid preparers had errors. The IRS auditor will likely direct questions to the tax preparer on how they calculated basis to support the loss at the shareholder/partner level (GAO Report GAO-10-195).

    PRACTICE POINTER: To prevent this issue, tax practitioners should:

- Ensure the shareholder/partner tax preparer is responsible for basis/loss computations.

- Do the basis calculations.

- Correctly interpret debt basis issues.

- Watch for at-risk limitations and passive activity rules.

¶ 109 CONSTRUCTION INDUSTRY

The construction industry is another focus area for IRS audits. Unreported income is an issue, as the construction industry can have complicated accounting methods. Other issues relevant to audits of construction clients include worker status, capitalization of costs to long-term contracts, cash payments, depreciation, and auto expenses.

Tax practitioners may be working with general contractors, subcontractors, and developers in both commercial and residential construction. According to an older IRS ATG for the construction industry, "residential construction is of particular interest because this group of taxpayers accounts for 73 percent of the return filings but reports only 10 percent of the gross receipts."

IRS data on common adjustments in construction audits are provided in the following chart:

Error Rate in IRS Construction Audits			
Issue	Schedule C	Form 1120S	Form 1065
Gross receipts	63%	47%	53%
Cost of sales	65%	No data given	57%
Depreciation	71%	73%	100%
Other deductions	78%	71%	86%
Car/truck expenses	74%	64%	No data given
Officer compensation	N/A	51%	N/A

Prevention of audit issues starts with good accounting systems. Tax professionals should pose the following questions to their construction clients:

- Are you a diligent recordkeeper?
- Should you be your own bookkeeper?
- If you are your own bookkeeper, do you understand your accounting method?
- How are you accounting for and paying subcontractors?

In an audit, tax professionals should give the IRS agent the big picture, including the properties developed, contracts worked, accounting procedures used, financial conditions for the year under examination, unusual items for the year, and an overview of the accounting system. It is best to do the work for the agent as much as possible. The IRS's Construction Industry ATG (updated in 2021 and found here: https://www.irs.gov/pub/irs-pdf/p5522.pdf) details construction industry issues and IRS audit techniques. Tax practitioners should always review the ATG and use it to prepare for the audit.

¶ 110 WORKER STATUS

In 2020, 27,212 employment tax returns were examined by the IRS (<0.1 percent coverage rate). The historical change rate is approximately 84 percent, and the average recommended additional tax per return was $18,044. However, it is a myth that the chances of an employment tax audit are very low. In reality, all IRS field audits include employment tax compliance checks. Based on 7.6 million employers, the audit coverage rate is actually much higher as all small business audits review employment tax compliance.

The main focus in most employment tax audits is worker status, that is, whether the worker is an independent contractor or an employee. The ultimate question to consider is: Who has the right to control and direct the individual performing services, the payer (W-2 employee) or the contractor (Form 1099 independent contractor)? The IRS uses three factors to determine control:

- **Relationship of the parties.** This includes the agreements between them, how they each perceive the relationship, and how they represent the relationship to others.
- **Behavior controls.** How much control does the business have over the worker?
- **Financial controls.** These include the worker's risk of loss and whether he or she has made a significant financial investment.

IRS Revenue Ruling 87-41 provides 20 common-law factors to examine to help make the determination:

- Instructions given to the worker
- Job-related training
- Integration of the worker's services into the business operations
- Services rendered personally
- Hiring, supervising, and paying assistants
- Continuing relationship
- Set hours of work
- Full time required
- Doing work on the employer's premises
- Order of sequence set
- Oral or written reports required
- Payment by hour, week, or month
- Payment of business and/or traveling expenses
- Furnishing of tools and materials
- Significant investment by the worker
- Realization of profit or loss by the worker
- Working for more than one firm at a time
- Making service available to the general public
- Right to discharge
- The worker's right to terminate

However, there is no bright-line test; rather, determining worker status is a facts-and-circumstances test and is fairly subjective. However, some precedents may help in this area. The court in *Atlantic Coast Masonry, Inc. v. Commissioner*, TCM 2012-233, considered whether masons were employees or contractors. An S corporation officer used a foreman to hire masons on a per-job basis. There were no contracts with the masons; the workers were paid per brick laid. The corporation officer met with the masons at the beginning of the project and during the project to approve their work and check on the quality of work performed. The masons worked eight-hour days and were paid weekly. They furnished their own tools and were an essential part of the business. They had a transitory relationship but mostly worked for the S corporation.

Using the common-law factors, the court weighed in favor of "employee" status for the masons because they were paid like employees, had little investment in the facilities (they used their own tools, but the expensive parts, such as heavy machinery and construction materials, were purchased or reimbursed for them), had no opportunity for profit or loss (no additional profit if the project came in under budget, and no loss if it came in over budget), and the corporation had the right to discharge them at any time.

The court also noted that the workers were an integral part of and had a continuing relationship with the corporation.

Audit Defenses

The first defense in a worker status audit is to prove that the worker is an independent contractor. If applicable, if the worker is likely an employee, the tax professional should determine if the client is entitled to Section 530 relief or a classification settlement program (CSP).

Section 530 of the Revenue Act of 1978 provides relief for taxpayers who reasonably, but incorrectly, classify workers as independent contractors instead of employees. Section 530 is a safe harbor provision that allows a taxpayer to obtain relief from retroactive assessment of federal employment tax liabilities when the taxpayer has:

- Consistently treated the workers (and similarly situated workers) as independent contractors;
- Complied with Form 1099 reporting requirements with respect to the compensation paid to the workers for the tax years at issue; and
- Had a reasonable basis for treating the workers as independent contractors.

The CSP started in 1996 and is one of the only settlements that can be offered at the agent level. The closing agreement is available only if the taxpayer has filed Forms 1099 for its workers. If a taxpayer is under audit, it can request a CSP from the IRS. If it is not under audit, it should use Form 8952, *Application for Voluntary Classification Settlement Program (VCSP)*. The program is a settlement of worker status issues under which the taxpayer agrees to prospectively treat workers as employees. In turn, the employer does not have to pay the entire past payroll tax liabilities. The employer can obtain a reduced tax under Code Sec. 3509, which is interest-free if paid within 30 days of the agreement. Also, correction of past W-2s is not required.

> **PRACTICE POINTER:** To help business clients avoid compliance issues, when hiring a contractor, they should:
>
> - Always obtain the contractor's taxpayer identification number (TIN) before making payments.
> - Always timely file Forms 1099.
> - Document the contractor relationship.
>   - Obtain the contractor agreement and other business documentation (invoices, proof of insurance, copy of necessary business licenses, EIN, etc.).
>   - Avoid non-compete agreements.
>   - Pay by the job or project completion deliverable.
>   - Allow use of subcontractors and assistants.
>   - Have indemnification clauses.
>   - Treat the contractor as a vendor, not as an employee (employee events, separate contractor file, no benefits).

¶ 111 E-COMMERCE

With regard to e-commerce, revenue agents focus on unreported income (part of IRS minimum income verification requirements in an audit), hobby losses, personal deductions, and Form 1099-K reconciliation. Areas of interest include the taxpayer's online sales, customer payments online, advertising income, online tip jars, sales of customer lists, and referral fees.

In 2012, the IRS instituted mandatory audit techniques for businesses that have e-commerce activity. IRM 4.10.4.3.7.1 provides step-by-step audit techniques the IRS is using in the e-commerce area.

Tax professionals working with e-commerce clients must be confident that their clients are reporting income from all sources. They should test clients' digital cash transactions (cash, credit card, PayPal, etc.) and trace them back to their source. Practitioners should also perform a Form 1099-K litmus test, and if 1099-K discrepancies are found, they should attach a statement to the client's return with an explanation. In preparing for an audit, tax professionals should check the client's past website and e-commerce activity to anticipate the auditor's questions.

NOTE: Tax professionals can visit www.archive.org and use the Wayback Machine to see a client's website history.

¶ 112 RELATED RETURNS AND MULTIPLE YEARS

Small business audits are comprehensive in scope. Required filing checks include all returns open under statute, key partners/shareholders, contractors (tracing the vendor payments), employment tax compliance, information returns compliance, and pension plans.

Another trend in audits is more multiyear audits. Practitioners should look for the IRS to expand its audits into more than the year under exam if it finds an issue. IRS agents have been criticized recently by the Treasury Inspector General for Tax Administration (TIGTA) for missing prior and subsequent year issues.

In the audit, tax professionals should treat all open years as if they were under audit. They should prepare for multiple-year examinations, including prior and subsequent years; prepare for shareholder/partner returns to be examined; examine information statement filing compliance; and ensure the Form 2848, *Power of Attorney and Declaration of Representative*, has multiple years/forms included.

¶ 113 FORM 1099 NONCOMPLIANCE

According to GAO Report GAO-09-238, although there are many small businesses, few file Forms 1099. Therefore, in an audit, the IRS reviews payments for missing Form 1099 filings. Penalties for information statement errors include penalties under Code Sec. 6721 for failure to file correct information returns, under Code Sec. 6722 for failure to furnish correct payee statements, and under Code Sec. 6723 for failure to comply with other reporting requirements (e.g., supplying correct TIN). The maximum failure to file penalty with respect to Form 1099s and misclassification of workers is 25 percent.

During the audit, the IRS will review client records such as vendor files, accounts payable files, payments, Forms 1099 filed, and "B" notices received. The IRS will ask about the taxpayer's steps for identifying and issuing Forms 1099-MISC/NEC, and its controls for obtaining TINs for contractors (W-9 procedures). The IRS is looking for situations that require backup withholding (IRM 4.10.5.6.1).

To avoid Form 1099 noncompliance penalties, taxpayers should always obtain a contractor's taxpayer identification number (TIN) before making payments and always file the required Forms 1099.

¶ 114 PENALTIES

The last section discussed information return penalties, especially for nonfiling. This section reviews accuracy penalties and preparer penalties. Despite the fact that there recently have been fewer audits and CP2000 Notices, IRS accuracy penalty assessments remain high. There has been an 1154 percent increase in accuracy penalties in the past seven years, with only an 8 percent increase in the number of individual returns. Again, the IRS is trying to assert penalties to deter underreporting noncompliance—that is, inaccurate tax returns.

In the past several years, IRS agents have been encouraged to apply accuracy-related penalties to deter underreporting noncompliance. According to IRM 20.1.5.7.1, with regard to accuracy penalty determinations, "the most important factor in determining with reasonable cause is the taxpayer's effort to report the proper tax liability. . . . The determination is done on a case-by-case basis, taking into account all the relevant facts and circumstances." According to Treas. Reg. § 1.6664-4(b), a facts and circumstances test reveals an "honest misunderstanding of fact or law that is reasonable in light of all of the facts and circumstance."

Tax professionals should review accuracy penalty determinations closely. Accuracy penalties must be approved by an IRS manager (Code Sec. 6751(b)(1)) prior to issuing any written penalty determination (with the exception of a CP2000 Notice). In audits, many penalty determinations are proposed as an afterthought—so tax professionals should dig deeper to understand the IRS's reasons for penalty assertion. They should:

- Ask for the manager's written penalty approval document to get a closer understanding of the IRS's position and their understanding of the facts of the case that warrant penalty assertion.
- Consider using a Freedom of Information Act (FOIA) request if the document is not provided (IRM 20.1.1.2.3)
- Request a manager conference to dispute accuracy penalties.

There are three areas where the IRS has more closely pursued preparer penalties in small business audits: where there is a substantial understatement of income (Code Sec. 6662(b)(1)), rental properties adjustments, and losses taken in excess of basis on flow-through entities.

In small businesses, most fraud cases stem from unreported income. There are three common situations that would cause the IRS to pursue fraud related to unreported income:

- Omission of specific items of income, entire sources of income, or substantial amounts of income
- Unexplained increases in net worth
- Unexplained bank deposits

IRS agents are trained to look for "badges of fraud." Badges are indicators that fraud may be present, and the agent should dig further to find any willfulness to evade taxes.

Fraud Red Flags for the IRS
• More than one set of books and records
• False statements about material facts in an examination
• Attempts to hinder the investigation by failing or refusing to answer questions, canceling appointments, or refusing to supply records
• Employee testimony about irregular business practices
• Destruction of books and records
• Transfers of assets for purpose of concealment

Tax practitioners should be alert to the following signs that an IRS agent is looking for a firm indication of fraud:

- The issues and IDRs are related to unreported income, and multiple years are under examination.
- The IRS is using many third-party audit techniques.

- The IRS is using summons techniques.
- The IRS wants documented interviews and signed affidavits.
- The IRS has not issued a RAR, and the assessment statute is imminent.

The agent will make a fraud referral when there are firm indications of fraud and the fraud meets criminal criteria. Criminal criteria are defined in the IRS Law Enforcement Manual (LEM), which is not available to the public.

> **PRACTICE POINTER:** If tax professionals suspect a client may be subject to a fraud referral, they should use their professional judgment, consult an attorney, advise the client to hire legal counsel, and inform the client that communications with them are not privileged.

¶ 115 OTHER SMALL BUSINESS AUDIT ISSUES

Other issues that can arise in small business audits involve small business accounting software, rental properties, and personal expenses.

Small Business Accounting Software

Most small and midsize businesses use small business accounting software. Requesting a small business's electronic accounting records is standard operating procedure in an IRS audit, and this practice has been upheld by the courts. An IRS agent's initial IDR typically includes a request for small business accounting backup files, and some agents are trained in QuickBooks and Sage/Peachtree (see IRM 4.10.4.3.7.5, August 9, 2011).

Controversy arises because the backup file is not limited to the year under audit. Because the IRS gets the entire file—errors, deletions, voids, and all—professionals should consider whether the audit trail may reflect poorly on the client's internal control. The tax professional should provide a detailed explanation to the auditor and explain how they corrected any errors made by the client. In many cases, the IRS will accept an alternative to the backup files, such as spreadsheets or financial statements.

Rental Income

Another issue is misreporting rental income. In a 2008 study (GAO-08-956), the GAO reviewed rental property reporting and found it to be a significant area of noncompliance. The GAO's findings include the following:

- 53 percent of taxpayers misreport rental income and expenses. The most prevalent issue is overstating expenses.
- Data showed that noncompliance is mainly on individuals. The most likely noncompliant profiles are self-managed properties with little or no information reporting the rental income.
- The GAO found that four out of five rental real estate taxpayers use a professional tax preparer. Therefore, tax preparers must be extra careful when reporting a client's rental properties.

Personal Expenses

The IRS is projected to hire several thousand new revenue agents over the next few years, and one of their tasks will be to audit businesses that have many personal expenses, such as travel and entertainment, automobiles, cell phones and computers, and legal and professional fees.

According to Code Sec. 162, such expenses must be ordinary and necessary in carrying on a trade or business. Tax professionals should ensure their clients have the proper substantiation for such expenses, such as Code Sec. 274 for travel and entertainment expenses, mileage logs for automobile expenses, and so on. There are many mobile apps available that can be helpful with tracking and substantiating personal expenses.

¶ 116 FINAL TIPS

This chapter has discussed the IRS's and tax professional's perspective in the audit process. Understanding the IRS agent's tasks in this process highlights why tax professionals need to prepare well for the audit. The IRS agent has a lot to do in 46 hours. With no background or history, the agent must learn about the taxpayer, including:

- The big picture of the people/entities involved
- Business operations
- Industry issues
- Books and records
- Tax return positions
- Related entities

The agent must also develop, propose, and conclude adjustments to the tax return and all related returns. In addition, the agent will propose a change in 9 of 10 exams, on average.

TOP 10 SMALL BUSINESS FIELD AUDIT TIPS:

- Be a facilitator in the audit.
- Prepare well (do a mock audit).
- Provide the big picture.
- Anticipate questions and issues.
- Focus on income and the "most important IRS issue."
- Google your client.
- Examine income closely prior to the audit.
    — Do the "big three" income tests.
- Communicate with the auditor.
    — Follow up with a written summary.
- Use your informal and formal appeal rights.
- Contest penalties.

It is also a good idea to get a second perspective in an audit. Field audits have been rare, but they are likely to increase in the future. Tax professionals may not get enough repetitions in this area to stay practice-savvy, and the costs of an audit can be high. For these and other reasons, asking another professional for their perspective can be invaluable.

Key Takeaways from This Chapter

- Tax gap data concludes that small businesses are the most noncompliant taxpayer segment.
- The IRS traditionally focuses on common issues in small business audits. However, one issue is most important: unreported income.
- Small business audits can be very comprehensive in scope.

- Awareness of these issues is beneficial in your due diligence. Preparation is the key to a successful audit outcome.

- Although the number of small business audits has decreased over the past 10 years, they are about to be a focus area again as IRS enforcement increases.

STUDY QUESTIONS

4. If you receive a mail audit on Schedule C expenses, you will likely do any of the following, *except:*

    a. Request a reconsideration if you miss the 30 and/or 90-day letters.

    b. Use Form 1040X to respond.

    c. Follow up by phone for status.

    d. Always request an appeal if the IRS disagrees.

5. Which of the following identifies the error rate found in IRS construction audits on Form 1065 related to depreciation?

    a. 47 percent

    b. 53 percent

    c. 65 percent

    d. 100 percent

6. Which of the following is *not* one of the fraud red flags for the IRS?

    a. Increased depreciation deductions compared to prior year

    b. More than one set of books and records

    c. False statements about material facts in an examination

    d. Employee testimony about irregular business practices

7. A 2008 GAO study revealed that more than 50 percent of taxpayers misreport rental income and expenses. What is the most prevalent misreporting issue?

    a. Understating the expenses

    b. Overstating the expenses

    c. Using a professional tax preparer

    d. Failing to substantiate the expenses

MODULE 1: BUSINESS—Chapter 2: Payroll Tax Returns Deluged with Change

¶ 201 WELCOME

This chapter explains the payroll tax changes made by Congress as part of the COVID-19 tax-relief programs.

¶ 202 LEARNING OBJECTIVES

Upon completion of this chapter, you will be able to:

- Recognize how coronavirus pandemic relief programs affect payroll tax
- Identify employee retention credit (ERC) and Families First Coronavirus Response Act (FFCRA) credits, and Paycheck Protection Program (PPP) forgiveness wage absorption

¶ 203 INTRODUCTION

Employment tax returns have been pummeled by a flood of congressional pandemic relief changes. First, there was the deferral of employer Old Age, Survivors, and Disability Insurance (OASDI) until 2021 and 2022. Next, sick pay and family leave to employees under the Families First Coronavirus Response Act (FFCRA) was offset by all federal employment taxes. The Paycheck Protection Program (PPP) then blitzed America with intricate employment tax interplay. Then, the president allowed the deferral of employee OASDI. Subsequently, the employee retention credit (ERC) burst on the scene to retroactively coexist alongside PPP loans and forgiveness, but not on the same wages. Next, Congress changed the employee retention credit (ERC)/ employment tax interplay prospectively. After all of this, the IRS weighed in. This chapter reviews these and other changes.

¶ 204 FAILURE TO DEPOSIT PENALTY

In Notice 2020-22, the IRS provided that there is no Code Sec. 6656 failure to deposit penalty for an employer's failure to deposit employment taxes if:

1. FFCRA qualified leave (or ERC eligible) wages are paid,
2. The amount of payroll tax deposits not made equals or exceeds the anticipated FFCRA (and/or ERC) credit(s), and
3. No advance is requested on Form *7200, Advance Payments of Employer Credits due to COVID-19.*

   NOTE: If Form 7200 is used to obtain an advance payment, the penalty abatement provision does not apply.

   According to the IRS, if taxpayers received an errant penalty notice after they reduced deposits beyond employer OASDI, the IRS will take action to correct the issue: https://www.irs.gov/newsroom/failure-to-deposit-penalties-on-some-employers-claiming-new-tax-credits

   For Forms 941 and related employment tax deposits, the normal due dates and normal deposit due dates apply. However, Code Sec. 6656 failure to deposit penalties may be waived on a case-by-case basis in connection with a federally declared disaster (T.D. 8911 (2001-3 IRB p. 322 (01/16/01)), such as the COVID-19 pandemic.

¶ 205 PAYROLL TAX RETURNS

The FFCRA credit is summarized in the following table:

FFCRA Summary			
	FFCRA Round 1 4/1 – 12/31/20	FFCRA Round 2 1/1 – 3/31/21	FFCRA Round 3 4/1 – 9/30/21
Form 941* (or 941-X Retroactive) Claim FFCRA	Yes	Yes	Yes
FFCRA Offset Against Employer OASDI	Yes	Yes	No
FFCRA Offset Against Employer Medicare	No	No	Yes
Form 7200 Available with Quarter	Yes	Yes	Yes
Form 7200 Advance Available at Beginning of Quarter	No	No	No
Form 7200 After Close of Quarter	No	No	No

Claiming the ERC

The following table demonstrates how the ERC is claimed against federal employment tax returns:

Claiming the ERC: Federal* Employment Tax Returns (Same for 2020 and 2021)		
	Original Return	Amended Return
Most Employers	Form 941 Quarterly	Form 941-X Amended
Annual Employment Tax Return (seldom used)**	Form 944	Form 944-X
Agriculture	Form 943	Form 943-X
Railroad Companies	CT-1	CT-1-X
Advance of Credit (only used through due date of return of quarter credit generated from)	Form 7200	Instructions to 7200 do not discuss or make available amended return
* Fed Form 940 and state employment tax returns are unaffected. ** Form 944 is used if annual OASDI, Medicare, and FIT combined is greater than $1,000.		

The ERC is claimed against payroll tax returns up through the end of 2021. It will be offset, at least the non-refundable portion, against employer Social Security tax, but for the last two quarters of this program, it will be offset against employer Medicare tax.

Claiming the ERC: Payroll Tax Returns			
	ERC Round 1 3/13 – 12/31/20	ERC Round 2 1/1 – 6/30/21	ERC Round 3 7/1 – 12/31/21
Form 941 (or 941-X Retroactive) to Claim ERC	Yes	Yes	Yes
ERC Offset Against Employer OASDI	Yes	Yes	No
ERC Offset Against Employer Medicare	No	No	Yes

Claiming the ERC: Payroll Tax Returns			
	ERC Round 1 3/13 – 12/31/20	ERC Round 2 1/1 – 6/30/21	ERC Round 3 7/1 – 12/31/21
Form 7200 Available within Quarter	Yes	Yes	Yes
Form 7200 Advance Available at Beginning of Quarter	No	Yes	Yes
Form 7200 After Close of Quarter	No	No	No

¶ 206 COVID-19 RELIEF: MANY ROADS LEAD TO PAYROLL TAX RETURNS

The Coronavirus Aid, Relief, and Economic Security (CARES) Act, the Consolidated Appropriations Act of 2021 (CAA), the FFCRA, and the American Rescue Plan Act (ARPA) contain a flood of COVID-19 relief provisions affecting payroll tax. The following chart lists some of these provisions with their duration and order of application:

COVID-19 Relief for Payroll Tax		
COVID-19 Relief Provision	Duration of Relief	Order of Application
Deferral of Employer OASDI (CARES Act Sec. 2302)	2020 Employer OASDI Half deferred to 12/31/21 Half deferred to 12/31/22	Applies before COVID-19 ERC
Deferral of Employee OASDI (Notice 2020-65, CAA, (Taxpayer Uncertainty Relief Act of 2020, Sec. 274))	Employee OASDI (9/1/20 to 12/31/20) deferred to 12/31/21	Applies before COVID-19 ERC
FFCRA (Families First Coronavirus Response Act) (Extended for voluntary continuation by CAA and ARPA)	4/1/20 – 12/31/20 mandatory 1/1/21 – 9/3/21 voluntary	Applies before COVID-19 ERC
Non-COVID-19 Disaster ERC (CAA Sec. 303)	Federally declared disasters from 1/1/20 – 2/25/21	Not available on same wages used for COVID-19 ERC
COVID-19 Disaster ERC (CARES Act, CAA, ARPA)	Qualified wages paid 3/13/20 – 12/31/21	Applies after FFCRA and deferral of employer and employee FICA

¶ 207 EMPLOYEE RETENTION CREDIT

The COVID-19 ERC is claimed on the taxpayer's applicable federal employment tax return. To claim the ERC, an employer must (IRS Notice 2021-20, Q&A number 50) reduce otherwise required federal employment tax deposits (including trust fund taxes withheld), and, for a credit exceeding federal employment tax deposits otherwise due, file:

- During the quarter, Form 7200 to request an advance payment;
- Form 941 after the close of the quarter; or
- Form 941-X to amend a previously filed Form 941.

   EXAMPLE: In the third quarter of 2020, an employer pays $10,000 in qualified wages. After a $2,000 deferral of its OASDI (half to 2021 and half to 2022), the employer is required to deposit $8,000 in federal employment taxes during the same quarter. The employer has no FFCRA credit. The employer can keep up to $5,000 (50% of the qualified wages) of the $8,000 it was otherwise required to deposit, without penalty. The $5,000 can be accounted for later on the employer's Form 941.

EXAMPLE: Assume that an employer has $10,000 of Form 941 tax in the third quarter of 2020. After a $2,000 deferral of employer OASDI (half to 2021 and half to 2022), the required deposit for the quarter is $8,000. The employer has no FFCRA credit. It has $20,000 in ERC wages for the quarter and thus a $10,000 ERC credit ($20,000 × 50 percent). The employer need not deposit $8,000 of that amount. It can file Form 7200 for a $2,000 refund or wait to claim it on the Form 941.

In June 2021, the IRS issued Draft Form 941 for 2021: *Employer's Quarterly Federal Tax Return*. Note that this draft version is for the first quarter of 2021; there will be a different version for the second quarter. The draft form accommodates recent legislative changes made by the American Rescue Plan Act (ARPA):

- FFCRA emergency sick pay and family leave credits extended by ARPA,
- COBRA employment tax credits created by ARPA,
- Seasonal employer ERC qualification changes, and
- The new start-up business ERC qualification rule.

There is a way to get an advance payment on Form 7200 (Notice 2021-20, Q&A numbers 52 and 53). A taxpayer must have a minimum credit of $25. The form is not mailed to the IRS but instead must be faxed to the number provided in the Form 7200 instructions. The last day to file is the due date of Form 941 (e.g., for the second quarter of 2020, the due date was July 31, 2020).

Advance of COVID-19 Employer Credits		
	ERC Round 1 3/13/20 – 12/31/20	**ERC Rounds 2 and 3 1/1/21 – 12/31/21**
Advance of ERC* available (For 2021 rule changes, see CAA 2021 and Taxpayer Uncertainty Relief Act of 2020, Sec. 207(g))	Yes – For all employers	Yes – For employers with no more than 500 full-time employees (employed in 2019) (30/hours week = full time)
When available	During quarter must reduce deposits before requesting advance	Same as 2020, but also: Advance credit obtainable as quarter begins
Amount of advance credit	No maximum advance (other than amount of ERC eligible to be claimed)	Same as 2020, but also up to 70 percent of average quarterly wages in 2019 (2020 if employer did not exist in 2019)
How advance credit is obtained	Form 7200	Form 7200
Recovery if advance too high	Increase in employment tax for quarter on Form 941	Increase in employment tax for quarter on Form 941

Form 7200: Who Can Sign

According to IRS Notice 2021-20, Form 7200 can be signed by the following:

- For corporations: the president, vice president, or other principal officer duly authorized
- For partnerships (including limited liability companies [LLCs] taxed as partnerships) or unincorporated organizations: a responsible and duly authorized partner, member, or officer having knowledge of the entity's affairs
- For single-member LLCs (disregarded for federal income tax): the owner or a principal officer duly authorized
- For trusts or estates: the fiduciary
- In addition, a duly authorized agent of the taxpayer if a valid power of attorney (Form 2848) is on file and attached

Common Costly Errors in Claiming COVID-19 Payroll Tax Credits

According to the IRS, taxpayers should note the following tips to avoid common but costly errors when filing taxes or claiming credits (COVID Tax Tip 2021-64, May 10, 2021):

- Report advance credits actually received, not merely requested payments. There is a line on Forms 941 and 941-X to indicate if you have asked for an advance on Form 7200. However, according to the IRS, that line should not be filled out if the advance has not yet been received.
- Complete all lines on amended tax returns. Due to the length of the form, some taxpayers are failing to fill out all the lines.
- Use Form 7200 to request the advance payment of a credit only, not for claiming the credit. Form 941 or Form 941-X must be filed to claim the credit.
- Report the number of employees correctly on Form 941, Line 1.
- Inform third-party payers or reporting agents of a requested and received advance payment of credits.
- Use the fractions of cents line correctly for fractions of cents, due to rounding for the employee share of Social Security and Medicare taxes.

Delay in Deposit of Employment Taxes

According to CARES Act Section 2302, taxpayers may delay the deposit of the 2020 employer share of Social Security (OASDI) taxes. Tax incurred from March 27, 2020, through December 31, 2021, is eligible for deferral. The employer's share of Medicare tax is not eligible for deferral. This constitutes an "interest- and penalty-free loan" if paid back on time. Half is required to be deposited by the end of 2021, and the other half by the end of 2022. A self-employed individual may delay one half of the self-employment tax, the OASDI (but not the Medicare) portion.

Deferral of Employee OASDI

In August 2020, President Trump signed an Executive Order permitting employers to not withhold and submit the employee share of OASDI from September 1, 2020, to December 31, 2020. It was originally due to be paid back by April 1, 2021. The CAA extended repayment until January 3, 2022. No penalty or interest applies along the way. After not being initially withheld from employees by the employer, the employee share of OASDI must be recovered from employees by the employer. See also the IRS Small Business/Self-Employed Division Memo, *Update to Procedures for Mitigating CARES Act and Notice 2020-65* (SBSE-05-0421-0021), dated April 27, 2021.

FFCRA Credits: Expanded and Extended

The FFCRA was signed into law on March 18, 2020, and contains the following:

- The Emergency Paid Sick Leave Act (EPSLA)
- The Emergency Family and Medical Leave Expansion Act (EFMLEA)
- Dollar-per-dollar reimbursement of forced EPSL and EFML employee pay by tax credits for paid sick and paid family and medical leave

The FFCRA applies to government agencies, private employers with fewer than 500 employees, household employers, and self-employed individuals. It forces employers to pay sick leave and medical leave to workers afflicted by COVID-19 who are unable to work, or who have family who are afflicted by COVID-19 or cannot go to school or daycare because it is closed due to the pandemic. It was effective beginning on April 1, 2020 and ending on December 31, 2020.

FFCRA: Self-Employed Individuals

Self-employed individuals (with the same qualifying standards as for employees) are also entitled to FFCRA sick and family leave benefits through tax credits. The FFCRA credits for self-employed individuals (and general partners in partnerships) are claimed against Form 1040 self-employment tax (employer share of OASDI of self-employment tax) via Form 7202. Taxpayers may use prior year rather than current year earnings to compute the credit. Under the FFCRA, a self-employed individual (or general partner) may refrain from making self-employment tax payments to get the credit in advance. The amount of the credit is not included in the income of the self-employed individual. For more information on the mechanics and nuances of this provision, see https://www.irs.gov/newsroom/special-issues-for-employees#specific-provisions-related-self-employed-individuals

FFCRA Voluntary Extension for First Quarter 2021

The CAA provided a voluntary first quarter extension of credits for FFCRA paid employee sick and family leave. The sick and family leave mandates ended on December 31, 2020, yet employers may voluntarily continue them (two and/or 12-week benefit periods) and get credits for doing so. Both non-refundable and refundable credits for paid sick and family leave can be continued through March 31, 2021.

For self-employed individuals, the self-employment tax credit was extended for the first quarter of 2021. Taxpayers could elect to use prior year (2020, not 2021) net earnings from self-employment to compute 2021 FFCRA self-employment tax credits.

ARPA: FFCRA Credit Voluntary Extension, Reset, and Expansion for Second and Third Quarter 2021

The FFCRA credits were extended (only on a voluntary basis) and expanded to September 30, 2021 (ARPA Sections 9641 through 9650, creating new Internal Revenue Code Sections 3131 through 3133). This change incentivizes employers to continue (or start) offering FFCRA sick pay (ESPL) and family leave (EFML) that was previously mandatory. Voluntary payment by the employer of sick pay and family leave (offset by employment tax credits) is made available from April 1, 2021, through September 30, 2021. Sick pay benefits reset as of April 1, 2021 (i.e., no carryover is required of benefits used up before that date) (Code Sec. 3131(b)(2)(B)). The ARPA resets each employee's possible EPSL to a fresh two weeks starting on April 1, 2021, even if the employee had used up some leave before. There is no similar reset for family leave pay (Code Sec. 3132).

Under ARPA Sections 9641 through 9650, beginning on April 1, 2021, both sick and family leave are expanded for an employee's covered time away from work to include receiving the COVID-19 vaccine, suffering a physical reaction to (side effects of) the COVID-19 vaccine, and awaiting the results of a COVID-19 test or diagnosis.

The family leave maximum was expanded from $10,000 to $12,000, and the first two weeks are no longer unpaid (ARPA Section 9641, Code Sec. 3132). The new total maximum per employee is $17,110 (plus a sick pay reset amount). The maximum amount is similarly extended and expanded for self-employed individuals (ARPA Sections 9642 and 9643).

The ARPA also adds an anti-discrimination rule to prevent the voluntary FFCRA credit from being available only to highly compensated, full-time, or tenured employees; it must be offered to all employees.

¶207

The credits allowed by Code Secs. 7001 and 7003 shall be increased by the amount of employer Medicare taxes (imposed by Code Secs. 3111(a) and (b) and 3221(a)) on qualified sick leave wages or qualified family leave wages. These provisions are effective for the second and third quarters of 2021 for employers and the self-employed.

NOTE: The FFCRA is a federal law only. Taxpayers should also check their state or local law rules for paid leave.

FFCRA Scope After the CAA and ARPA		
	Sick Pay	**Family and Medical Leave**
Applies To	Government or business with fewer than 500 employees **Same**	Government or businesses with fewer than 500 employees **Same**
Required	Pay sick pay for two weeks **Same**	Pay family and medical leave for 10 weeks (first two weeks [10 days] unpaid; after 10 days, must pay for 10 weeks **Total of 12 weeks (first two weeks also paid) (only for 4/1–9/30/21)***
Full-Time Employee	80 hours (10 days) **Same**	Employee must be on payroll for at least 30 days **Same**
Part-Time Employee	Typical number of hours worked in two-week period **Same**	Typical number of hours worked in two-week period **Same**

* For self-employed, family and medical leave increased from 50 to 60 days.

FFCRA: Employees Eligible After CAA and ARPA		
	Sick Pay	**Family and Medical Leave**
Eligible Employee	Employee unable to work (or telework) due to: • Federal, state, or local quarantine or isolation order • Self-quarantining under advice of healthcare provider due to COVID-19 concerns • Obtaining diagnosis due to COVID-19 symptoms • Assisting a family member quarantined under order or advice of healthcare provider • Caring for child if school closed or child care provider closed or unavailable due to COVID-19 • Additional categories added by Department of Health and Human Services **From 4/1/21 to 9/30/21, additional covered events:** • **Obtaining a COVID-19 vaccine** • **Recovering from a reaction to COVID-19 vaccine** • **If employee was exposed to COVID-19 or employer requested test (or diagnosis), seeking or awaiting result (of test or diagnosis)**	Employee unable to work (or telework) due to: • Caring for child if school closed • Caring for child if child care provider closed or unavailable due to COVID-19 **From 4/1/21 to 9/30/21, additional covered events:** • **Obtaining a COVID-19 vaccine** • **Recovering from a reaction to COVID-19 vaccine** • **If employee was exposed to COVID-19 or employer requested test (or diagnosis), seeking or awaiting result (of test or diagnosis)**

FFCRA Amount of Credit After CAA and ARPA		
	Sick Pay	**Family and Medical Leave**
Amount	Full compensation up to $511/day ($5,110/employee cap)	Two-thirds of compensation up to $200/day ($10,000/employee cap) **($12,000/employee cap) (4/1–9/30/21)**
	Total possible/employee = $5,110 (plus reset)	Total possible/employee - $12,000
Amount	If to care for family member with coronavirus or child after school or daycare closing, then $200/day ($2,000/employee cap)	–
Relation to Existing Programs	FFCRA sick leave is in addition to sick leave already offered by employer (whether required by law or not)	–
Credit Available for	100 percent of sick pay + Employer's health insurance plan expenses (per employee)	100 percent of family and medical leave pay + Employer's health insurance plan expenses (per employee)

FFCRA Sick and Family Leave Credits

The IRS issued frequently asked questions (IR 2021-28, 6/11/21) to clarify how extended and changed FFCRA sick and family leave credits offset against payroll taxes. The two sets of FAQs provide information on eligibility, computing the credit amounts, and how to claim these tax benefits. See: https://www.irs.gov/newsroom/new-faqs-available-to-aid-families-and-small-business-under-the-american-rescue-plan#:~:text=IR-2021-128%2C%20June%2011%2C%202021%20WASHINGTON%20–%20The%20Internal,claiming%20credits%20under%20the%20American%20Rescue%20Plan%20%28ARP%29.

The FFCRA mandatory sick and family leave pay ended on December 31, 2020. The ARPA extends the voluntary FFCRA employer participation/offset against payroll tax available under the CAA through September 30, 2021. The ARPA also expands employee (and self-employed) qualifying conditions eligible for FFCRA benefits/credits.

COBRA Subsidies in 2021 for Terminated Employees

After an employee loses his or her job, the employee may continue to maintain coverage under the prior employer's health plan through COBRA coverage by paying up to 102 percent of the prior employer's cost of such coverage. ARPA Section 9501 now mandates that the cost of COBRA coverage from April through September of 2021 for any employee whose employment has involuntarily terminated (called an assistance eligible individual, or AEI) is wholly paid for by the U.S. government.

The former employer first pays the premium cost and then is reimbursed by the federal government via a payroll tax credit against Medicare tax. Any excess portion is a refundable credit (ARPA Sec. 9501(b), Code Sec. 6432(a)). The employer must provide notice to eligible individuals. Otherwise, eligible individuals who did not elect COBRA coverage have 60 days after receiving notice to elect coverage (ARPA Sec. 9501(a)(4)(A)).

The former employer adds back to 2021 income the amount of such credit. The COBRA subsidy is not included in the AEI's gross income (ARPA Sec. 6720C(c)(4), Code Sec. 139I (effective after March 11, 2021)).

STUDY QUESTIONS

1. The Emergency Paid Sick Leave Act is part of which of the following?

    a. FFCRA

    b. CAA

    c. ARPA

    d. COBRA

2. Which of the following IRS forms relates to advance payments of employer credits due to COVID-19?

    a. Form 1065

    b. Form 1023

    c. Form 1120

    d. Form 7200

3. Mandatory sick and family leave provided under which of the following programs ended on December 31, 2020?

    a. CARES

    b. FFCRA

    c. PPP

    d. HEROES

ERC Extension and Modifications

The goal of the ERC was to help businesses keep their employees on the payroll during and after the pandemic. The ARPA extended the ERC to the third and fourth quarters of 2021 (ARPA Sec. 9651, Code Sec. 3134). Effective for the third and fourth quarters of 2021, the ERC can be offset against employer Medicare tax (1.45 percent); it is not offsettable against employer OASDI (6.2 percent), as was the case for all of 2020 and the first and second quarters of 2021.

At slower absorption rate (1.45 percent versus 6.2 percent) to soak the ERC against employment tax deposits, it will take longer to reap a cash flow benefit. Thus, filing Form 7200 will be more advantageous for employers for the third and fourth quarters of 2021.

The statute of limitations for IRS assessment of an ERC claim is five years (instead of the usual three years) after the date of the original return (e.g., Form 941) was filed or treated as filed. The usual rule is that Form 941 for any quarter of 2020 is treated as filed on April 15, 2021, so the IRS may examine these claims as late as April 15, 2024. The usual rule applies for all quarters of 2020 and the first two quarters of 2021. The special rule for the ERC is for the third and fourth quarters only, and the statute of limitations expires on April 15, 2027 (i.e., five years after April 15, 2022).

Recovery Start-up Businesses and Severely Distressed Employers

Under the ARPA, if a taxpayer started a recovery start-up business after February 15, 2020, and its average annual gross receipts for the last three years is less than $1 million, the taxpayer qualifies for the ERC, regardless of whether the taxpayer is otherwise qualified. The taxpayer does not have to show a drop in gross receipts or government suspension. Such taxpayers can obtain an ERC of up to $50,000 per quarter. Since they will not have a three-year history, they can use the time period the business is in existence.

¶207

The ARPA also includes a provision for severely financially distressed employers, defined as those that experienced a decline in gross receipts of 90 percent or more for the third or fourth quarter of 2021 compared to the same calendar quarter in 2019. Those who qualify can treat wages (paid to both workers not currently providing services and those currently providing services) as ERC qualifying. This provision applies even if the employer has fewer than 500 employees.

Availability of ERC (or Wages for ERC)	
Double Dip?	**ERC**
Claim on same wages?*	
If taxpayer claims FFCRA Form 941 tax credit	Can't use ERC on same wages (FFCRA comes first)
If taxpayer claims family leave income tax credit (Code Sec. 45S)	Cannot claim ERC on same wages (Code Sec. 45S credit comes first)
ERC if the taxpayer received Paycheck Protection Program (PPP) forgiveness, or a Shuttered Venue Operator Grant (SVOG) or Restaurant Revitalization Grant (RRG)*?	**Yes, but not on same wages**
Research and Development (R&D) Form 941 tax credit**	Not on same wages
Veterans Form 941 tax credit**	Not on same wages
Work Opportunity Tax Credit, Empowerment Zone Employment, and Indian Employment Credits**	Not on same wages
* For PPP, CAA 2021, Taxpayer Uncertainty and Disaster Relief Act of 2020, Sec. 207(f)); and for PPP Second Draw, SVOG, and RRG, ARPA Sec. 9651 (Code Sec. 3134) ** ARPA Sec. 9651, Code Sec. 3134(c)(2)(D)	

The following example illustrates a basic ERC calculation:

> **EXAMPLE:** ABC Co. has 10 employees. Each employee earns $40,000. The company's receipts dropped 55 percent for each quarter in 2020 (from 2019) and dropped 30 percent for each quarter in 2021 (from 2019).
>
> **For 2020:** Assuming ABC has no competing PPP loan, its ERC = $50,000. Computation: For each employee, wages of $10,000/year × 50 percent credit rate = $5,000. 10 employees × $5,000 = $50,000.
>
> **For 2021:** Assuming ABC has no competing PPP loan, its ERC = $280,000.

Computation

> **Pre-ARPA:** For each employee, wages of $10,000/quarter × 2 quarters × 70 percent credit rate = $14,000. 10 employees × $14,000 = $140,000.
>
> **Under ARPA (now 4 quarters):** Wages of $10,000/ quarter × 4 quarter × 70 percent credit rate = $28,000.
>
> 10 employees × $28,000 = $280,000.
>
> Even if ABC Co. received a PPP loan, if there are plenty of wages to go around, it may get the full ERC and full PPP forgiveness.

Effect of ERC on Income Tax Return		
	Tax Break	**Effect on Income Tax**
Employee Retention Credit (ERC)	ERC [(Round 1 (2020)) = 50 percent × up to $10,000 compensation cost] [(Round 2 (2021)) = 70 percent × up to $20k compensation cost] offset against employer OASDI [(Round 3 (2021)) = 70 percent × up to $20k compensation cost] offset against employer Medicare	Income tax deduction for wages reduced by amount of credit taken (CARES Act Sec. 2301(e), FAQ 85). Reduce wages in year ERC generated. For example, if wages paid in 2020 and credit received in 2021, reduce wages on 2020 return (CARES Act Sec. 2301(e), Code Sec. 280C, Reg. § 1.280C-1)
		For example, $10,000 ERC wages in 2020. $5,000 ERC. Deductible wages for 2020 are only $5,000.
M-1 Adjustment?		Yes (for expense recorded on books, but not on tax return)

The CARES Act created the 2020 ERC, but not for PPP borrowers. The CAA opened up the ERC retroactively for PPP borrowers, but not on same wages. The CAA extended the ERC to the first and second quarters of 2021 and increased the ERC wage base to $10,000 per quarter and the credit rate to 70 percent for the first two quarters of 2021. The ARPA extended the ERC to the third and fourth quarters of 2021. It also expanded ERC eligibility for certain small start-up companies, only for the last two quarters of 2021. The ARPA changed the payroll tax absorption for Q3 and Q4 2021 from employer OASDI to employer Medicare.

Eligibility for the ERC		
	ERC Round 1 3/13/20 – 12/31/20	**ERC Rounds 2 and 3 1/1/21 – 12/31/21**
Eligibility	Gross receipts (GR) drop -or- Full or partial suspension	Gross receipts (GR) drop -or- Full or partial suspension
Initial gross receipts drop	ERC eligible for a 2020 quarter if GR drop (for such quarter) by more than 50 percent from same quarter in 2019	ERC eligible for a 2021 quarter if GR drop (for such quarter) by more than 20 percent from same quarter **in 2019**
	Example: Taxpayer would qualify if it had a 2Q 2020 52 percent drop in GR compared to 2Q 2019 GR Would not qualify if it had a 2Q 2020 47 percent drop in GR compared to 2Q 2019 GR	Example: Taxpayer would qualify if it had a 1Q 2021 drop in GR of 22 percent compared to 1Q 2019 GR Would not qualify if it had a 1Q 2021 15 percent drop in GR compared to 1Q 2019 GR

Eligibility for ERC: Drop in Gross Receipts		
	ERC Round 1 3/13/20 – 12/31/20	**ERC Rounds 2 and 3 1/1/21 – 12/31/21**
Eligibility	Gross receipts (GR) drop -or- Full or partial suspension	Gross receipts (GR) drop -or- Full or partial suspension
Initial gross receipts drop	Gross receipts drop more than 50 percent from same quarter in 2019	ERC eligible for quarter if 2021 gross receipts drop more than 20 percent from same quarter **in 2019**

Eligibility for ERC: Drop in Gross Receipts		
	No safe harbor	If taxpayer does not meet GR drop test, second chance: Election to use prior quarter's gross receipts: [Safe harbor (SH)] Look at previous quarter and compare it to same quarter in 2019 (to see if gross receipts drop by more than 20 percent) Example: For 1Q 2021, if taxpayer does not have GR drop of more than 20 percent, look to 4Q 2020 and compare to 4Q 2019 (to see if there is a more than 20 percent GR drop)
Duration of qualification	Through quarter of drop by less than 20 percent of gross receipts (GR). Example: Taxpayer has a 2Q 2020 drop in GR of 52 percent compared to GR of 2Q 2019, and a 3Q 2020 GR drop only 17 percent. ERC eligible for Q2 and Q3 2020, but not Q4 2020.	For quarter of qualification and any other quarter it qualifies for. Example: Taxpayer has a 1Q 2021 drop in GR of 22 percent compared to GR of 1Q 2019. In this example, also qualifies for 2Q 2021 (applying safe harbor test), but does not automatically qualify for 3Q 2021.
"	For 2020, if a taxpayer gets initial quarter, it gets at least two (If taxpayer qualifies for one quarter of qualification, it also qualifies for the next—but not necessarily the one after that.)	For 2021, if the taxpayer gets initial quarter under GR test only, then automatically qualifies for the next (under second-chance safe harbor). However, if qualifies under safe harbor, it does not automatically get the next.
Eligibility	Gross receipts (GR) drop -or- Full or partial suspension	Same as 2020
Availability of credit for employers not in existence for all of 2019	Not available if qualifying for ERC based on drop in gross receipts	For drop in GR, for any calendar quarter, if employer not in existence at beginning of same calendar quarter in calendar year 2019, substitute 2020 for 2019
"	Eligibility for ERC alternatively available if qualifying based on full or partial suspension	Same as 2020

Gross Receipts Wage Range (Wide)		
	ERC Round 1 3/13/20 – 12/31/20	**ERC Rounds 2 and 3** 1/1/21 – 12/31/21
"Gross receipts" ERC wage range	Entire quarter for which it qualifies	Same as for 2020

ERC Wages Paid vs. Incurred		
	ERC Round 1 3/13/20 – 12/31/20	**ERC Rounds 2 and 3** 1/1/21 – 12/31/21

ERC Wages Paid vs. Incurred		
Wages qualifying for ERC: Cash vs. Accrual	If qualifying for drop in GR, all wages *paid* within qualifying time period qualify for ERC Wages must be actually *paid*, not merely accrued (CARES Act Sec. 2301(c)) (No IRS guidance yet) Example: Wages earned prior to ERC qualifying period paid inside (at beginning of qualifying period) appear to qualify for ERC. Example: Texas shut down non-essential businesses on 3/19/20. Payroll checks cut on 3/20/20 for 3/1–3/14.	Same as for 2020

Gross Receipts

For purposes of the ERC, *gross receipts* for a business has the same meaning as under Code Sec. 448(c). Gross receipts include:

- Total sales (net of returns and allowances);

- All amounts received for services; and

- Income from investments and incidental or outside sources, including interest (including original issue discount and tax-exempt interest under Code Sec. 103), dividends, rents, royalties, and annuities, regardless of whether such amounts derived in the ordinary course of the taxpayer's trade or business.

To determine gross receipts for purposes of the ERC, taxpayers should utilize their usual method (e.g., cash or accrual) of accounting for tax purposes. Gross receipts do not include the repayment of a loan, or sales tax if the tax is legally imposed on the purchaser of the good or service, and the taxpayer merely collects and remits the sales tax to the taxing authority. According to the IRS (FAQ number 41), an employer does not need to prove that a significant decline in gross receipts is related to the COVID-19 crisis.

According to IRS Notice 2021-20, Q&A number 25, gross receipts for tax-exempt organizations include the following (Code Sec. 6033):

- The gross amount received by the organization from all sources without a reduction for costs or expenses, including cost of goods or assets sold, cost of operations, or expenses of earning, raising or collecting.

- This includes the gross amount received as (from):

    — Contributions, gifts, and grants;

    — Dues or assessments from members or affiliated organizations;

    — Gross sales or receipts from business activities (including business activities unrelated to the organization's exempt purpose);

    — Gross receipts from sale of assets without a reduction for cost or other basis and expenses of sale; and

    — Investment income, such as interest, dividends, rents, and royalties.

Eligibility for ERC Full or Partial Suspension		
	ERC Round 1 3/13/20 – 12/31/20	**ERC Rounds 2 and 3** 1/1/21 – 12/31/21
Full or partial suspension	Operations suspended due to order from government authority limiting commerce, travel, or group meetings (commercial, social, religious or other)	Same as 2020

Eligibility for ERC Wage Range (Narrow)		
	ERC Round 1 3/13/20 – 12/31/20	**ERC Rounds 2 and 3** 1/1/21 – 12/31/21
"Full or partial suspension" ERC wage range	ERC for only wages paid during time of suspension (not entire calendar quarter)	Same as 2020

C Corporation or S Corporation Ownership

The wages of owners of C corporations or S corporations (regardless of their ownership percentage) do qualify for the ERC. Likewise, the wages of the spouses of owners of C or S corporations (regardless of the owner's ownership percentage) qualify for the ERC. However, according to Notice 2021-49, this is only the case if the owner and the spouse do not have any other family members, as defined by IRC section 267(c)(4).

Additionally, the wages of non-spouse relatives of more than 50 percent owners of C corporations and S corporations do *not* qualify for the ERC. The wages of non-spouse relatives of 50 percent (or less) owners *may* qualify for the ERC, depending on the total percentage ownership and the application of the attribution rules under IRC section 267.

ERC Wage Availability: Related-Party Rules

According to IRS FAQ number 59, wages paid by an employer to employees who are related individuals are not considered qualified wages. Wages paid to related individuals, as defined by Code Sec. 51(i)(1), are not taken into account for the ERC. A related individual is any employee who has any of the following relationships to an individual (shareholder who owns more than 50 percent of the corporation):

- A child or a descendant of a child
- A brother, sister, stepbrother, or stepsister
- The father or mother or ancestor of either
- A stepfather or stepmother
- A niece or nephew
- An aunt or uncle
- A son-in-law, daughter-in-law, father-in-law, mother-in-law, brother-in-law, or sister-in-law

PPP versus ERC

The following table summarizes the availability of the PPP and the ERC to business owners for 2020 and 2021:

¶207

PPP versus ERC: Availability for Owners and Relatives				
ERC Wage Qualification	**PPP 2020**	**PPP 2021**	**ERC 2020**	**ERC 2021**
C or S corporation shareholder (regardless of ownership percent)	Yes	Yes	Maybe	Maybe
Shareholder's spouse	Yes	Yes	Maybe	Maybe
Non-spouse relative of more than 50 percent shareholder	Yes	Yes	No	No
Non-spouse relative of 50 percent (or less) shareholder	Yes	Yes	Maybe	Maybe
Sole proprietor or general partner profit comp? (No W-2)	Yes	Yes	No (except for pay to W-2 employees)	No (except for pay to W-2 employees)
Sole proprietor's or general partner's spouse	Yes	Yes	Yes	Yes
Non-spouse relative of sole proprietor or more than 50 percent general partner	Yes	Yes	No	No
Non-spouse relative of 50 percent (or less) general partner	Yes	Yes	Yes	Yes

¶ 208 AGGREGATION RULES

Entities are aggregated for the ERC for the following purposes (Notice 2021-20, Q&A number 7) (FAQ number 26):

- Determining whether the employer has business fully or partially suspended due to government orders related to the COVID-19 pandemic
- Determining whether there is a significant decline in gross receipts
- Determining whether there are more than 100 (or 500) full-time employees
- Determining the maximum amount of credit per employee

To determine whether the Code Sec. 448(c) gross receipts test is met, the aggregation rules under Code Sec. 448(c)(2) apply. The rules require combining companies and testing them as one for purposes of computing the ERC. There are four ways to get snagged by the Code Sec. 448(c) aggregation rules:

- Code Sec. 52(a): Controlled group of C corporations under Code Sec. 1563 (but with more than 50 percent relatedness for the parent-subsidiary)
- Code Sec. 52(b): Parent-subsidiary or brother-sister controlled group. This can be any entity, not just C corporations
- Code Sec. 414(m): Affiliated service group (employee benefit plans)

According to IRS FAQ number 25, all members of the aggregated group are treated as a single employer for purposes of the ERC. It states:

> Under the section 52 rules, corporate taxpayers may be required to aggregate as a parent-subsidiary controlled group, a brother-sister controlled group, or a combined group of corporations. . . . The section 52(b) aggregation rules apply to partnerships, trusts, estates, or sole proprietorships in businesses under common control. . . . Under section 414(m) of the Code, an "affiliated service group" is treated as a single employer based on rules related to the performance of services by one entity for another or by one entity in association with another for third parties, even if the entity does not have sufficient ownership or control of the other entity to form a controlled group.

For a plain English IRS explanation of similar attribution rules, see: https://www.irs.gov/newsroom/faqs-regarding-the-aggregation-rules-under-section-448c2-that-apply-to-the-section-163j-small-business-exemption

According to IRS FAQ number 75, each employer reports its own ERC on its own Form 941 without regard to its aggregation. The ERC is apportioned among members of the aggregated group based on each member's proportionate share of qualified wages giving rise to the ERC.

¶ 209 PAYROLL TAX RETURN MECHANICS

If a taxpayer "missed the party" and did not originally claim the ERC on Form 941, it should File Form 941-X to retroactively claim the ERC. A Form 941-X should be filed for each retroactive quarter claimed.

There is no special statute of limitations deadline. Note that it is too late to file Form 7200 if the taxpayer already filed Form 941. To claim the ERC on Form 941, the taxpayer should check the "Claim" box in Part 1 of Form 941. Because wages are not being adjusted (on page 1 of Form 941), the taxpayer should not check the box for "Adjusted employment tax return" on the form. In completing Form 941-X for an ERC claim, the taxpayer should not complete Part 2. Because the return is not an "adjusted employment tax return," Part 2 is irrelevant.

The nonrefundable portion of the ERC is limited to the employer share of Social Security tax (OASDI) reported on Form 941, lines 5a and 5b, after being first reduced by any:

- Form 8974 research credit for qualified small business payroll tax credit for increasing research activities,
- Form 5884-C work opportunity credit for qualified tax-exempt organizations hiring qualified veterans, and/or
- Form 941 credit for the nonrefundable portion of the credit for FFCRA qualified sick and family leave wages.

The refundable portion of the credit (line 26) is allowed after the employer share of Social Security tax is reduced to zero by nonrefundable credits.

STUDY QUESTIONS

4. Under the ARPA, the ERC is up to what amount per employee, per year?

    a. $2,000

    b. $5,000

    c. $7,000

    d. $28,000

5. For purposes of determining gross receipts with respect to the ERC, which of the following is included when calculating gross receipts?

    a. Sales, net of returns and allowances

    b. Employee retention credit

    c. Sales tax legally imposed on purchaser

    d. Repayment of a loan

6. Which of the following IRS Forms should be used to retroactively claim the ERC for each past quarter?

    a. Form 941

    b. Form 941-X

    c. Form 943

    d. Form 944

7. Which statement is correct regarding the aggregation rules for purposes of the ERC?

    a. Corporate taxpayers are never required to aggregate.

    b. The aggregation rules do not apply to trusts.

    c. Entities are not aggregated for purposes of determining whether there is a significant decline in gross receipts.

    d. All members of an aggregated group are treated as a single employer.

MODULE 1: BUSINESS—Chapter 3: Excess Business Losses under Code Sec. 461(l) and Net Operating Losses

¶ 301 WELCOME

This chapter reviews the Code Sec. 461(l) excess business loss rule and newly revamped net operating loss (NOL) limitation rules.

¶ 302 LEARNING OBJECTIVES

Upon completion of this chapter, you will be able to:

- Recognize the complexity in the Code Sec. 461(l) and net operating loss (NOL) rules
- Identify loss limitation hurdles post–Tax Cuts and Jobs Act
- Describe non–C corporation excess business losses
- Describe the changes to the tax treatment of NOLs as a result of the Tax Cuts and Jobs Act
- Explain the provisions of Code Sec. 461(l)
- Describe the qualified business income deduction
- Recognize which entities are ineligible for the qualified business income deduction

¶ 303 INTRODUCTION

The goal of this chapter is to explain the excess business loss rules of Code Sec. 461 (l) and also the net operating loss rules themselves. It discusses how the Coronavirus Aid, Relief, and Economic Security Act (CARES Act) postponed, retroactively changed, and scrambled both the excess business loss and the NOL 80 percent absorption and carryforward/carryback rules. Other topics covered include whether it is necessary to file an amended return and/or redemptive 2020 return.

¶ 304 LOSS LIMITATION HURDLES

When a business has a legitimate business loss, it must overcome a series of hurdles in order to write off that loss. Three distinct time periods come into play in business losses: (1) prior law, before the 2017 Tax Cuts and Jobs Act (TCJA); (2) post-TCJA, or 2018 and after; and (3) post–CARES Act, which was enacted in March 2020.

Prior to the TCJA, businesses had to overcome the following four hurdles:

- Basis (Code Secs. 705 and 1367)
- At-risk (Code Sec. 465)
- Passive loss (Code Sec. 469)
- Net operating loss, or NOL (Code Sec. 172)

After passage of the TCJA, businesses had to jump two additional hurdles, for a total of six:

- Basis (Code Secs. 705 and 1367)
- Business interest expense (Code Sec. 163(j)) (expanded by the TCJA)

- At-risk (Code Sec. 465)
- Passive loss (Code Sec. 469)
- Excess loss (Code Sec. 461(l))
- NOL (Code Sec. 172) (major changes made by the TCJA)

A business had to review each set of rules before anything could emerge as a loss, and then confront the next hurdle. The Code Sec. 461(l) rules for excess losses became effective in 2018. Also in 2018, major changes came down the pike for NOLs.

¶ 305 EXCESS BUSINESS LOSSES

Code Sec. 461(l) applies to business losses of non–C corporations, including individuals, trusts, and estates. Congress passed the new rules on December 27, 2017; therefore, the first tax season for which they could have affected returns was 2018. IRS Form 461, *Limitation on Business Losses*, which will be reissued beginning for the tax year 2021, is used to figure the excess business loss reported on a noncorporate tax return.

According to Code Sec. 461(l), any excess business loss (EBL) equals the excess of aggregate deductions attributable to the trade or businesses, over the sum of aggregate gross business income or gain, plus a threshold amount. For 2018, that threshold amount is $500,000 for taxpayers who are married filing jointly (MFJ) and $250,000 for single taxpayers. For 2019, the threshold amounts are $510,000 and $255,000, and for 2020, they are $518,000 and $259,000, respectively.

The disallowed amount equals the EBL, and the EBL becomes the NOL carryover under Code Sec. 172. The following chart illustrates an example for 2018:

$500,000 Loss Allowed (MFJ Form 1040)		
Original Loss	**Computation**	**Loss Allowed (2018)**
2018 business* loss	$2,000,000	
Code Sec. 461(l) limit (MFJ)	–$500,000	$500,000
EBL becomes NOL carryforward to 2019 (not for farmers; farmers get a two-year carryback)	$1,500,000	
* Material participation – Not subject to Code Sec. 469 passive loss rules. 2018 nonbusiness income exceeding $500,000 will (may) be subject to tax.		

What Code Sec. 461(l) primarily accomplishes is a short-term deferral in ability to write off a currently generated business loss. Code Sec. 461(l) itself is vague, with sparse legislative history, and little, if any, guidance has been provided by the Department of the Treasury or the IRS. As a result, practitioners must make up their own stories; it is best to have "substantial authority" (i.e., a well-reasoned argument) to back up your position or "reasonable basis" and disclosure.

> **EXAMPLE:** If a MFJ taxpayer had $700,000 in non-passive business loss generated in 2018, $500,000 would be allowed and $200,000 disallowed. The EBL ($200,000) becomes part of the NOL carryforward.

Code Sec. 461(l) can hurt a taxpayer with a sizeable current year non-passive business loss and also sizeable current year income from non-business sources.

> **EXAMPLE:** In 2018, a single individual in Boulder, Colorado, has investment income of $1 million and non-passive business loss. Code Sec. 461(l) limits the loss absorption to $250,000. That means $750,000 of income remains exposed to income tax, and 2018 estimated tax payments must be made.

The Code Sec. 461(l) rules are also detrimental to an owner of property with a large passive activity loss (PAL) freed up on disposition.

EXAMPLE: An owner of Cheyenne, Wyoming, residential rental property with a $2 million PAL (accumulated over past 20 years) sells the property in 2018. The PAL is freed up on disposition. The excess of the PAL over gain on the sale of $150,000 is treated as if it freshly arose in 2018. Such loss is limited by Code Sec. 461(l).

Code Sec. 461(l) Limits "Freed Up" Passive Activity Loss		
$2 million 2018 PAL allowed on complete disposition (Code Sec. 469(g))*	Computation	**Loss Allowed (2018)**
2018 Code Sec. 1231 gain is $150,000*	$2,000,000 – $150,000 = $1,850,000	
Code Sec. 461(l) limit (single)	–$250,000	$250,000
NOL carryforward to 2019 (not farmer)	$1,600,000	
* Sale of rental business property – Former Code Sec. 469 passive activity. 2018 nonbusiness income exceeding $250,000 will (may) be subject to tax.		

A kissing cousin of Code Sec. 461(l) is the Code Sec. 461(j) excess farm limitation (enacted in 2008). Code Sec. 461(j) limits losses from farming businesses receiving certain agricultural subsidies. Note that Code Sec. 461(l) applies to a much broader range of taxpayers, and Code Sec. 461(l) and 461(j) each have distinct carryforward rules.

Business income and business losses land in Part I of Form 461; however, investment income and investment losses are covered in Part II. Part III states that if there is an excess business loss over business income, only $250,000 or $500,000 will be allowed, depending on the taxpayer's marital status.

Investment Income and Business Loss (MFS Form 1040)		
	Computation	**Loss Allowed (2018)**
2018 rental income (net lease commercial building) (investment property) of $800,000* Also, $800,000 net rental business loss	$800,000 – $800,000 = $0 (passive netting) However, no netting for Code Sec. 461(l)	
2018 business income	$0	
Code Sec. 461(l) limit (single)	–$250,000	$250,000
EBL becomes NOL carryforward to 2019 (not farmer)	$800,000 – $250,000 = $550,000	
* $800,000 investment income, plus $800,000 business loss. 2018 nonbusiness income exceeding $250,000 will (may) be subject to tax.		

The bottom line is that business losses offset only up to $500,000 ($250,000), but may offset unlimited business income. Thus, taxpayers want to have as much business income, not nonbusiness income, as possible to avoid this limitation.

The first question that comes to mind, then, is: Are wages business income? The original statute is unclear, and there was no Treasury guidance. In its Code Sec. 461(l) Instructions, the IRS noted that wages are business income. However, the Blue Book published by the Joint Committee on Taxation stated that wages are not business income. According to Code Sec. 179, wages are business income, but Code Sec. 199A notes that wages are not business income.

This confusion meant some taxpayers were going in one direction and others were going the other direction, resulting in chaos. According to the canon of statutory construction: "Where Congress includes particular language in one section of a statute, but omits it in another . . . it is generally presumed Congress acted intentionally and purposefully in the disparate inclusion or exclusion" (*Keene Corp v. U.S.*, 508 U.S. 200, 208 (1993)). This bodes well for the position that wages are Code Sec. 461(l) business income. The following example chart illustrates the substantial difference in income tax if wages are/are not considered business income:

2018 Single Taxpayer: $200,000 Wages, $525,000 Business Loss		
	Wages Are Business Income	**Wages Are *Not* Business Income**
2018 Code Sec. 461(l) computation	$200,000 business loss absorbed against W-2 wages (business of being an employee) + $250,000 = $450,000 business loss allowed	$0 business loss absorbed against business income. Only $250,000 business loss allowed.
Carryover to 2019 (nonfarmer)	$525,000 business loss – $450,000 allowed = $75,000 EBL (NOL carryforward to 2019)	$525,000 business loss – $250,000 allowed = $275,000 EBL (NOL carryforward to 2019)
Difference in 2018 income tax (32 percent effective rate)	$64,000 less	$64,000 more

CARES Act Section 2304 included a technical correction stating that in the EBL computation, W-2 wages are *not* Code Sec. 461(l) business income. This change applies retroactively to 2018, 2019, and 2020, and to all future years.

Some argue that losses from the disposition of business property are not subject to the Code Sec. 461(l) EBL limit. The premise is that Code Sec. 461(l) refers to deductions, income, and gains, but not losses. This argument is supported by similar statutory language in and pro-taxpayer interpretation of Code Sec. 461(j) (farm losses) in its implementing Worksheet for Form 1040, Schedule F. If there are net gains, such gains are arguably taken into account in computing EBL.

The substantial difference in income tax if losses from the disposition of business property are or are not subject to the Code Sec. 461(l) limit is outlined in the following chart:

2018 Single Taxpayer: $300,000 Dividend Income, ($300,000) Code Sec. 1231 Loss		
	Disposition Loss Included in Code Sec. 461(l) Computation	**Disposition Loss *Not* Included in Code Sec. 461(l) Computation**
2018 Code Sec. 461(l) computation	($300,000) business loss limited to $250,000 current deductibility	($300,000) business loss fully absorbed against investment income
Carryover to 2019 (non-farmer)	$300,000 business loss – $250,000 allowed = $50,000 EBL ($50,000 NOL carryforward to 2019)	$300,000 business loss fully allowed No carryforward to 2019
Difference in 2018 income tax (32 percent effective rate)	$16,000 more	$16,000 less

CARES Act Section 2304 also includes the following technical correction: In the EBL computation, capital gains are only included to extent of the lesser of net capital gain attributable to trade or business or capital gain net income. This change applies retroactively to 2018, 2019, and 2020, and to all future years.

Taxpayers who filed a return in 2018 and/or 2019 consistent with the idea that in the EBL computation, wages are not business income, do not need to go back and make a change. However, if they filed the return on the premise that wages *were* business income, it appears that now an amended return is mandatory. Along similar lines, in the EBL computation, if the taxpayer included capital gains to offset a loss, if they were generated inside the business context, then it is only to the extent of the lesser of that net capital gain generated (or basically capital gain net income across the board). All capital gains and losses net against each other. Again, an amended return should be filed.

Business versus Nonbusiness

How will each of the following be treated?

- Gain (loss) from sale of partnership interests or S corporation stock
- Interest expense allocable to acquisition of partnership interest or S corporation stock
- Debt financed distributions from partnership or S corporation
- Cancellation of debt (COD) income
- Guaranteed payments for capital or services
- Interest income (business or investment)
- Self-charged items

Code Sec. 461(l) EBL limits apply to partners and S corporation shareholders at the owner level; the limits do not apply at the pass-through entity level.

Guidance Needed

Guidance is lacking on a number of issues associated with the Code Sec. 461(l) rules, including the following:

- Treatment of NOLs, passive activity losses, and other carryovers from before 2018
- For foreign individuals and trusts, whether the EBL applies only to income (loss) effectively connected with a U.S. business
- Computational effects on the Code Sec. 1402 self-employment tax and Code Sec. 1411 net investment income tax
- Interactions with Centralized Partnership Audit (CPAR) rules
- Code Sec. 461(l) reporting requirements

These and other issues highlight that Congress has created something that should have been defined more carefully. Much guidance is needed and will likely be issued in the near future. Consequently, tax practitioners must stay on top of this topic and related updates.

Alternative Minimum Tax

The TCJA repealed the alternative minimum tax (AMT) for C corporations (for tax years beginning after December 31, 2017), but not for individuals, trusts and estates. Regular tax NOLs and EBLs may (or likely will) differ from AMT NOLs and EBLs. The differences stem from depreciation, percentage depletion, Code Sec. 174 research and development (R&D) expenditures for non-materially participating investors, private activity bond interest, Code Sec. 421 incentive stock options (ISOs), and others.

Although under Code Sec. 199A, they are computed the same for both regular tax and AMT, when it comes to these different types of NOL carryovers, there very well could be a different regular tax EBL from an AMT EBL.

Trusts and Estates

As mentioned earlier, Code Sec. 461(l) applies to trusts and estates. A nongrantor trust (or estate) may deduct $250,000 of business losses against the trust's (or estate's) own nonbusiness income. The trust (or estate) is taxed as an individual. The trust's or estate's nonbusiness income is presumably after the distributable net income (DNI) deduction (Code Sec. 651 or 661).

Multiple taxable trusts set up to game the system may be treated as one under Code Sec. 643 (or future anti-abuse rules) if the trusts have the same grantor(s) and same primary beneficiary(ies), and their principal purpose is the avoidance of income tax. Taxpayers must be careful, because they will often not have a business reason to have more than one trust.

Tax-Exempt Businesses

For tax-exempt businesses that happen to have losses, the interplay between Code Sec. 461 (l) and 512(a)(6) is unclear. Currently, there is no guidance on this issue. Unrelated business taxable income is computed separately for each trade or business.

State Conformity

Some states conform to Code Sec. 461(l), whereas others do not. In the nonconforming states, individuals may have higher business losses for state tax purposes than for federal. This may lead to state/federal NOL mismatches, including both regular tax and AMT NOL mismatches. There is a growing list of states that have balked at the Code Sec. 461(l) rules.

State of Confusion

To put it simply, Code Sec. 461(l) is a colossal mess. Consequently, practitioners should think in terms of "substantial authority" for pro-taxpayer positions; that is, whether they have at least a 40 percent chance of success for the position they have taken. If they do not have substantial authority, they should determine whether they have at least a "reasonable basis" for the position and consider attaching a disclosure in Form 8275 to reduce the sting of any potential substantial understatement penalty.

With the lack of guidance, the best advice for tax practitioners is to see how tax software approaches Code Sec. 461(l) and stay tuned for any newly issued guidance.

CARES Act

The CARES Act layers on top of everything discussed so far with regard to Code Sec. 461(l). The Act postpones the effective date of the Code Sec. 461(l) EBL limitation from years beginning after December 31, 2017, to years beginning after December 31, 2020 (CARES Act Section 2304).

As mentioned earlier, if a 2018 or 2019 return was filed reporting EBL, an amended return (possibly generating a refund) is available. Technical corrections in the CARES Act note that in the EBL computation:

- Wages are not business income.

- Capital gains are only included to the extent of the lesser of net capital gain attributable to trade or business or capital gain net income.

On Form 1065, Schedule K-1, Box 20, Code AH; and Form 1120S, Schedule K-1, Box 17, Code AC, all reporting Code Sec. 461(l) information, disclosures are not needed for 2018, 2019, and 2020. The Code Sec. 461(l) rules and changes discussed in this section are summarized in the following chart:

¶305

Non-C Corporation Excess Business Losses *Timeline of Code Sec. 461(l)*			
	Pre-TCJA	**TCJA**	**CARES Act**
Effective date	Prior to 2018	After 2017 and before 2026	After 2020
CARES Act reshuffle	N/A	Deletes Code Sec. 461(l) for 2018, 2019, and 2020	Reinstates Code Sec. 461(l) for after 2020
CARES Act re: wage income	N/A	Wages income = Business income?*	Wage income is *not* business income
CARES Act re: capital gain income generated in a business	N/A	Capital gain inside business = Business income?	Capital gain inside business = Business income
Form 1065 and 1120S K-1 disclosures re: Code Sec. 461(l)	N/A	After postponement, not needed for 2018, 2019, and 2020	Back on table in 2021
*Code Sec. 461(l) is silent; IRS Instructions say "yes"; Blue Book says "no."			

¶ 306 NET OPERATING LOSSES

In SBSE-04-0419-0006 (04/17/19), the IRS Standard Explanation of Computation of NOLs, the IRS states: "Net operating loss deductions (NOLD) and net operating loss carryovers, for losses arising in tax years beginning after December 31, 2017, are limited to 80 percent of your taxable income. We adjusted your allowable net operating loss deduction as shown in the attached computation."

Pre-TCJA, NOLs generated before 2018 offset 100 percent of taxable income in the year carried to. However, the TCJA stated that NOLs generated in years beginning after 2017 may only offset 80 percent of taxable income of the year the NOL is carried to.

NOL Carrybacks and Carryforwards

With regard to carrybacks and carryforwards, pre-TCJA, NOLs could be carried back two years and carried forward 20 years. However, Code Sec. 172(b)(1) allowed for three-year loss carryback periods for casualty, theft, and farmers. Under the TCJA, for NOLs generated in years beginning after 2017, there are no more NOL carrybacks (except two years for farmers and insurance companies). NOLs indefinitely carry forward.

In SBSE-04-0419-0006 (04/17/19), the IRS Standard Explanation of Period for NOL Carryback is as follows: "We disallowed your net operating loss carryback. In general, for tax years beginning after December 31, 2017, net operating losses cannot be carried back but can be carried forward indefinitely."

The following chart illustrates NOL carrybacks and carryforwards under the TCJA before the CARES Act changed them:

Losses Generated in Calendar Year 2018 80 Percent NOL Absorption (MFJ Form 1040)		
Original Loss	**Computation**	**Loss Allowed (2018)**
Calendar year 2018 business loss	$2,000,000	
Code Sec. 461(l) limit (MFJ)	–$500,000	$500,000
NOL carryforward to 2019 (not farmer)	$1,500,000	
NOL	**Computation**	**Loss Allowed (2019)**
NOL carryforward to 2019	$1,500,000	

Losses Generated in Calendar Year 2018 80 Percent NOL Absorption (MFJ Form 1040)		
80 percent × 2019 taxable income of $1 million (80 percent × $1 million)	$800,000	$800,000
NOL carryforward to 2020	$700,000	

Farming Businesses

There are special rules for farming businesses. Code Sec. 263A(e)(4) defines a farming business as a business that performs the following:

- Cultivation of land or raising or harvesting of any agricultural or horticultural commodity
  - Examples: Growing crops; operating a nursery or sod farm; raising of or harvesting trees bearing fruit, nuts, or other crops; raising of most ornamental trees
- Raising, shearing, feeding, caring for, training, and management of animals
- Processing activities normally incident to growing, raising, or harvesting of agricultural or horticultural products (Reg. § 1.263A-4(a)(4)(i), (ii))

Under the TCJA, the NOL carryback for farming businesses is limited to 80 percent, detailed in the following example:

Calendar Year Farmer: <$300> Farming Loss, no Code Sec. 461(l), no NOLs		
	Pro-Taxpayer Method*	Blue Book Method*
2018 taxable income: <$300>	<$300> farming loss carried back 2 years to 2016	<$300> farming loss carried back two years to 2016
2016 taxable income: $100 (before NOL)	$80 NOL absorbed (80 percent × $100)	$80 NOL absorbed (80 percent × $100)
2017 taxable income: $200 (before NOL)	$160 NOL absorbed (80 percent × $200)	$160 NOL absorbed (80 percent × $200)
2019: $60 NOL available	$60 NOL available (i.e., $300 – $80 – $160)	$60 NOL available (i.e., $300 – $80 – $160)
* The pro-taxpayer method and Blue Book method yield same result because this fact pattern does not involve both prior law and TCJA NOLs.		

TCJA NOL Changes: Controversy

The lack of Treasury guidance on some of these changes has resulted in NOL computation controversies. For example, the interaction of the charitable contribution carryover and NOL carryover for C corporations is unclear. The current IRS method (ILM 201928014) converts a longer lived NOL carryover to a shorter lived charitable contribution carryover by forcing the taxpayer to compute a Code Sec. 170(d)(2)(B) charitable contribution carryover adjustment for each year an NOL carryover is absorbed. The pro-taxpayer method would not do so.

In addition, there is confusion about the interplay between NOLs and Code Sec. 512(a)(6) where a tax-exempt organization has more than one business and NOL carryovers are flowing in.

AMT NOLs

AMT NOLs remain unchanged at a 90 percent absorption rate. The AMT remains for non–C corporations (individuals, trusts, and estates) after 2017, whereas the C corporation AMT has been eliminated for years beginning after 2017.

STUDY QUESTIONS

1. Which of the following identifies a new loss limitation hurdle post-TCJA?

    a. Code Sec. 163(j)

    b. Basis

    c. At-risk

    d. Passive loss

2. When calculating excess business losses, which of the following identifies the threshold amount in 2020 for single taxpayers?

    a. $255,000

    b. $259,000

    c. $510,000

    d. $518,000

3. Which of the following statements is correct regarding non–C corporation excess business losses?

    a. The CARES Act removed Code Sec. 461(l) for all years.

    b. Form 1065 disclosures regarding Code Sec. 461(l) were removed by the CARES Act starting in 2021.

    c. It is effective after 2020 based on the CARES Act.

    d. Capital gain income does not equal business income.

CARES Act NOL Changes

CARES Act Code Sec. 2303 repeals the 80 percent limit for years beginning before January 1, 2021. This helps C corporations that generated NOLs in 2018, 2019, or 2020. It may help or hurt non–C corporations, depending on the tax rate brackets then, now, and in the future.

Also under the CARES Act, NOLs arising in years after December 31, 2017, and before January 1, 2021, are allowed as carrybacks to each of the five years prior. This helps C corporations that generated NOLs in 2018, 2019, or 2020 to get refunds at up to a 35 percent rate if amended returns are filed. The C corporation AMT existed prior to 2018. This may help or hurt non–C corporations, again depending on the tax rate brackets. They may waive the NOL carryback (the deadline is one year after March 27, 2020). The following chart summarizes the NOL details before and after the TCJA, and in light of the CARES Act:

Net Operating Losses			
	Pre-TCJA	**TCJA**	**CARES Act**
Time frame	Pre-2018	Tax years beginning after 2017*	Retroactive to after 2017
Regular tax absorption rate	100 percent of taxable income in year carried to	80 percent of taxable income in year carried to	100 percent of taxable income in year carried to
Carrybacks	Back two (or three), years, unless elect not to	Back two years (farmers), unless elect not to	For 2018, 2019, 2020, back five years, unless elect not to (elect within one year after March 27, 2020)
Carryforwards	20 years	Forever	Forever

Net Operating Losses			
AMT absorption rate	90 percent of AMTI in year carried to	90 percent of AMTI in year carried to	90 percent of AMTI in year carried to
* As corrected by the CARES Act.			

IRS Guidance on NOLs under the CARES Act

The IRS provides guidance on NOLs under the CARES Act in IR 2020-67 (April 9, 2020). Rev. Proc. 2020-24 outlines the procedures for NOLs carried back (for five years) under the CARES Act.

- For 2018, 2019, and 2020: Taxpayers can waive a carryback period for NOLs arising in a year beginning after December 31, 2017, and before January 1, 2021.

- For the TCJA transition fiscal year: Taxpayers can waive a carryback period, reduce a carryback period, or revoke an election to waive a carryback period for a year beginning before January 1, 2018, and ending after December 31, 2017.

The rules for making elections to waive carrybacks under Code Sec. 172(b)(3) for NOLs arising in taxable years beginning in 2018 or 2019 are as follows (Rev. Proc. 2020-24):

- Taxpayers may elect under Code Sec. 172(b)(3) to waive the carryback period for an NOL arising in year beginning in 2018 or 2019.

- The election must be made no later than the due date, including extensions, for filing the income tax return for the first year ending after March 27, 2020.

- A taxpayer makes the election by attaching to the return filed for the first year ending after March 27, 2020, a separate statement for each of years 2018 or 2019 for which the taxpayer intends to make the election.

- The election statement must state that the taxpayer is electing to apply Code Sec. 172(b)(3) under Rev. Proc. 2020-24 and the year for which the statement applies.

- Once made, the election is irrevocable.

IRS Notice 2020-26 provides a six-month extension to file forms for tentative carryback adjustments (Code Sec. 6411) regarding NOLs arising in 2018 (i.e., NOLs that arose in a year beginning in 2018 and that ended on or after June 30, 2019). To request a quick tentative carryback adjustment, individuals, trusts, and estates file IRS Form 1045; corporations file Form 1139.

To take advantage of the extension of time for requesting a tentative refund based on a 2018 NOL carryback, taxpayers should file the form no later than 18 months after the close of the year in which the NOL arose (no later than June 30, 2020, for a tax year ending December 31, 2018). They should include at the top of the applicable form: "Notice 2020-26, Extension of Time to File Application for Tentative Carryback Adjustment."

Calendar Year*	Due Date	Effect of Notice 2020-26
2018	June 30, 2020	Extended six months
2019	December 31, 2020	Regular due date
2020	December 31, 2021	Regular due date
* For tax years beginning before January 1, 2018, and ending after December 31, 2017, the tentative NOL carryback filing deadline is July 25, 2020. (CARES Act Section 2303(d)(4)(A) providing 120 days after CARES Act date of enactment.)		

¶306

Providing Proof

Because the TCJA allows NOLs to carryforward forever, a taxpayer must be in a position to prove that NOLs carried forward actually exist in the real world. If a taxpayer has an old NOL carrying into a new year, it must be prepared to provide the IRS with the old tax return and backup records that prove the tax return that produced that NOL was valid.

For this and other reasons, old tax returns should not be discarded. According to *Internal Revenue Manual* 4.11.11.13, when the amount of an NOL is material, it constitutes a large, unusual, or questionable item. It is important to determine the correct taxable income in the source year as well as all earlier years that gave rise to the NOL carryforward.

The IRS may redetermine correct taxable income in a closed year to ascertain either the amount of the NOL, or the amount of the NOL absorbed in the closed year to determine the correct NOL deduction for the open year. Code Sec. 7602(a) states: "For purpose of ascertaining correctness of any return, IRS is authorized to examine any books, papers, records or other data which may be relevant or material to such inquiry."

Attaching the NOL Schedule to the Return

Taxpayers must attach an NOL schedule to their tax return showing exactly what year the NOL arose, where it went, how much was absorbed, how much was not used, where it went next, and so forth. According to Reg. § 1.172-1(c): "Every taxpayer claiming a NOL deduction shall file with return a concise statement setting forth amount of NOL deduction claimed and all material and pertinent facts, including a detailed schedule showing the computation of NOL deduction." Failure to attach that schedule can result in the IRS disallowing the NOL on that tax return.

In fact, in *Mark D. Jasperson* (unpublished 11th Circuit memorandum dated 08/31/16), aff'g TCM 2015-186 (09/22/15), Code Sec. 172 NOLs from the operation of an S corporation were disallowed because they were not proven. The court found that the taxpayer failed to attach the detailed NOL schedule to the Form 1040. Backup proof would have been considered, had it been submitted.

¶ 307 QUALIFIED BUSINESS INCOME DEDUCTION (QBID)

The QBID under Code section 199A, which is available for non–C corporations, is a 20 percent deduction for "qualifying pass-through income" (QBI) from S corporations, partnerships, trusts, estates, and sole proprietorships. The QBID is available only to individuals (Form 1040) and trusts and estates (Form 1041); it is not available to C corporations (Form 1120).

The QBID only reduces the income tax effective rate. It does *not*:

- Reduce self-employment income or self-employment tax
- Reduce investment income (Code Sec. 1411)
- Reduce basis in a partnership interest
- Reduce basis in S corporation stock or AAA
- Increase NOLs

The taxpayer need not separately compute the QBID for AMT. Negative QBI (qualified business loss carryover (QBL) reduces QBI in both the current and following year(s).

QBI and Losses

With regard to previously suspended losses, losses or deductions disallowed in years before 2018 (and later allowed) do not reduce QBI in a later year. These include suspended losses (basis limitations), suspended at-risk losses, and suspended passive losses. According to final regulations, such pre-2018 losses are used up in first-in first-out (FIFO) order. However, for 2018 and later years, such losses do reduce QBI in the year allowed on the tax return.

In general, NOLS do not reduce QBI. However, excess business losses under Code Sec. 461(l) (which become part of the NOL carryover) do reduce QBI in the year later allowed.

Provision	Proposed	Final
Portion of loss disallowed under Code Sec. 461(l) excess net loss rule offsets QBI in year later allowed	Yes	Yes
Two types of NOLs to track: 1. NOL (does not offset QBI) 2. QBINOL (EBLNOL) (Code Sec. 461(l) induced) (offsets QBI)	Yes	Yes

¶ 308 CODE SEC. 163(J) BUSINESS INTEREST EXPENSE LIMIT

Under Code Sec. 163(j)(1), for years beginning after December 31, 2017, the deduction for business interest expense (BIE) cannot exceed the sum of:

- Business interest income (BII),
- 30 percent of adjusted taxable income (ATI; cannot be less than zero); and
- Floor financing interest expense (vehicle dealers) (Code Sec. 163(j)(9))

Taxpayers use IRS Form 8990, *Limitation on Business Interest Expense Under Section 163(j)*, to calculate the amount of business interest expense they can deduct and the amount to carry forward to the next year. Exempt small business or excepted business are not subject to the limit.

Code Sec. 163(j) Business Interest Expense Limit		
Interest expense		$4 million
Allowed (limit)	($8 + 2 = $10 mil. (ATI) × 30 percent)	–$3 million
Excess (disallowed) business interest expense carryforward		$1 million

¶ 309 CODE SEC. 163(J): PARTNERSHIPS AND PARTNERS

Code Sec. 163(j) makes retroactive changes that can affect the NOL computation. Partnership income (loss), net of $3 million allowed BIE, passes through Schedule K-1 to the partners. It is not subject to a further Code Sec. 163(j) limit at the partner level.

Code Sec. 163(j) ATI Limit: TCJA Example Partnership – Year 1

For example, assume $1 million of excess (disallowed) business interest expense (EBIE) is split 50/50 ($500,000 each) between the two equal partners. Each partner's basis is reduced by $500,000. EBIE stacks (siloes) the $500,000 at the partner level. The siloed EBIE carryforward for each is offset later only by future ETI and/or EBII from the same partnership.

Code Sec. 163(j) Business Interest Expense Limit		
Interest expense		$4 million
Allowed (limit)	($8 + 2 = $10 million (ATI) x 30%)	–$3 million
EBIE carryforward		$1 million

Code Sec. 163(j) ATI Limit: TCJA Example Partnership – Year 2

Assume the partnership income (loss), net of $4 million allowed BIE, passes through the Schedule K-1 to the partners and is not subject to a further Code Sec. 163(j) limit at the partner level. The $4 million BIE passed through as non-separately stated income (loss) reduces basis in the partnership interest. There is no further Code Sec. 163(j) limitation at the partner level. The $2 million ETI passes to the partners 50/50, $1 million each. It soaks up the siloed $500,000 (from year 1) for each partner from the same partnership.

Code Sec. 163(j) Business Interest Expense Limit		
BIE (includes EBIE)	Year 2: $4 million + EBIE $0	$4 million
Limit	($18 + 2 deprec. = $20 million (ATI) × 30 percent)	$6 million
ETI	$6 million cap – $4 million BEI	$2 million
EBIE carryforward	No EBIE at partnership level	$0

CARES Act Changes to Code Sec. 163(j)

For years beginning in 2019 and 2020, the CARES Act increased the 30 percent of ATI limit to 50 percent (CARES Act Section 2306). Taxpayers can elect out of the 50 percent rule. There is a special rule for partnerships: 50 percent of 2019 excess business interest expense allocated by the partnership to the partner that is deductible by the partner in 2020 is not subject to the Code Sec. 163(j) limit. Partnerships and partners can elect for this rule not to apply.

	2018	2019	2020
BIE Deduction Limit	30 percent × ATI	50 percent × ATI, unless elect out to 30 percent	50 percent ATI, unless elect out to 30 percent
Partnerships	Partnership level EBIE siloed until future ETI from same partnership	Partnership level EBIE siloed until future ETI from same partnership	Partnership level EBIE siloed until future ETI from same partnership. However, 50 percent of siloed BIE from 2019 is allowed, unless elect out

¶ 310 CODE SEC. 168(K) QUALIFIED IMPROVEMENT PROPERTY (QIP)

QIP includes improvements to the interior of a commercial building placed in service after the building was placed in service. It does not include residential, exterior, expansion, or structural improvements, nor elevators and escalators.

The TCJA did not include QIP as bonus-eligible in 15-year property. However, the CARES Act fixed this, retroactively to 2018 and later. The following charts detail the timelines for QIP changes in the TCJA and CARES Act:

Qualified Improvement Property (QIP): TCJA Timeline			
	2015	2016–2017	2018 and Later
39-year property	N/A	Yes	Yes
Bonus eligible	N/A	Yes	No (botched attempt)
Elect out if don't want	N/A	Yes	N/A

Qualified Improvement Property (QIP): TCJA Timeline			
15-year property	N/A	No	No (botched attempt)
Code Sec. 179 eligible	N/A	No	Yes
Elect in if want	N/A	No	Yes

Qualified Improvement Property (QIP): CARES Act Sec. 2307 Timeline			
	2015	2016–2017	2018 and Later
39-year property	N/A	Yes	Yes
Bonus eligible	N/A	Yes	Yes
Elect out if don't want	N/A	Yes	Yes
15-year property	N/A	No	Yes
Code Sec. 179 eligible	N/A	No	Yes
Elect in if want	N/A	No	Yes

Prior to the TCJA, there were three categories of 15-year property:

- Qualified leasehold improvement property (QLIP)
- Qualified retail improvement property (QRIP)
- Qualified restaurant property (QRP)

In the TCJA, Congress collapsed these three categories into QIP. They were intended to be 15-year property (bonus eligible) but inadvertently became 39-year property (not bonus eligible). The CARES Act (CARES Act Section 2307), retroactive to property placed in service after December 31. 2017, renders QIP as 15-year property (20-year ADS [alternative depreciation system]), and bonus eligible under Code Sec. 168(k) (if all bonus requirements are met).

A CARES technical correction notes that used QIP is not eligible for the bonus depreciation; the 15-year recovery period and bonus depreciation only apply to improvements made by the taxpayer (the property must be new QIP).

EXAMPLE: If a taxpayer buys a building containing QIP (that was depreciable by seller), the taxpayer cannot bonus such QIP.

	Post-2017 QIP Before CARES Act	Post-2017 QIP CARES Act	
		Amended Return	Current Year and Forward Form 3115
39-year property	Yes	No	No
15-year property	No	Yes	Yes
Bonus eligible – automatic	No	Yes	Yes
Stay in bonus, bonus elect out, or revoke elect out	N/A	Yes	Yes
Retro via amended return	N/A	Yes*	—
Current year forward via Form 3115	N/A	—	Yes**
Code Sec. 179 eligible	Yes	Yes	Yes
Code Sec. 179 change amended return	Yes	Yes	Yes

* May generate refund of prior year tax.
** Does not generate refund of prior year tax.
For both * and **, the general deadline to file for change is October 15, 2021.

QIP Under the CARES Act: 20-Year ADS Depreciation Retroactive to 2018

CARES Act Section 2307, retroactive to property placed in service after December 31, 2017, renders QIP as 15-year property (20-year ADS). ADS depreciation may be elected or required ADS is required for tax-exempt use property, tax-exempt bond-financed property, property used outside the United States, and other types of property. ADS is required for the following:

- Nonresidential real property, residential real property, and QIP held by an electing real property trade or business (Code Sec. 163(j)(7)(B), Rev. Proc. 2019-8, IRB 2019-3).
- Property with a GDS (general depreciation system) recovery period of 10 years or more held by an electing farming business (Code Sec. 163(j)(7)(C), Rev. Proc. 2019-8, IRB 2019-3).

Rev. Proc. 2020-22 allows taxpayers who previously elected out of Code Sec. 163(j) to make a late election, or withdraw an election under Code Sec. 163(j)(7)(B) or Code Sec. 163(j)(7)(C), as applicable, on an amended federal income tax return, amended Form 1065, or administrative adjustment request (AAR) under Code Sec. 6227.

QIP Placed in Service by a Partnership

Partnerships under the Centralized Partnership Audit (CPAR) regime, also known as BBA (Bipartisan Budget Act) partnerships, file AAR with adjustments taken into account in 2020 by partners who owned interest in the BBA partnership in the year the relevant QIP was placed in service. However, for year 2018 (or later), if the partnership on Form 1065 elected out of the CPAR, then:

- If only 2018 Forms 1065 were filed, an amended Form 1065 is available
- If both 2018 and 2019 forms were filed before the QIP was retroactively claimed, then it appears (for now) that Form 3155 must be filed, making adjustments on such returns filed.

In Rev. Proc. 2020-23, the IRS allows BBA partnerships (those that did not elect out of CPAR) to file amended 2018 and 2019 Forms 1065 (or Form 3115 per usual protocol; watch for IRS guidance as to whether amended return may be filed for 2018 if both 2018 and 2019 have been filed) to retroactively benefit from claiming QIP for property placed in service after 2017 and other tax benefits.

Loss Limitation Hurdles

QIP retroactive changes kick in before any of the following six TCJA loss limitation hurdles (2018 and after):

- Basis (Code Secs. 705 and 1367)
- Code Sec. 163(j) (newly expanded) (amended by the CARES Act)
- At-risk (Code Sec. 465)
- Passive loss (Code Sec. 469)
- Excess loss (Code Sec. 461(l)) (amended by the CARES Act)
- NOL (Code Sec. 172) (major changes by the TCJA) (amended by the CARES Act)

STUDY QUESTIONS

4. Which of the following statements regarding NOLs is correct as a result of the TCJA?

    a. There are no carrybacks for all types of NOLs.

    b. The carryover is limited to 25 years.

    c. The carryover is limited to 75 percent of taxable income.

    d. For NOLs arising in tax years ending after December 31, 2017, the two-year carryback and the special carryback provisions were repealed.

5. The new QBID under TCJA allows for a deduction on qualifying business income of what percentage?

    a. 5 percent

    b. 15 percent

    c. 20 percent

    d. 30 percent

6. The Code Sec. 163(j) deduction for business interest expense cannot exceed the sum of all of the following, *except:*

    a. Business interest income

    b. 30 percent of adjusted taxable income

    c. 15 percent of gross income

    d. Floor financing interest expense

7. Which statement is true regarding qualified improvement property (QIP) under the CARES Act?

    a. QIP is 15-year property.

    b. QIP is 39-year property.

    c. QIP includes elevators and escalators.

    d. Used QIP is eligible for bonus depreciation.

CPE NOTE: When you have completed your study and review of chapters 1-3, which comprise Module 1, you may wish to take the Final Exam for this Module. Go to **cchcpelink.com/printcpe** to take this Final Exam online.

MODULE 2: COVID-19 UPDATES—Chapter 4: The American Rescue Plan Act of 2021: COVID-19 Pandemic Recovery

¶ 401 WELCOME

This chapter reviews the most important tax-related provisions of the American Rescue Plan Act of 2021 as well as provisions of prior stimulus bills that have been extended.

¶ 402 LEARNING OBJECTIVES

Upon completion of this chapter, you will be able to:

- Describe the key features of the American Rescue Plan Act of 2021 that apply to businesses and individual taxpayers
- Explain how provisions of these acts apply in common factual scenarios
- Identify how to determine whether taxpayers are eligible for provided benefits under the new legislation
- Recognize how the American Rescue Plan Act stimulus package applies
- Identify the interest rate on Paycheck Protection Program loans per year

¶ 403 INTRODUCTION

The American Rescue Plan Act of 2021 (ARPA) is a $1.9 trillion stimulus package designed to help America recover from the coronavirus pandemic. Key provisions include allocation of funds for vaccine distribution, schools, small businesses, and anti-poverty programs. The new law extends certain features of the Coronavirus Aid, Relief, and Economic Security (CARES) Act and Consolidated Appropriations Act (CAA), including Paycheck Protection Program (PPP) loans, supplemental unemployment benefits, and employee retention tax credits, as well as adds important new tax provisions such as an expanded child tax credit. The law also provides an immediate direct payment to taxpayers at and below certain income levels.

¶ 404 EXPANDED UNEMPLOYMENT BENEFITS

Although each state administers its own unemployment insurance (UI) program, the states generally follow federal guidelines. Each state UI program determines its eligibility levels; benefit amounts; duration of benefits; whether benefits are charged to employer accounts; and whether UI is available for individuals who are self-employed, unable to work, quit, were fired for misconduct, or refused to accept a job without a good reason (generally, UI is not available in these instances).

Federal Pandemic Unemployment Compensation (FPUC)

The CARES Act created the FPUC program, which is available to individuals who, as determined by the applicable state unemployment agency, meet that state's usual criteria to receive UI benefits. The program provided an increase of a flat payment of $600 per week to the amount regularly available for unemployment under state law, that lasted through July 31, 2020 (approximately four months).

The CAA provided an increase of a flat payment of $300 per week to the amount regularly available for unemployment under state law, from December 26, 2020, though March 14, 2021. The ARPA extended the flat payment of $300 per week to September 6, 2021.

The CAA also created a new program for Mixed Earners Unemployment Compensation (MEUC). The MEUC program is an optional $100 per week supplement to FPUC for individuals who:

- Have received at least $5,000 of self-employment income in the most recent taxable year,
- Are receiving a form of unemployment compensation other than Pandemic Unemployment Assistance, and
- Submit documentation substantiating the claimed self-employment income. MEUC payments are available for weeks of unemployment between December 27, 2020, and March 14, 2021.

The ARPA extended the MEUC program through September 6, 2021.

Pandemic Unemployment Assistance (PUA)

PUA is available to individuals who are not usually eligible for unemployment benefits, including those who are furloughed or out of work as a direct result of COVID-19, self-employed and independent contractors, and those who have exhausted all rights to regular or extended UI benefits under state or federal law.

> **NOTE:** PUA is not available to individuals who have the ability to telework with pay and those who are receiving paid sick leave or other paid benefits (even if they otherwise satisfy the following criteria to receive assistance under the new law).

The CAA extended PUA through April 5, 2021, though no new applicants were eligible for weeks after March 14, 2021. Individuals who were already receiving benefits and had not yet exhausted their entitlement under these programs remained eligible for benefits through April 11, 2021. The ARPA extends these benefits through September 6, 2021.

Applicants for PUA must provide self-certification that they are (1) partially or fully unemployed or (2) unable and unavailable to work for specified reasons. The CAA increased the maximum total benefits from 39 weeks to 50 weeks. The ARPA provides up to 79 weeks of unemployment benefits (and up to 86 weeks for individuals in states with high levels of unemployment).

Unemployment Fraud Prevention

To combat fraud, the CAA requires a claimant to substantiate earnings and employment (as opposed to providing only a self-certification) and directs states to implement a process to verify the claimant's identity. For individuals filing claims on or after January 31, 2021, the claimant must provide documentation substantiating employment or self-employment. Claimants must also provide a self-certification that their unemployment, partial unemployment, or inability to work are attributable to a qualifying reason under the CARES Act and identify the specific reason for each week that PUA is claimed. In addition to these claimant-based obligations, States must prepare and implement procedures for identity verification to validate PUA claims.

Pandemic Emergency Unemployment Compensation (PEUC)

The PEUC program provides additional assistance to those individuals who have exhausted their state law unemployment benefits. Under the CARES Act, the benefits provided eligible individuals up to 13 weeks of benefits and was set to expire on December 31, 2020. The CAA extended benefits to up to 24 weeks and through March 14, 2021. The ARPA extends benefits up to 53 weeks and through September 6, 2021.

¶ 405 BUSINESS TAX PROVISIONS

The CAA and ARPA include several business tax measures to help businesses that are struggling due to the coronavirus pandemic.

Net Operating Loss (NOL) Carrybacks—Farmers

The CAA allows farmers who elected a two-year net operating loss carryback prior to the CARES Act to elect to retain that two-year carryback rather than claim the five-year carryback provided in the CARES Act. It also allows farmers who previously waived the election to carry back a net operating loss to revoke the waiver. These clarifications eliminate unnecessary compliance burdens for farmers. The provision applies retroactively as if included in Section 2303 of the CARES Act.

Real Estate Depreciation

A "real property trade or business" may elect out of the limitation on the deductibility of business interest imposed by Code Sec. 163(j) that was enacted as part of the Tax Cuts and Jobs Act of 2017 (TCJA).

If a real property trade or business makes this election, it is required to use the longer cost recovery periods under the alternative depreciation system (ADS). When the TCJA was enacted, the ADS cost recovery period for residential rental property was reduced from 40 to 30 years. However, due to a drafting error, this reduction in the cost recovery period for residential rental properties applied only to buildings placed into service or acquired in 2018 or later with the result that a real property trade or business with a residential rental property at the end of 2017 that elected out of the limitation on the deductibility of business interest would be required to use the 40-year cost recovery period.

The CAA retroactively corrected the error so that the 30-year cost recovery period is available for all residential rental property regardless of when it was placed into service.

Meals Deduction

The TCJA limited the deductibility of business meal expenses to 50 percent of the cost for food and beverages provided by a restaurant. The CAA permits businesses to deduct 100 percent of these business meals expenses during 2021 and 2022.

Extension of Limitation on Excess Business Losses of Noncorporate Taxpayers

Code Sec. 461(l) was amended to provide that the limitation on the deduction for excess business losses will continue to apply to noncorporate taxpayers for taxable years beginning after December 31, 2017, and before January 1, 2027 (previously January 1, 2026).

Generally, Code Sec. 461(l)(3)(A) provides that an *excess business loss* is the excess of the (1) taxpayer's aggregate trade or business deductions for the tax year over (2) the sum of the taxpayer's aggregate trade or business gross income or gain plus $250,000 (as adjusted for inflation).

Repeal of Election to Allocate Interest on a Worldwide Basis

The ARPA repeals Code Sec. 864(f) in its entirety. Code Sec. 864(f), which first went into effect in the 2021 tax year, would have allowed multinational taxpayers to allocate interest expense on a worldwide basis, altering the computation of the foreign tax credit limitation under Code Sec. 904, which provides for the allocation and apportionment of deductions between U.S.-source and foreign-source income. The repeal of this election will result in the continuation of the pre-2021 policy for allocating interest expense.

"Gig" Reporting Requirements for Third-Party Network Transactions

The ARPA amends Code Sec. 6050W to provide that increased reporting will be required (with a reporting trigger point of $600 instead of the prior law's $20,000 threshold) on IRS Form 1099-K, *Payment Card and Third Party Network Transactions*, starting for payments in 2022. Form 1099-K is an informational return used to report certain payment transactions to the IRS to improve voluntary tax compliance. These amendments will result in an increase in reporting to the IRS by so-called gig economy companies, with the expected corresponding result of an increase in federal taxes paid.

Code Sec. 162(m) Limitation Expanded

Applicable to tax years beginning after December 31, 2026, the ARPA provides a change in the law whereby publicly traded companies are denied deductions for compensation in excess of $1 million for the eight highest-paid employees, plus the chief executive officer and chief financial officer. Under current law, the deduction is denied only for the three highest-paid employees, plus the chief executive officer and chief financial officer. The five additional so-called covered employees will not become permanent covered employees merely because they are included in this next five.

¶ 406 INDIVIDUAL TAX ISSUES

This section reviews several ARPA and other provisions that affect individual taxpayers.

Direct Payment

The ARPA authorizes a third round of COVID-19 stimulus payments, up to $1,400 per eligible individual. These payments are treated as tax credits and therefore are not includible in the recipient's 2021 taxable income.

The stimulus begins to phase out for single taxpayers with adjusted gross income (AGI) between $75,000 and $80,000, heads of household filers with AGI between $112,500 and $120,000, and joint filers without children with AGI between $150,000 and $160,000. No stimulus payment is offered for any taxpayers with AGI greater than the phaseout limits.

Individuals with an AGI of $80,000 or more (or couples with an AGI of $160,000 or more) will not be eligible to receive stimulus payments. Qualifying dependents may include full-time students younger than 24 and other adult dependents. The IRS scheduled over $90 million in stimulus payments to be sent out by March 17, 2021.

Earned Income Tax Credit

For tax year 2021 only, the ARPA will increase the availability of the earned income tax credit (EITC) for childless households, effectively making more taxpayers eligible to claim the EITC. Pursuant to the ARPA, individual taxpayers (with no qualifying children) will see changes to the computation of their EIC, including increases in the phaseout percentage, the earned income amount, and the phaseout amount. The maximum amount of EITC for childless households will increase from $540 to $1,500.

The ARPA includes a provision intended to strengthen the EITC for the 2021 taxable year for individuals with no qualifying children by generally allowing such taxpayers who are age 19 and older (previously age 25 and older) to claim the credit. Additionally, the act, for the 2021 taxable year, eliminates the current maximum age of 64 for receiving the EITC for such taxpayers.

For taxpayers with no qualifying children in the 2021 taxable year, the provision also increases both the credit percentage and phaseout percentage from 7.65 percent to 15.3 percent, as well as increases the EITC amount from $4,220 to $9,820 and the phaseout amount from $5,280 to $11,610.

For purposes of calculating the 2021 EITC, individual taxpayers may choose to use their 2019 income if it was higher than their 2021 income. For all future tax years, including tax year 2021, married individual taxpayers who are separated may be treated as not married for the purpose of the EITC if, and only if, such married individual taxpayers do not file a joint tax return.

Child Tax Credit Changes for 2021

With the intent of bringing more children out of poverty, the ARPA expanded the child tax credit, allowing taxpayers with qualifying children who are 17 or younger to claim the credit for the 2021 taxable year (changed from 16 or younger). In addition, the act increases the credit amount for each qualifying child for the 2021 taxable year from $2,000 to $3,000 ($3,600 for qualifying children who have not attained age 6 as of the close of the calendar year in which the taxable year of the taxpayer begins). As with the stimulus payments, the credit begins to phase out at $150,000 for joint returns or surviving spouses, $112,500 for heads of household, and $75,000 in any other case. The per-child credit amount is reduced by $50 for every $1,000 of modified AGI exceeding the above listed amounts.

Dependent Care Assistance

For 2021 only, the ARPA adjusted the calculation for the credit for dependent care assistance employment expenses. The amount of eligible expenses has been increased, in the case where the taxpayer has one dependent, from $3,000 to $8,000, and where the taxpayer has two or more dependents, from $6,000 to $16,000. The act also increases the percentage of these expenses that may be claimed as a credit from 35 percent to 50 percent. This means a maximum credit of $4,000 in the case of one dependent, or $8,000 for two or more.

The credit begins to phase out when an individual's AGI exceeds $125,000. (There are additional phaseout guidelines for "high-income individuals," those with AGI of more than $400,000). Also for the 2021 taxable year, the credit is refundable.

For taxpayers who receive reimbursements from their employer, there is an exclusion from an individual's gross income of amounts paid by an employer for dependent care assistance; the act increases this exclusion amount from $5,000 to $10,500 (or from $2,500 to $5,250 for a separate return filed by a married individual). This change applies only to the 2021 taxable year.

Exclusion of Unemployment Benefits

The ARPA provides that, for taxpayers whose 2020 modified AGI is less than $150,000, the first $10,200 of unemployment compensation received in 2020 is not included in the taxpayer's 2020 gross income. In the case of a joint return, the first $10,200 per spouse is not included in gross income

Some taxpayers had already filed their returns before the ARPA passed. If taxpayers had included unemployment compensation in their gross income, the IRS will automatically refund those who had already filed their tax returns starting in May of 2021. Taxpayers will not have to amend returns or do anything else for this change. The IRS released instructions on how to calculate and report the excluded amounts, with a special Unemployment Compensation Exclusion Worksheet; see www.irs.gov/forms-pubs/new-exclusion-of-up-to-10200-of-unemployment-compensation.

Student Loan Debt

Federal student loans have been in a forbearance period since March 2020 (scheduled to continue until October 2021). The Biden Administration is also expected to move to cancel some portion of existing federal student loan debt, though it is unclear what amount will be cancelled or when such a move will be made.

The ARPA provides further relief for those with student loans by temporarily changing the income tax treatment of student loan debt cancellation. As part of student loan reform, the act excludes from gross income certain student loans discharged after December 31, 2020, and before January 1, 2026. The provision applies to student loans provided by the federal government, state governments, and eligible educational institutions, as well as certain private education loans as defined in the Truth in Lending Act.

Under prior law, any amount of private or federal student loan debt that is cancelled or forgiven is treated as gross income for the debtor. The ARPA amends Code Sec. 108(f) to exclude any amount of private or federal student loan debt forgiven after December 31, 2020. The ARPA did not make this change permanent, and the revision to Code Sec. 108(f) is scheduled to sunset as of January 1, 2026.

Charitable Contributions

Generally, AGI is gross income less certain deductions (above-the-line deductions). Charitable deductions are itemized deductions that further reduce AGI. They are known as below-the-line-deductions.

The CARES Act added new charitable deductions to the calculation of gross income for tax years beginning in 2020, making them above-the-line deductions. The limit is $300 for individuals; the CARES Act did not address married couples. Under the CAA, a married couple, for contributions paid in calendar year 2021, will be allowed to take such deduction up to $600. This provision is permanent.

The general rule is that individuals are allowed a deduction for cash contributions to certain charitable organizations, subject to AGI limitations. The AGI limitation was increased under the TCJA to 60 percent of AGI in the tax year. The excess can be carried forward for five years. The CARES Act provides that for 2020 only, "qualified contributions" are disregarded in applying the 60 percent AGI limitation on cash contributions to qualifying charitable organizations. The CAA extends this to 2021 only. This means that there is no AGI limitation on charitable contributions for these years.

Retirement Plan Distributions and Loans

The CAA allows a qualified disaster distribution of up to $100,000 to be made from most defined contribution retirement plans (401(k), IRA, etc.) even if the participant does not satisfy the usual hardship distribution rules. No penalty applies.

A *qualified disaster distribution* means any distribution from an eligible retirement plan made on or after the first day of the incident period of a qualified disaster and before the date that is 180 days after the date of the enactment of the CAA (approximately June 25, 2021), and to an individual whose principal place of abode at any time during the incident period of such qualified disaster is located in the qualified disaster area with respect to such qualified disaster and who has sustained an economic loss by reason of such qualified disaster.

¶406

A *qualified disaster* means, with respect to any qualified disaster area, the disaster by reason of which a major disaster was declared with respect to such area.

A *qualified disaster area* is any area with respect to which a major disaster was declared, during the period beginning on January 1, 2020, and ending on the date that is 60 days after the date of the enactment of the CAA (approximately February 25, 2021).

The distribution is not subject to mandatory income tax withholding or the 10 percent penalty tax even if the participant is younger than age 59½. The participant may repay the distribution to the plan (or an IRA) within three years without being taxed on it. If not repaid, the distribution is treated as regular income spread equally over the three-year period from the date of the distribution for federal income tax purposes.

Participants may receive retirement plan loans of up to $100,000 (or 100 percent of their account balance in the plan, if less). The payments may be put on hold for one year, but interest continues to accrue on the loan during the one-year grace period on repayment.

COBRA Subsidy

The Consolidated Omnibus Budget Reconciliation Act (COBRA) allows workers and their families who lose group health benefits for a qualifying reason to continue their health benefits generally for up to 18 months after a qualifying event. Employees typically are responsible for bearing the costs of the extended insurance premiums during the period covered by COBRA.

The ARPA, however, provides a 100 percent subsidy, for up to six months, of the health insurance premiums under COBRA (including any permitted administrative fees) for eligible employees who lost insurance coverage due to an involuntary reduction in hours or involuntary termination. The subsidy period runs from April 1, 2021, until September 30, 2021 (but the period ends sooner if the employee becomes eligible for coverage under another group health plan or the employee's COBRA period ends). The subsidy does not extend an employee's maximum period of COBRA coverage but does allow for qualified employees to retain COBRA coverage at no cost during the subsidy period.

The COBRA subsidy is available to: (1) any eligible individual who is enrolled in COBRA (or will enroll in COBRA) for coverage during the subsidy period; and (2) any former employee (who is otherwise an eligible individual) who did not elect COBRA coverage or dropped COBRA coverage prior to April 1 but would otherwise be within the employee's 18-month COBRA coverage during the subsidy period. Premiums for COBRA-qualified beneficiaries who are eligible for the COBRA subsidy will be paid by the federal government through payroll tax credits against employers' quarterly Medicare taxes.

Obamacare Premium Subsidies

For 2021 and 2022 taxable years, the ARPA increases the subsidies for eligible taxpayers with coverage purchased on the Affordable Care Act (ACA) marketplaces by making the insurance indexing adjustments inapplicable to the 2021 and 2022 tax years. This reduces the applicable premium percentages that are considered when calculating the premium assistance amount. Also for 2021 and 2022, the act further expands the number of taxpayers eligible for assistance by allowing households with taxable income over 400 percent of the poverty line to claim assistance.

¶406

Health Savings Accounts (HSAs) and Flexible Spending Accounts (FSAs)

For plan years ending in 2020 or 2021, the CAA permits cafeteria plans offering health care FSAs and/or dependent care FSAs to include a carryover feature. For plan years ending in 2020, the FSA may allow participants to carry over unused amounts remaining in the FSA at the end of the plan year to the plan year ending in 2021. For plan years ending in 2021, the FSA may allow participants to carry over unused amounts remaining in the FSA at the end of the plan year to the plan year ending in 2022.

For plan years ending in 2020 or 2021, the CAA permits cafeteria plans offering health care FSAs and/or dependent care FSAs with a grace period to extend the grace period to 12 months after the end of the plan year. This increases the maximum grace period length from two months and 15 days to 12 months.

The ARPA further expanded dependent care FSA flexibility by increasing the maximum annual contribution amount from $5,000 ($2,500 for a married individual filing separately) to $10,500 ($5,250 for a married individual filing separately). This is the first time in 35 years that the dependent care FSA maximum has been increased, but for now it only applies to the 2021 plan year. Like the changes described earlier, this is an optional increase for plan sponsors to consider.

Reduction in the Medical Expense Deduction Floor

The CAA permanently reduced the threshold for the medical expense deduction to 7.5 percent of adjusted gross income. Without this provision, the 7.5 percent threshold was set to revert to 10 percent in 2021.

STUDY QUESTIONS

1. The American Rescue Plan Act (ARPA) of 2021 is a _____ trillion stimulus package designed to help America recover from the coronavirus pandemic.

    a. $1.9

    b. $2.3

    c. $3.4

    d. $4.9

2. Regarding unemployment rules, state programs determine each of the following, *except:*

    a. Eligibility levels

    b. Deductibility on federal returns

    c. Benefit amounts

    d. Duration of benefits

3. Which of the following statements is correct regarding federal pandemic unemployment assistance?

    a. It is available to individuals who, as determined by the applicable state unemployment agency, meet that state's usual criteria to receive UI benefits.

    b. The CARES Act provided an increase of a flat payment of $200 per week to the amount regularly available for unemployment under state law.

    c. The CAA provided an increase of a flat payment of $600 per week to the amount regularly available for unemployment under state law.

    d. The ARPA extends the flat payment of $300 per week to December 31, 2021.

4. Regarding pandemic unemployment assistance, the CAA increased the maximum total benefits from 39 weeks to how many weeks?

    a. 42

    b. 46

    c. 50

    d. 75

5. In 2020, a non-itemizing taxpayer can claim an above-the-line charitable contribution (in cash) of up to _____.

    a. $150

    b. $300

    c. $750

    d. $999

6. Based on the CAA, disaster-related retirement plan loans up to what amount may be withdrawn by eligible employees?

    a. $100,000

    b. $150,000

    c. $250,000

    d. $500,000

7. Which of the following tax provisions was made permanent by the CAA?

    a. Treatment of mortgage insurance premiums as qualified residence interest

    b. Personal residence energy improvements

    c. Qualified fuel cell motor vehicle credit

    d. Reduction in the medical expense deduction floor

¶ 407 LOANS AVAILABLE FOR BUSINESSES

The Paycheck Protection Program (PPP) initially provided $349 billion of loan funds to support small businesses and other eligible entities impacted by the COVID-19 pandemic. Eligible expenses included funds to pay workers, interest on mortgage obligations, rent, insurance, paid sick or medical leave, utilities, and payroll related costs incurred from February 15, 2020, to December 31, 2020.

Applicants could apply for a loan up to a maximum of $10 million, from participating lenders. Loan amounts are based on previous payroll and covered cost amounts (2.5 times the average total monthly "payroll costs," up to $10 million). Up to 24 weeks of eligible expenses during the covered period can be forgiven from the loan principal as long as the employer maintains previous payroll counts during this emergency. Other details about PPP loans are as follows:

- The interest rate is 1 percent per annum with term of two years.
- There are no fees for borrowers to apply, and no prepayment fees.
- Loan repayments will be deferred for six months.
- Entities had to be operational by February 15, 2020, had payroll, and paid taxes.
- The covered loan period was from February 15, 2020, to December 31, 2020.

- If the business has already received Small Business Administration (SBA) Economic Injury Disaster Loan (EIDL) and chooses to refinance that loan with a PPP Loan, the outstanding EIDL loan amount can be added to the loan amount, subject to the $10 million cap.
- Applicants generally could apply until August 8, 2020. (Subject to replenishment of depleted funds by Congress).

Borrowers were required to make a good-faith certification that the loan proceeds will be used for:

- Payroll costs
- Costs related to the continuation of group health care benefits during periods of paid sick, medical, or family leave, and insurance premiums
- Employee compensation
- Business-related mortgage interest payments (not principal), lease payments, or utility payments
- Interest on any other business debt obligations that were incurred prior to February 15, 2020

Borrowers are eligible for loan forgiveness equal to the amount spent by the borrower during a 24-week period (8 weeks for borrowers who borrowed early in the program) after the origination date of the PPP loan, for qualified expenditures. The following could be included in the PPP loan forgiveness amount:

- Payroll costs
- Interest payment on a mortgage or debt that originated prior to February 15, 2020
- Payment of rent on a lease that began prior to February 15, 2020
- Payment on any utility for which service began before February 15, 2020

Amounts forgiven may not exceed the principal amount of the loan and accrued interest. Loan proceeds used for any other purposes will not be forgiven, and any cancelled indebtedness will not be included in the borrower's taxable income. No more than 40 percent of nonpayroll costs can be forgiven. The SBA and U.S. Department of the Treasury have offered a great deal of guidance on the specifics of loan forgiveness.

PPP Loans: Round 2

The eligibility for first-time borrowers is largely unchanged from previous guidance, except the bill also expands eligibility to certain 501(c)(6) organizations, which include "destination marketing organizations" and chambers of commerce. For a 501(c)(6) organization to qualify, it must have no more than 300 employees, not receive more than 15 percent of gross receipts from lobbying, and not spend more than $1 million on lobbying activities during the most recent tax year that ended prior to February 15, 2020.

The CAA added operational costs to continue serving customers, such as costs for personal protective equipment (PPE), and administrative costs like cloud computing, software, and consulting to assist with PPP compliance as PPP forgiveness eligible expenses. Further, if an existing borrower has not yet applied for forgiveness, they may also include these types of costs. Borrowers must still spend at least 60 percent of the PPP loan on eligible payroll expenses in order to qualify for full forgiveness.

The CAA allows qualified first-time borrowers as well as second-time borrowers that meet stricter qualifications to obtain a new PPP loan. In addition, if a borrower has returned a portion of funds but has not yet applied for forgiveness, they can reapply to receive the maximum allocation.

A borrower that previously received a PPP loan can obtain a second loan of up to $2 million if they have 300 or fewer employees and can demonstrate a 25 percent reduction in gross receipts in any 2020 calendar quarter, compared to the same quarter in 2019. The maximum loan amount for a second draw will be the same as the first round (2.5 times monthly average payroll), except for businesses in the accommodations and food service sector, which will be eligible for 3.5 times monthly average payroll.

The CARES Act originally provided for an 8-week covered period (time in which borrower must use loan proceeds to qualify for forgiveness) beginning on the day loan proceeds were disbursed; subsequent amendments allowed borrowers to alternatively elect for a 24-week covered period. PPP Round 2 borrowers will be permitted to choose the length of their covered period provided it is no less than 8 weeks and no more than 24 weeks.

Eligible expenses. Previously, PPP proceeds were to be used for payroll, rent, covered mortgage interests, and utilities in order to qualify for 100 percent forgiveness. Pursuant to the CAA, PPP proceeds may also be allocated to the following expenses:

- **Operation expenditures:** Software and cloud computing service payments used to facilitate, without limitation, business operations, service or product delivery, payroll, processing, billing, accounting, inventory and human resources (HR) functions.

- **Supplier costs:** Payments to suppliers of goods that are essential to operations at the time made pursuant to an order or contract in effect prior to the covered period (or in effect at any time during the covered period if goods are perishable).

- **Property damage:** Costs related to any public disturbances that occurred in 2020, to the extent not covered by insurance or other compensation.

- **Worker protection costs:** Costs related to compliance with regulations issued by the Centers for Disease Control and Prevention (CDC), the Department of Health and Human Services (HHS), the Occupational Safety and Health Administration (OSHA), or any state or local government authority after the period beginning on March 1, 2020, and ending on the date when the national emergency declared by the president related to COVID-19 safety measures expires.

Expenses deductible. During 2020, the IRS issued Notice 2020-32, which allowed a forgiven PPP loan to be nontaxable but barred a taxpayer from deducting expenses used toward forgiveness. The IRS confirmed the position in November. The CAA clarifies that for both original and subsequent PPP loans, "no deduction shall be denied, no tax attribute shall be reduced, and no basis increase shall be denied, by reason of the exclusion from gross income provided" by Section 1106 of the CARES Act.

Simplified forgiveness. The CAA creates a simplified forgiveness application for loans of $150,000 or less. The form is to be no longer than one page and would require a borrower to certify use of the funds without providing any documentation to the bank at the time of the application. The SBA and the Treasury Department recently published updated loan forgiveness guidance and forms, including a one-page application for borrowers that received a PPP loan of $150,000 or less. (Form 3508S). No documentation is required to be submitted with this form, but borrowers must retain supporting info for potential loan review or audit.

The SBA and the Treasury also released two other new PPP loan forgiveness applications, Form 3508 and Form 3508EZ. The CAA also reverses previous legislation that required a borrower's PPP forgiveness to be reduced by any EIDL advance received.

¶407

PPP Loans: Round 3

The original deadline to apply for PPP loans under the ARPA was March 31, 2021. However, the PPP Extensions Act was passed by Congress and the president signed it into law on March 30, 2021, extending the deadline to apply for PPP loans to May 31, 2021.

The eligibility requirements for small business and nonprofit PPP loans under the ARPA are essentially the same as they were under the CARES Act. Under the ARPA (and the CARES Act), most small businesses or nonprofit organizations are potentially eligible to receive a PPP loan if the organization employs 500 employees or fewer. However, some entities could benefit from elevated employee caps established by the SBA for certain industries.

The ARPA also provides that small businesses or nonprofit organizations with more than one physical location are eligible to receive a PPP loan if they employ no more than 500 employees *per physical location.* This is an important expansion of PPP eligibility that creates a new class of potential beneficiaries.

Under the CAA and ARPA, businesses are now eligible to take the employee retention credit even if they previously received PPP funding and loan forgiveness, as long as the payroll and expenses identified for the employee retention credit were not paid using PPP funds.

¶ 408 EMPLOYER FILING DEADLINE DEFERRALS AND CREDITS

Under the CARES Act, the employee retention credit is a refundable tax credit against certain employment taxes equal to 50 percent of the qualified wages an eligible employer pays to employees after March 12, 2020, and before January 1, 2021. Eligible employers can get immediate access to the credit by reducing employment tax deposits they are otherwise required to make. Also, if the employer's employment tax deposits are not sufficient to cover the credit, the employer may get an advance payment from the IRS.

For each employee, wages (including certain health plan costs) up to $10,000 can be counted to determine the amount of the 50 percent credit. Because this credit can apply to wages already paid after March 12, 2020, many struggling employers can get access to this credit by reducing upcoming deposits or requesting an advance credit on Form 7200, *Advance of Employer Credits Due to COVID-19.*

Employers, including tax-exempt organizations, are eligible for the credit if they operate a trade or business during calendar year 2020 and experience either of the following:

- The full or partial suspension of the operation of their trade or business during any calendar quarter because of governmental orders limiting commerce, travel, or group meetings due to COVID-19; or

- A significant decline in gross receipts.

The CAA made the following changes to the employee retention credit:

- The credit is extended through June 30, 2021 (wages paid January 1 to June 30).

- The credit percentage is increased from 50 percent to 70 percent.

- The per employee limitation is increased from $10,000 in total to $10,000 per quarter.
- The threshold for the change in treatment of qualified wages is raised to more than 500 employees.
  - Employers with more than 500 employees can claim the credit only for employees who are paid *not* to work.
- An eligible quarter requires a gross receipts decline of more than 20 percent instead of more than 50 percent.
- There is an election to use the prior quarter's gross receipts for purposes of determining if the company's gross receipts were less than 80 percent of gross receipts compared to the same quarter in 2019. IRS Notice 2021-23 (April 2, 2021) provides that this election to use the prior quarter's gross receipts is exercised by claiming the employee retention credit for the quarter using the alternative quarter to calculate gross received.
- Rules are provided allowing new employers that were not in existence for all or part of 2019 to be able to claim the credit.

The preceding changes apply to calendar quarters beginning after December 31, 2020. Employees who receive PPP loans may still qualify for this credit with respect to wages that are not paid with forgiven PPP proceeds (retroactive to the effective date of the CARES Act).

The ARPA made several changes to the credit as well. Under the act:

- The credit is extended through December 31, 2021 (wages paid July 1 through Dec 31).
- The credit percentage stays at 70 percent (including cost of health benefits).
- An eligible quarter requires a gross receipts decline of more than 20 percent.
- The election to use the prior quarter's gross receipts for purposes of determining if the company's gross receipts were less than 80 percent of gross receipts compared to the same quarter in 2019 is extended to the third and fourth quarters of 2021. Under this election, a company could use its second quarter 2021 gross receipts compared to its second quarter 2019 gross receipts to determine credit eligibility for the third quarter, and could use its third quarter 2021 gross receipts to determine credit eligibility for the fourth quarter 2021.
- The ARPA allows a recovery startup business (RSB) to take the credit (subject to a maximum credit of $50,000 per quarter) even if neither of the above conditions occur. An RSB is a business that (1) began business on or after February 15, 2020; (2) has no more than $1,000,000 in average annual gross receipts over the prior three years; and (3) is not otherwise eligible for the credit because the business was not shut down per a COVID-19 lockdown order and did not have a significant reduction in gross receipts compared to the same quarter in 2019.
- The 500-employee threshold as in the CAA continues, but the ARPA adds a new category, severely financially distressed employer (SFDE). This is a company whose gross receipts for the quarter are less than 10 percent of gross receipts for the same quarter in 2019 (i.e., a reduction in gross receipts of more than 90 percent). A SFDE is allowed the credit if its employees are performing services, even if it had more than 500 employees in 2019. This would potentially apply to companies in severely distressed industries, such as the cruise, hospitality, and entertainment industries. Because the effective date of the ARPA is July 1, 2021, however, a SFDE will only be eligible to claim the credit for the second two quarters of 2021.

Tax Credits for Providing Leave

The CAA does not extend the December 31, 2020, expiration date for mandated paid-leave obligations under the Families First Act (FFA). As of January 1, 2021, employers are no longer required to provide paid sick leave or expanded Family and Medical Leave Act (FMLA) paid leave to their employees related to the COVID-19 pandemic, and employees are no longer entitled to paid leave under the Families First Coronavirus Response Act (FFCRA).

However, for employers who voluntarily extend the FFA paid leave benefits, the CAA extends through March 31, 2021, the period in which employers can claim a payroll tax credit for such leave. The tax credit is only available to paid leave that would otherwise qualify under the FFA. Employers may choose to continue providing paid leave under the FFA (including emergency paid sick leave and/or expanded FMLA paid leave) through March 31 and continue taking a payroll-tax credit up to the daily and aggregate limits under the FFCRA. As noted, employers are not *required* to provide additional paid leave after December 31.

The ARPA extends this period from April 1, 2021, to September 30, 2021. In addition to the reasons for paid sick leave under the FFCRA and CAA, the ARPA includes two additional qualifying circumstances:

- An employee seeking or awaiting the results of a diagnostic test for, or a medical diagnosis of, COVID–19, and such employee has been exposed to COVID–19, or the employee's employer has requested such test or diagnosis, or

- The employee is obtaining immunization related to COVID-19 or recovering from any injury, disability, illness, or condition related to such immunization.

The tax credit is available for a new bank of 80 hours of emergency paid sick leave (EPSL) for full-time employees beginning April 1, 2021. For part-time employees, the employer may use the work hours averaged over two weeks. The credit is up $200 per day for individuals caring for an individual in quarantine or due to school closures and daycare provider closures and up to $511 for all other reasons.

How to get the credits. According to the IRS, eligible employers that pay qualifying sick and/or child-care leave will be able to retain an amount of federal payroll taxes equal to the amount of qualifying sick and child-care leave payments rather than depositing the federal payroll taxes with their quarterly payroll tax returns to the IRS. Per the IRS release, the payroll taxes available for retention are withheld federal income taxes, the employee share of Social Security and Medicare taxes, and the employer share of Social Security and Medicare taxes "with respect to all employees."

In the event that the amount of payroll taxes retained is insufficient to cover qualifying sick and child-care leave payments made by an employer, an employer will be able to file a request for an accelerated payment from the IRS, which the IRS expects to process within two weeks or less. Under the examples provided by the IRS, the amount of qualifying leave credit is deducted from the amount of payroll taxes withheld and payable to the IRS.

Local governments. Previously, state and local government employers were not eligible for these tax credits. Now, state and local public employers can apply the wages paid for sick leave and family leave as a credit against their employer contributions for Social Security and Medicare taxes (FICA taxes). These credits must be applied to leave taken after April 1 and before Sept. 30.

Under the ARPA, agencies or instrumentalities of the U.S. government are not able to receive tax credits for EPSL and EFMLA payments. However, state or local governments are not agencies or instrumentalities of the U.S. government. Rather, they are political subdivisions of their particular state. Previously, the FFCRA stated, "this credit shall not apply to the Government of the United States, the government of any State or political subdivision thereof, or any agency or instrumentality of any of the foregoing." By the plain language, local public employers are not precluded from using tax credits.

STUDY QUESTIONS

8. To combat fraud, the CAA requires a claimant to substantiate earnings and _____.

   a. Employment

   b. Age

   c. Citizenship

   d. Intent

9. Which of the following Internal Revenue Code Sections related to the limitation on the deduction for excess business losses was amended as a result of the ARPA?

   a. Code Sec. 864(f)

   b. Code Sec. 6050W

   c. Code Sec. 162(m)

   d. Code Sec. 461(l)

10. Which of the following statements is correct regarding the ARPA direct payment to individuals?

   a. Qualifying dependents may include full-time students younger than 24 and other adult dependents.

   b. The payments are treated as taxable income.

   c. The ARPA authorizes a third round of COVID-19 stimulus payments, up to $2,700 per eligible individual.

   d. The stimulus begins to phase out for single taxpayers with adjusted gross income between $150,000 and $175,000.

11. Which of the following statements is correct regarding the earned income tax credit (EITC)?

   a. The maximum amount of EITC for childless households will increase to $5,500.

   b. For the tax year 2021 only, the ARPA will increase the availability of the earned income tax credit for childless households.

   c. For taxpayers with no qualifying children in the 2021 taxable year, the provision does not increase the credit percentage and phaseout percentage.

   d. For purposes of calculating the 2021 EITC, individual taxpayers may choose to use their 2018 income if it was higher than their 2021 income.

¶ 409 MISCELLANEOUS PROVISIONS

There are other provisions in the stimulus legislation as well. For example, federal rental assistance is included for families affected by COVID-19, applicable to past-due rent, future rent payments, and utility and energy bills. Pandemic assistance grants will be made to eligible businesses serving food or drinks, including restaurants and food trucks. In addition, new targeted EIDL grants will be available for eligible small businesses in low-income communities.

Direct Aid to State and Local Governments

The ARPA provides a total of $350 billion in assistance to states, counties, municipalities, territories and tribal governments to cover expenses, make up for lost revenue and ease the overall economic impact from the COVID-19 pandemic. Funds allocated from each of the State Fiscal Recovery Funds and Local Fiscal Recovery Funds may be used to:

- Respond to the COVID-19 emergency and address its economic effects, including through aid to households, small businesses, nonprofits, and impacted industries such as tourism and hospitality.
- Provide premium pay to essential employees of state or local governments or make grants to the employers of essential employees. Premium pay may not exceed $13 per hour or $25,000 per worker.
- Provide government services to the extent of any revenue reduction resulting from COVID-19.
- Make investments in water, sewer, and broadband infrastructure.

All funds must be spent on costs incurred on or before December 31, 2024. State and local governments cannot use the funds to make pension payments. States also cannot use the funds to offset revenue losses resulting from any tax cut, tax delay, or tax rebate enacted after March 3, 2021 (this may be subject to change).

Deadlines Extended to May 17, 2021

Individual taxpayers could postpone federal income tax payments for the 2020 tax year due on April 15, 2021, to May 17, 2021, without penalties and interest, regardless of the amount owed. Individual taxpayers would automatically avoid interest and penalties on the taxes paid by May 17.

This relief did not apply to estimated tax payments that were due on April 15, 2021. These payments were still due on April 15.

In extending the deadline to file Form 1040 series returns to May 17, the IRS automatically postponed to May 17, 2021, the deadline for individuals to make 2020 contributions to their individual retirement arrangements (IRAs and Roth IRAs), HSAs, Archer medical savings accounts (Archer MSAs), and Coverdell education savings accounts (Coverdell ESAs).

EIDL

The ARPA provides another $15 billion for EIDL advance grants. Small businesses in low-income communities are eligible for EIDL grants of up to $10,000; $5 billion is reserved for $5,000 grants to businesses that experienced a revenue loss of more than 50 percent and have no more than 10 employees. EIDL loans are provided directly to small businesses by the SBA and can reach up to $2 million over 30 years.

> **NOTE:** In a Procedure Notice issued on June 19, 2020, the SBA noted the following regarding the intersection between EIDL and PPP loans:
>
> - If a business received an SBA EIDL loan from January 31, 2020, through April 3, 2020, and its EIDL loan was not used for payroll costs, then its EIDL loan is not required to be refinanced with its PPP loan.

¶409

- If a business received an SBA EIDL loan from January 31, 2020, through April 3, 2020, and its EIDL loan was used for payroll costs, then its PPP loan must be used to refinance the full amount of its EIDL loan.

- If a business received an SBA EIDL loan before January 31, 2020, or after April 3, 2020, then its EIDL loan may not be refinanced with its PPP loan.

The amount of the EIDL loan to be refinanced does not include the amount of any EIDL "advance" (also referred to as an EIDL "grant") received by the business, because the EIDL advance does not need to be repaid.

¶ 410   AID TO PARTICULAR INDUSTRIES

The ARPA appropriates $28,600,000,000 for fiscal year 2021 to struggling restaurants, to be administered by the SBA. Eligible entities include restaurants or other specified food businesses, including such businesses operating in an airport terminal. It does not include a state or local government operated business, or a company that as of March 13, 2020, operates in more than 20 locations, whether or not the locations do business under the same name. It also does not include any business that has a pending application for, or has received, a grant under the Economic Aid to Hard-Hit Small Businesses, Non-Profits and Venues Act.

Restaurant Revitalization Program

To qualify for assistance under this program, an applicant must be one of the following:

- A restaurant

- A food stand

- A food truck or food cart

- A caterer

- A saloon, inn, tavern, bar, lounge, brewpub, tasting room, or licensed facility or premise of a beverage alcohol producer where the public may taste, sample or purchase products

- Another place of business in which the public or patrons assemble for the primary purpose of being served food or drink.

Eligible entities can qualify for a grant amount of the pandemic-related revenue loss. Pandemic-related revenue loss is calculated using gross receipts, as established using such verification documentation as the SBA may require, of the eligible entity during 2020 subtracted from the gross receipts of the entity in 2019.

If the entity was not in operation for the entirety of 2019, then the calculation is the difference between (1) multiplying the average monthly gross receipts in 2019 by 12 and (2) multiplying the average monthly gross receipts in 2020 by 12. There may be other formulas determined by the SBA.

NOTE: The calculated amount of the grant will be *reduced* by unrepaid PPP loans (not reduced by EIDLs or employee retention credits).

An *affiliated business* is defined as "a business in which an eligible entity has an equity or right to profit distributions of not less than 50 percent, or in which an eligible entity has the contractual authority to control the direction of the business, provided that such affiliation shall be determined as of any arrangements or agreements in existence as of March 13, 2020."

Grants provided from the Restaurant Revitalization Fund will equal the pandemic-related revenue loss of the eligible entity with a cap of $10 million for each eligible entity (together with affiliated businesses) and $5 million per physical location for each eligible entity. To receive a grant, eligible entities must certify as follows:

- The uncertainty of current economic conditions makes necessary the grant request to support the ongoing operations of the eligible entity.
- The eligible entity has not applied for or received a grant under Section 324 of the Economic Aid to Hard-Hit Small Businesses, Nonprofits, and Venues Act.

Restaurant Revitalization Fund grants can be used for the following expenditures during the covered period (currently February 15, 2020–December 31, 2021):

- Payroll costs
- Mortgage principal or interest (except for prepayment of principal)
- Rent (excluding prepayment of rent)
- Utilities
- Maintenance expenses, including construction of outdoor seating and furniture, fixtures and equipment
- Supplies, including protective equipment and cleaning materials
- Food and beverage expenses (not yet clear whether alcohol counts)
- Covered supplier costs
- Operational expenses
- Paid sick leave
- Other expenses that the SBA determines to be essential to maintaining the eligible entity

Funds not used for these purposes must be repaid.

An eligible entity can use grant funds for eligible expenses incurred from February 15, 2020, until December 31, 2021. The SBA may extend this covered period an additional 14 months, until March 11, 2023, and has the authority to extend it up to two years after enactment of the Restaurant Revitalization Fund Grant (RRFG) program. If an entity cannot use all grant funds or permanently ceases operations on or before December 31, 2021 (or a date extended by SBA), the entity must return the unused funds to the U.S. Department of Treasury.

The following can disqualify an entity from RRFG eligibility:

- As of March 13, 2020, the entity owns or operates (together with any affiliated business) more than 20 locations, regardless of whether those locations do business under the same or multiple names.
- The entity has received a Shuttered Venues Operations Grant (SVOG) or has a pending SVOG application.
- The entity is a publicly traded corporation or is majority owned and controlled by a publicly traded corporation.
- The entity does not have a place of business located in the United States, does not operate primarily within the United States, and does not make a significant contribution to the U.S. economy through payment of taxes or use of American products, materials, or labor.
- The entity is a state- or local government-owned or operated business.
- The entity is permanently closed.

- The entity filed for bankruptcy under Chapter 7 or is liquidating under Chapter 11.

- The entity has filed for bankruptcy under Chapter 11, 12, or 13 but does not have an approved plan for reorganization.

Gross receipts mean all revenue in whatever form received or accrued from whatever source, including from the sales of products or services, interest, dividends, rents, royalties, fees, or commissions, reduced by returns and allowances. Generally, receipts are considered *total income* (or in the case of a sole proprietorship, gross income) plus *cost of goods sold* as these terms are defined and reported on IRS tax return forms—these include Form 1120 for corporations; Form 1120-S for S corporations; Form 1120, Form 1065, or Form 1040 for limited liability companies (LLCs); Form 1065 for partnerships; and Form 1040, Schedule C for other sole proprietorships.

Receipts do not include net capital gains or losses; taxes collected for and remitted to a taxing authority if included in gross or total income, such as sales or other taxes collected from customers and excluding taxes levied on the concern or its employees; proceeds from transactions between a concern and its domestic or foreign affiliates; and amounts collected for another by a travel agent, real estate agent, advertising agent, conference management service provider, freight forwarder or customs broker.

Subcontractor costs, reimbursements for purchases a contractor makes at a customer's request, investment income, and employee-based costs such as payroll taxes are not excluded from receipts. Currently, it is unclear whether other COVID-19 stimulus funds will be included.

Shuttered Venue Operators Grant (SVOG) Program

The SVOG program includes over $16 billion in grants to shuttered venues, such as live venue operators or promoters, theatrical producers, live performing arts organization operations, museum operators, motion picture theater operators, and talent representatives.

To be eligible, applicants generally must have experienced not less than a 25 percent reduction in gross earned revenue between corresponding quarters in 2019 and 2020 and must have been "fully operational" on February 29, 2020. The proposed regulations outline additional eligibility requirements for each business type, as well as characteristics that make an entity ineligible related to funding, ownership, and more.

Eligible applicants may qualify for SVOGs equal to 45 percent of their 2019 gross earned revenue, with the maximum amount available for a single grant award of $10 million. (Applicants that began operations after January 1, 2019, may qualify for the lesser of $10 million or their average monthly gross earned revenue for each full month in operation during 2019 multiplied by six.)

The amount of $2 billion is reserved for eligible applications with up to 50 full-time employees. The proposed regulations state that the SBA will review complete applications in the order in which it receives them, based on the availability of funds and priorities related to the extent of the applicant's revenue loss.

Use of funds. Grant funds must be used for the following:

- Payroll costs

- Certain covered rent, utility, or scheduled mortgage or debt payments (not including prepayment of principal)

- Defined "covered worker protection expenditures"

- Payments to independent contractors as reported on Form 1099-MISC, "not to exceed a total of $100,000 in annual compensation for any individual employee of an independent contractor"
- Other "ordinary and necessary business expenses," including:
  — Maintenance expenses
  — Administrative costs, including fees and licensing costs
  — State and local taxes and fees
  — Operating leases in effect as of February 15, 2020
  — Insurance payments
  — "Advertising, production transportation, and capital expenditures related to producing a theatrical or live performing arts production, concert, exhibition, or comedy show, except that a grant under this section may not be used primarily for such expenditures."

Grant funds *cannot* be used:

- To purchase real estate
- To make investments or loans
- For payments of interest or principal on loans originated after February 15, 2020
- "For contributions or expenditures to, or on behalf of, any political party, party committee, or candidate for elective office"
- "For any other use as may be prohibited by the Administrator."

Under the CAA, businesses that applied for or received a PPP loan prior to December 27, 2020, were eligible to apply for a SVOG, but if a business applied for a first- or second-draw loan on or after that date, it would not be eligible for a SVOG, unless the PPP loan was declined.

The ARPA changed the rules so that an entity that receives a first-or second-draw PPP loan after December 27, 2020, can apply for a SVOG, though its SVOG grant would be reduced by the amount of any PPP loans received after that date. (Amounts received before December 27, 2020, do not reduce the SVOG amount.) However, if the business is approved for a SVOG before it receives a PPP loan number, it is then ineligible for the PPP loan.

Applications. Preliminary application checklists are available on the SBA website at: https://www.sba.gov/sites/default/files/2021-03/3-11-21%20SVOG%20application%20checklist-508.pdf. All applicants need financial documents, corporate documents, a written statement of need, and a certification that the uncertainty of current economic conditions makes the grant necessary to support the ongoing operations of the eligible person or entity, among other assurances related to operations and use of funds. Also, other detailed information is required depending on the type of applicant.

SVOG applications are accepted on a first-in, first-out basis, and funds are allocated to applicants to the respective priority periods as applications are received. The first 14 days of SVOG awards, which were expected to begin being paid out in late April, were to be dedicated to entities that suffered a 90 percent or greater revenue loss between April and December 2020 due to the COVID-19 pandemic.

The second 14 days (days 15–28) were to include entities that suffered a 70 percent or greater revenue loss between April and December 2020. Following those periods, SVOG awards will include entities that suffered a 25 percent or greater revenue loss between one quarter of 2019 and the corresponding quarter of 2020.

¶410

Aid to Affected Industries

The stimulus legislation also includes aid to other industries affected by the pandemic. The aerospace industry was offered payroll support, and loans were made available to socially disadvantaged farmers and ranchers. Aid for the healthcare sector includes vaccine distribution funding, Medicare reimbursements, and direct grants. There were also direct grants available for higher education and some student loan forgiveness. Indian Tribal governments could apply for direct grants as well.

STUDY QUESTIONS

12. Which of the following statements is correct regarding PPP Round 3 under the ARPA?

    a. The ARPA provides that small businesses with more than one physical location are eligible to receive a PPP loan if they employ no more than 500 employees per physical location.

    b. The eligibility requirements for small business and nonprofit PPP loans under ARPA are very different compared to the CARES Act.

    c. Under the ARPA, most small businesses or nonprofit organizations are potentially eligible to receive a PPP loan if the organization employs 5,000 employees or fewer.

    d. Under the CAA and ARPA, businesses are ineligible to take the Employee Retention Credit if they previously received PPP funding and loan forgiveness.

13. The ARPA provides a total of _____ billion in assistance to states, counties, municipalities, territories and tribal governments to cover expenses, make up for lost revenue and ease the overall economic impact from the COVID-19 pandemic.

    a. $248

    b. $350

    c. $475

    d. $568

14. Which of the following identifies the approximate amount appropriated to struggling restaurants to be administered by the SBA?

    a. $13.4 billion

    b. $28.6 billion

    c. $34.6 billion

    d. $47.5 billion

15. Which of the following statements is correct regarding the SVOG program?

    a. It includes nearly $45 billion in grants to shuttered venues.

    b. To be eligible, applicants generally must have experienced not less than a 50 percent reduction in gross earned revenue between corresponding quarters in 2019 and 2020.

    c. $2 billion is reserved for eligible applications with up to 50 full-time employees.

    d. Eligible applicants may qualify for SVOGs equal to 75 percent of their 2019 gross earned revenue.

CPE NOTE: When you have completed your study and review of chapter 4, which comprises Module 2, you may wish to take the Final Exam for this Module. Go to **cchcpelink.com/printcpe** to take this Final Exam online.

MODULE 3: TAX DEVELOPMENTS AND UPDATES—Chapter 5: Cryptocurrency and Taxes

¶ 501 WELCOME

This chapter presents a basic overview of cryptocurrency. It outlines the history of virtual currencies, explains how they work, and outlines the advantages and disadvantages of using them. The IRS rules for tracking and reporting cryptocurrency transactions for tax purposes are also discussed.

¶ 502 LEARNING OBJECTIVES

Upon completion of this chapter, you will be able to:

- Describe cryptocurrency
- Identify the tax implications of using cryptocurrency
- Recognize characteristics of blockchain technology
- Recognize which federal agencies want to regulate initial coin offerings
- Differentiate which type of virtual currency wallet is the safest from online hacking
- Recognize how the IRS requires virtual currencies to be reported

¶ 503 INTRODUCTION

As our world becomes more digital, the use of virtual currencies is on the rise. Although there are still challenges to the widespread adoption of virtual currencies, an increasing number of governments, businesses, and individuals are investigating the use of virtual currency transactions.

¶ 504 WHAT IS VIRTUAL CURRENCY?

Virtual currency can be defined as virtual money. It is issued by its developers and used within a given virtual community. The European Banking Authority defines virtual currency as "a digital representation of value that is neither issued by a central bank or a public authority, nor necessarily attached to a fiat currency, but is accepted by natural or legal persons as a means of payment and can be transferred, stored or traded electronically."

The definition of virtual currency from the Financial Crimes Enforcement Network (FinCEN) of the U.S. Department of the Treasury is similar: "a medium of exchange that operates like a currency in some environments, but does not have all the attributes of real currency." In particular, virtual currency does not have legal tender status in any jurisdiction. The IRS defines virtual currency as property, not as a currency.

There are different types of virtual currencies. *Closed virtual currencies* are used in a closed community, most commonly multiplayer online games. The currency is fictional and has no value outside the game. Game rules often prohibit players from buying and selling the currency outside of the game.

Single flow virtual currencies are similar to coupons. Common examples are frequent flyer miles with airlines and Amazon Coin. The currency can be purchased, or provided with a purchase, and can be used to purchase goods and services from a provider but cannot be purchased or exchanged on an open market.

Convertible virtual currencies can be purchased and sold on exchanges and used to complete transactions with individuals, businesses, and governments. Bitcoin is the most well-known convertible virtual currency.

A *cryptocurrency* is a digital currency using cryptography to secure transactions and to control the creation of new currency units. Not all virtual currencies use cryptography, so cryptocurrencies are a subset of virtual currencies.

Although there are many advantages to using virtual currencies, there are disadvantages as well. These are listed in the following table:

Advantages and Disadvantages of Using Virtual Currencies	
Advantages	**Disadvantages**
• No intermediary	• Volatility and risk
• Anonymity	• Hacking and theft
• Transparency	• Growth industry (bugs)
• Low fees	• Wallets can be stolen
• Irreversible transactions	• No buyer protections
• Worldwide use and access	• No guarantee of value
• No tracking	• No physical form
• No third-party seizure	

Blockchain

Virtual currencies are based on a technology known as blockchain. Blockchains are lists of records held on diverse computers (nodes) that are used to record and verify data. There are two types of blockchain platforms, *public* and *private*.

A public blockchain, such as the one used to power Bitcoin and other cryptocurrencies, is on all kinds of computers all over the world. Anybody who is mining Bitcoins or other cryptocurrency is allowing the use of their computer to record these transactions. They are acting as a node, and they get paid in the cryptocurrency for allowing their computer to be used as a node. Public blockchains are all over the world. Nobody is controlling who is involved in the network; it is usually an open source network.

Private blockchains, on the other hand, are held by organizations. For example, banking institutions might set up private blockchains for a companywide cryptocurrency. The blockchain works within the banking system, and all the data is stored on the bank's computers.

Blockchain transactions are recorded on nodes all over the world, and virtually anybody can see them. If the transactions are encrypted, criminals may be able to see the data but may not be able to decrypt it and see what is in the file itself. How is cryptocurrency transferred? There are two keys: a public key and a private key. When these two keys match up, users get a digital signature that allows them to transfer the ownership of some or all the cryptocurrency that they have stored on the blockchain. Note that the cryptocurrency doesn't transfer; it stays at the same place on the blockchain. Only the right to access the cryptocurrency transfers.

The public key is stored on the blockchain itself, so the public key is always available. The private key is what someone keeps in their wallet. The private key allows them to access the cryptocurrency. You match up the private key to the public key. And they're not the same, obviously, but the two of them together combine to allow someone to complete a transaction with that cryptocurrency.

Because the public key is a long string of alphanumeric characters, it is very difficult for anyone to guess it, even using computer speeds. It is not easy to circumvent that piece of security.

History of Bitcoin

Bitcoin, the first cryptocurrency, was released in 2009. Today, there are thousands of different types of crypto coins on the market. According to legend, Satoshi Nakamoto began working on the Bitcoin concept in 2007. Although he is on record as living in Japan, it is speculated that Nakamoto may be a collective pseudonym for more than one person. The following paragraphs present a timeline of important developments in the history of Bitcoin:

2009. The first Bitcoin was mined on January 3, 2009, and the first Bitcoin transaction occurred three days later. An exchange rate for Bitcoin versus U.S. dollars was established on October 5, 2009.

2010. On February 6, 2010, the first Bitcoin exchange was established. Mt. Gox, a Bitcoin exchange based in Japan, was established later that year on July 1. On August 15, 2010, a vulnerability in the Bitcoin system that causes Bitcoins to be improperly verified was discovered and exploited, resulting in the generation of 184 billion Bitcoins.

The Financial Action Task Force, an intergovernmental group that develops and promotes policies to prevent money laundering and funding of terrorists, published a report titled "Money Laundering Using New Payment Methods" in October of 2010 to warn about the use of digital currencies to finance terrorist groups.

2011. In this year, Silk Road, a Bitcoin marketplace, launched an illicit marketplace for drug deals, called the eBay for drugs. The largest ever Bitcoin theft was reported on June 13, 2011. Bitcoin Forum member allinvain claimed that 25,000 BTC were stolen from his wallet. At the time, the exchange rate put the amount close to US$375,000.

Also, in June 2011, Mt. Gox suffered a significant breach of security that resulted in fraudulent trading and required the site to be shut down for seven days. The breach compromised the Mt. Gox database with a leak of the user table that contained user names, email addresses, and password hashes of 60,000 accounts. An admin account was accessed from which sell orders were issued for hundreds of thousands of Bitcoins, which forced down the Mt. Gox price from US$17.51 to US$0.01 per Bitcoin.

2012. On September 24, 2012, Bitcoin Savings and Trust was investigated for running a Ponzi scheme. Phillip Moustakis, a senior attorney in the Enforcement Division of the U.S. Securities and Exchange Commission (SEC), announced an investigation of Bitcoin Savings and Trust after allegations were made that the Ponzi scheme decreased the value of Bitcoins by as much as 30 percent.

2013. This year was a busy one for Bitcoin developments.

- On March 18, 2013, FinCEN published its "Application of FinCEN's Regulations to Persons Administering, Exchanging, or Using Virtual Currencies," which defined its position on virtual currencies.
- Bitcoin Central was hacked on April 20, 2013, with hackers making away with "a few hundred" Bitcoins that the site's owners agreed to fully cover.
- On May 2, 2013, the first Bitcoin ATM in the world debuted in San Diego, California.
- A few weeks later, on May 14, the U.S. Department of Homeland Security seized more than US$2.9 million from a Dwolla account that belonged to a subsidiary of Mt. Gox because it allegedly "failed to register as a 'money transmitting business' in accordance with 18 U.S. Code 1960."

¶504

- On May 18, 2013, PrimeDice.com launched as an online casino platform that accepts Bitcoin wagers.

- In response to a claim by Trendon Shavers, founder of Texas-based Bitcoin Savings and Trust, that Bitcoins are not real money in an attempt to sidestep SEC charges of misappropriation of funds, Federal Magistrate Judge Amos Mazzant of the Eastern District of Texas ruled on August 6, 2013, that "Bitcoin is a currency or form of money, and investors wishing to invest in BTCST provided an investment of money."

- On October 2, 2013, the FBI shut down the infamous online drug marketplace Silk Road, seizing $3.6 million worth of Bitcoins.

- Bitcoin's daily transaction volume surpassed that of Western Union on November 19, 2013.

- December 2, 2013, saw the biggest heist in history when 96,000 Bitcoins were stolen from Sheep Marketplace, an online drug site. The thief's transfer of the funds from wallet to wallet could be viewed on the Internet.

2014. By the end of February, Mt. Gox had filed for bankruptcy protection in Japan amid reports that 744,000 Bitcoins had been stolen.

2016. In July, researchers published a paper showing that by November 2013, Bitcoin commerce was no longer driven by "sin" activities but instead by legitimate enterprises.

2018. On June 11, 2018, the price of Bitcoin slumped more than 7 percent after South Korea's Coinrail announced that it had been targeted by cyberthieves. In a statement, the exchange said that it had suffered a security breach in which hackers stole about 30 percent of its virtual currencies.

A June 13 study from the University of Texas in Austin suggested that at least half of the meteoric rise in cryptocurrency valuation in the previous year could be reflective not of market demand but of a motivated campaign of price manipulation.

2020. An NFL player had in his contract that half of his salary would be paid in Bitcoin.

2021. El Salvador adopted Bitcoin as legal tender for the country (note that the World Bank opposes this.) In 2021, Bitcoins and other cryptocurrencies are being sold at 7-11 and other convenience stores, although the author does not recommend asking the clerk for investment advice. Also, in 2021, Wyoming became the first state to charter a cryptocurrency bank.

Initial Coin Offerings

Bitcoins are not the only cryptocurrency being used on the Internet. There are a multitude of initial coin offerings (ICOs) being sold to investors. Many organizations are looking to profit from the popularity of cryptocurrency, and investors hope they will get rich quick with the new virtual currency.

On June 8, 2018, Jay Clayton, the head of the SEC, announced that the SEC would consider all tokens or digital assets that were used to raise funds for a venture or company with an expectation of profit, either given by the company formed or exchangeable on a secondary market, as securities, meaning that most ICOs would fall under the definition of securities.

The SEC announced on May 29, 2018, that it was suing Titanium Blockchain Infrastructure Services, Inc., for a $21 million ICO fraud. The ICO was based on social media marketing that deceived investors with purely fictional claims.

¶504

Hard Forks

A *hard fork* refers to a radical change to the protocol of a blockchain network that effectively results in two branches, one that follows the previous protocol and one that follows the new version. In a hard fork, holders of tokens in the original blockchain will be granted tokens in the new fork as well, but miners must choose which blockchain to continue verifying. A hard fork can occur in any blockchain, and not only Bitcoin (where hard forks have created Bitcoin Cash and Bitcoin SV, among several others, for example).

As mentioned earlier, there are thousands of cryptocurrencies in existence. The following chart lists several of them:

Other Digital Currencies	
• Ripple or RTXP	• Megacoin
• Litecoin	• Novacoin
• Darkcoin	• Quarkcoin
• Peercoin	• Worldcoin
• Dogecoin	• Infinitecoin
• Primecoin	• BBQcoin
• Namecoin	• Terracoin
• Megacoin	• Goldcoin
• Protoshares	• Zetacoin
• Feathercoin	• Luckycoin

STUDY QUESTIONS

1. Airline frequent flyer miles are an example of a _____.

    a. Closed virtual currency

    b. Single flow virtual currency

    c. Convertible virtual currency

    d. Public virtual currency

2. In May of 2013, Bitcoins were first used in which of the following?

    a. Online casinos

    b. Money laundering

    c. Illegal online purchases

    d. Terrorist funding

3. Which of the following events did *not* occur in 2013?

    a. Judge rules Bitcoin is a currency.

    b. Bitcoin surpasses Western Union.

    c. The FBI seizes Silk Road.

    d. Mt. Gox files for bankruptcy.

¶ 505 VIRTUAL CURRENCY FRAUDS

Cryptocurrency scams and frauds exist, and just as other types of fraud, they involve criminals trying to steal someone else's money and put it in their pocket. A 2018 *Forbes* article (https://www.forbes.com/sites/thomasbrewster/2019/01/23/ether-scammers-made-36-million-in-2018double-their-2017-winnings/#669c49a52c16) reported on cryptocurrency scammers who made $36 million by using a classic Ponzi scheme to trick the owners of Ether to part with their currency. The article highlighted a sharp rise in virtual currency scams from 2017 to 2018, looking at the total revenue that the scammers sold and the number of people they stole money from.

Another article, from Coindesk (https://www.coindesk.com/crypto-scams-pose-more-risk-than-payments-fraud-report-suggests), noted that cryptocurrency scams in 2019 posed more risk than payment fraud. In April 2020, the FBI reported (https://www.fbi.gov/news/pressrel/press-releases/fbi-expects-a-rise-in-scams-involving-cryptocurrency-related-to-the-covid-19-pandemic) that it expected a rise in scams involving cryptocurrency due to the COVID-19 pandemic. And the FBI was right—there was indeed a huge increase in crypto frauds, as well as frauds in general, as fraudsters who were social distancing at home committed their cybercrimes via the Internet.

New scams continue to surface. Another fraud to be aware of is *cryptojacking*, which is when scammers use a victim's computer or smartphone processing power to "mine" cryptocurrency for their own benefit, without the victim's permission. Scammers can put malicious code onto a victim's device simply by the victim visiting a website. Then they can help themselves to the victim's device processor without the victim knowing. Criminals mine the cryptocurrency using a company's computers or a victim's individual computer as nodes, and they're getting the benefit—they're getting paid for it.

In response to these types of frauds, in January 2021 the IRS requested $32 million in funding to help prevent the misuse of cryptocurrency and enhance its enforcement efforts. The IRS plans to spend the money on the hardware and software needed to fight these crimes, as well as on compensation for information technology (IT) specialists in crypto and cybersecurity.

¶ 506 VIRTUAL CURRENCY WALLETS

A virtual currency "wallet" is needed to buy, store, and use virtual currencies. A wallet is a software program that stores private and public keys and interacts with the virtual currencies' blockchain.

The wallet doesn't store the virtual currencies or coins; it only maintains the information that allows users to access the information for their transactions on the blockchain.

When a virtual currency transaction occurs, nothing is actually transferred. Rather, when an individual sends a virtual currency to someone, they are signing over the ownership of the Bitcoin. The public and private keys are compared, and if they match, the ownership is transferred and the transaction is recorded on the blockchain.

There are several types of virtual currency wallets. A user can create a paper wallet by printing a hard copy of the private key and the public key or by writing them down on paper. An advantage of a printed wallet is that it is safe from hackers. However, most people store the keys on their desktop or laptop, or on a mobile device like a cell phone. Other options include a jump drive, a wallet stored on a CD or DVD, or on the web or in the cloud.

¶ 507 VIRTUAL CURRENCIES AND TAXES

As mentioned earlier, for federal tax purposes, virtual currency is treated as property. Therefore, general tax principles for property transactions apply to transactions using virtual currency. Virtual currency cannot be reported as a currency transaction, and no foreign currency gain or loss can be claimed on a U.S. tax filing. A taxpayer who receives virtual currency as payment for goods or services must, in computing gross income, include the fair market value of the virtual currency, measured in U.S. dollars, as of the date that the virtual currency was received. See IRS Publication 525, *Taxable and Nontaxable Income*, for more details.

Currently, the IRS considers single flow virtual currency transactions (e.g., award programs from hotels, airlines, etc.) to be taxable, and therefore taxes are due when points are awarded or exchanged for trips or other awards. The IRS has not pursued a tax enforcement program with respect to promotional benefits such as frequent flyer miles because of the issue of valuing and reporting the awards.

The basis of virtual currency that a taxpayer receives as payment for goods or services is the fair market value of the virtual currency in U.S. dollars as of the date of receipt. See IRS Publication 551, *Basis of Assets*.

Taxpayers must choose a valuation methodology for record keeping to determine the tax basis for virtual currencies. Methods include:

- First in first out (FIFO): The first Bitcoin the taxpayer purchased is the first one they sell.

- Last in first out (LIFO): The most recent Bitcoin the taxpayer purchased is one the taxpayer sells.

- Specific identification: The taxpayer tracks every cryptocurrency or partial cryptocurrency, and specifically identifies what they are buying or selling and what they still have in their ownership (IRS preferred method).

- Average cost: The taxpayer uses the average value of the Bitcoin when it was acquired.

For U.S. tax purposes, transactions using virtual currency must be reported in U.S. dollars. Therefore, taxpayers are required to determine the fair market value of virtual currency in U.S. dollars as of the date of payment or receipt, even if the transaction occurred using a foreign currency.

If a virtual currency is listed on an exchange and the exchange rate is established by market supply and demand, the fair market value of the virtual currency is determined by converting the virtual currency into U.S. dollars (or into another real currency which in turn can be converted into U.S. dollars) at the exchange rate, in a reasonable manner that is consistently applied (similar to determining the basis for listed stocks).

If the fair market value of property received in exchange for virtual currency exceeds the taxpayer's adjusted basis of the virtual currency, the taxpayer has taxable gain. The taxpayer has a loss if the fair market value of the property received is less than the adjusted tax basis of the virtual currency. See IRS Publication 544, *Sales and Other Dispositions of Assets*, for information about the tax treatment of sales and exchanges, such as whether a loss is deductible.

The character of the gain or loss generally depends on whether the virtual currency is a capital asset in the hands of the taxpayer. A taxpayer generally realizes capital gain or loss on the sale or exchange of virtual currency that is a capital asset in the hands of the taxpayer.

A taxpayer typically realizes ordinary gain or loss on the sale or exchange of virtual currency that is not a capital asset in the hands of the taxpayer. See Publication 544 for more information about capital assets and the character of gain or loss. Capital gains and losses are reported on Schedule D of Form 1040.

> **NOTE:** Stocks, bonds, and other investment property are generally capital assets. Inventory and other property held mainly for sale to customers in a trade or business are examples of property that is not a capital asset.

¶507

For businesses that are using cryptocurrency, capital gains are taxed at the ordinary income level. They are not an investment, but rather a means of exchange. However, individuals who invest in cryptocurrency are using it to build wealth, as a long-term investment.

There are two types of capital gains: *short-term* and *long-term*. Short-term capital gains are owned for less than a year and are taxed at ordinary income tax rates. Long-term capital gains are owned for longer than one year and taxed at special capital gains tax rates. The following table lists the 2020 long-term capital gains tax rates for individuals.

Individual 2020 Long-Term Capital Gains Tax Rates				
Long-Term Capital Gains Tax Rate	Single Filers (Taxable Income)	Married Filing Jointly	Heads of Household	Married Filing Separately
0%	$0–$40,000	$0–$80,000	$0–$53,600	$0–$40,000
14%	$40,000–$441,450	$80,000–$496,600	$53,600–$469,050	$40,000–$248,300
20%	Over $441,450	Over –$496,600	Over $469,050	Over $248,300

When a taxpayer successfully "mines" virtual currency (e.g., uses computer resources to validate Bitcoin transactions and maintain the public Bitcoin transaction ledger), the fair market value of the virtual currency as of the date of receipt is includible in gross income. For more information on taxable income, consult IRS Publication 525, *Taxable and Nontaxable Income*.

If a taxpayer's mining of virtual currency constitutes a trade or business, and the mining activity is not undertaken by the taxpayer as an employee, the net earnings from self-employment (generally, gross income derived from carrying on a trade or business less allowable deductions) resulting from those activities constitute self-employment income and are subject to the self-employment tax.

Self-employment income includes all gross income derived by an individual from any trade or business carried on by the individual as other than an employee. Consequently, the fair market value of virtual currency received for services performed as an independent contractor, measured in U.S. dollars as of the date of receipt, constitutes self-employment income and is subject to the self-employment tax.

When compensating employees, the medium in which remuneration for services is paid is immaterial to the determination of whether the remuneration constitutes wages for employment tax purposes. The fair market value of virtual currency paid as wages is subject to federal income tax withholding, Federal Insurance Contributions Act (FICA) tax, and Federal Unemployment Tax Act (FUTA) tax and must be reported on Form W-2, *Wage and Tax Statement*.

A payment made using virtual currency is subject to information reporting to the same extent as any other payment made in property. A person who in the course of a trade or business makes a payment of fixed and determinable income using virtual currency with a value of $600 or more to a U.S. non-exempt recipient in a taxable year is required to report the payment to the IRS and to the payee on Form 1099.

NOTE: Examples of payments of fixed and determinable income include rent, salaries, wages, premiums, annuities, and compensation.

A person, or business, that in the course of a trade or business makes a payment of $600 or more in a taxable year to an independent contractor for the performance of services is required to report that payment to the IRS and to the payee on Form 1099-NEC, *Non-Employee Compensation*. Payments of virtual currency required to be reported on Form 1099-NEC should be reported using the fair market value of the

¶507

virtual currency in U.S. dollars as of the date of payment. The payment recipient may have income even if the recipient does not receive a Form 1099-NEC.

Payments made using virtual currency are subject to backup withholding to the same extent as other payments made in property. Therefore, payors making reportable payments using virtual currency must solicit a taxpayer identification number (TIN) from the payee. The payor must backup withhold from the payment if a TIN is not obtained prior to payment or if the payor receives notification from the IRS that backup withholding is required.

A third party that contracts with a substantial number of unrelated merchants to settle payments between the merchants and their customers is a third-party settlement organization (TPSO). A TPSO is required to report payments made to a merchant on a Form 1099-K, *Payment Card and Third Party Network Transactions*, if, for the calendar year, the gross amount of payments exceeds $600. This was changed with the American Rescue Plan Act of 2021.

Taxpayers may be subject to penalties for failure to comply with tax laws. For example, underpayments attributable to virtual currency transactions may be subject to penalties, such as accuracy-related penalties under Code Sec. 6662. In addition, failure to timely or correctly report virtual currency transactions when required to do so may be subject to information reporting penalties under Code Secs. 6721 and 6722.

¶ 508 COMMON QUESTIONS ABOUT CRYPTOCURRENCY

Here are a few frequently asked questions about cryptocurrency.

- Can taxpayers use the "wash sale" rules for cryptocurrencies?
    - No, the IRS limits the wash sale rule to securities and considers cryptocurrencies to be property, not taxes.
- Can taxpayers do a Section 1031 exchange for cryptocurrencies?
    - No, the Tax Cuts and Jobs Act limited Section 1031 exchanges to real property (i.e., real estate).
- Where are cryptocurrency transactions reported on Form 1040? Right below the address section on the form is the question, "At any time during 2020 did you receive, sell, send exchange, or otherwise acquire any financial interest in any virtual currency?" Taxpayers must answer this question yes or no.
    - Capital gains are reported on line 7 of Form 1040.
    - Other income, such as mining income, is reported on line 8, and on line 8 of Schedule 1.
    - Cryptocurrency transactions are reported individually on Form 8949.
    - Capital gains and losses are reported on Schedule D.

STUDY QUESTIONS

4. The IRS considers virtual currencies to be _____.

    a. Non-taxable

    b. Property

    c. Currency

    d. Securities

5. Although the IRS considers transactions in this type of virtual currency to be taxable, it does **not** enforce compliance of which of the following?

    a. Closed virtual currencies

    b. Single flow virtual currencies

    c. Convertible virtual currencies

    d. Cryptocurrencies

6. Which of the following valuation methodologies is preferred by the IRS for reporting gains/losses on virtual currencies?

    a. LIFO

    b. FIFO

    c. Specific identification

    d. Average cost

MODULE 3: TAX DEVELOPMENTS AND UPDATES—Chapter 6: Estate and Financial Planning Update

¶ 601 WELCOME

After a whirlwind period of legislation passed at breakneck speed, practitioners must stay informed of constant changes in the areas of estate and financial planning as the IRS issues notices and releases regulations impacting clients' estate and financial plans. This chapter reviews recent legislative, regulatory, and case law authority and how practitioners can advise individual taxpayers to ensure ongoing compliance and maximization of tax benefits.

¶ 602 LEARNING OBJECTIVES

Upon completion of this chapter, you will be able to:

- Summarize legislative developments affecting clients' estate and financial planning goals
- Recognize and analyze the potential tax impacts related to revenue rulings and case law decisions affecting estate tax and fiduciary income tax
- Recommend estate and financial planning ideas for clients looking to reduce tax liability while achieving estate planning goals

¶ 603 INTRODUCTION

Estate and financial planning is impacted not only by legislation passed since the beginning of 2020, but also by revenue procedures and rulings issued by the IRS in response to the legislation. Practitioners must stay on top of these developments, as well as new case law decisions, to best serve the estate and financial planning needs of their clients.

¶ 604 LEGISLATIVE DEVELOPMENTS

Recent legislative developments with which practitioners should become familiar include the passage of the Coronavirus Preparedness and Response Supplemental Appropriations Act, the Families First Coronavirus Response Act, the Coronavirus Aid, Relief, and Economic Security (CARES) Act, the Paycheck Protection Program (PPP) and Health Care Enhancement Act, the Heroes Act, the Consolidated Appropriations Act (CAA), and the American Rescue Plan Act (ARPA). This section reviews the ARPA provisions related to financial and estate planning.

The ARPA was introduced on February 24, 2021, passed the Senate on March 6, 2021, passed the House on March 10, 2021, and became law on March 11, 2021. Provisions relevant to estate and financial planning are detailed in the sections that follow.

Unemployment Compensation Deduction

Under the ARPA, up to $10,200 of unemployment compensation is not taxable at the federal level. The deduction applies only for taxpayers whose income is $150,000 or less. There is no differentiation in the income cap between single or married taxpayers, and no phaseout range. Taxpayers who filed their returns prior to the passage of the ARPA do not need to file amended returns to reduce their tax liability. However, they should consider filing an amended return if the reduction in income would qualify them for previously unclaimed credits based on gross income.

Note that some states have not been as generous as the federal government when it comes to the non-taxation of unemployment benefits. The justification for state-level reactions varies but includes the fact that some states do not link their state tax liability to the underlying federal tax liability. States that already tax unemployment compensation have also not uniformly proactively taken action to exclude unemployment from taxable income since such action could require state legislative or voter consent. Practitioners who prepare state-level income tax returns must check how the applicable states treat unemployment compensation and ensure that their software is tracking that information appropriately.

No Repayment of Excess Advance Premium Tax Credit

Eligible taxpayers have historically been permitted to claim a premium tax credit for health insurance coverage purchased through a Health Insurance Marketplace. Certain taxpayers may receive an advance credit to offset anticipated health insurance costs. Taxpayers file Form 8962, *Premium Tax Credit*, to compare their advance credit and eligible credit to determine if a refund or additional tax is due.

According to the ARPA, however, taxpayers with excess advance premium tax credit for 2020 are not required to file Form 8962 or to report an excess advance premium tax credit repayment on their 2020 Form 1040 or Form 1040-SR, Schedule 2, Line 2, when they file. This provides relief to taxpayers who received too much credit during the year by allowing them to skip repayment of the excess credit.

The IRS is proactively working to refund taxpayers who already paid back part of their advance premium tax credit; these taxpayers do not need to file an amended return but should keep an eye out for the refund due to them. Taxpayers who are owed a premium tax credit should still file Form 8962 to calculate the amount of credit due to them. So far, this provision is applicable only to 2020 individual tax returns and to taxpayers who actually purchase their health insurance through the marketplace. Practitioners should be mindful that these provisions could be extended by future legislation.

IRS Filing Deadline Extension

Notice 2021-21 extended the filing deadline for individual income tax returns (Form 1040) to May 17, 2021. The due date for payments owed with the 2020 individual return was also extended to May 17, 2021. The notice also postponed the deadline to make 2020 Individual Retirement Account (IRA), Health Savings Account (HSA), Archer Medical Savings Account (MSA), and Coverdell Education Savings Account (ESA) contributions to May 17, 2021. However, the first quarter estimated income tax payment for 2021 was still due on April 15, 2021, creating confusion and frustration on the part of tax preparers and taxpayers alike.

No official guidance was issued concerning the due date for Form 709, *United States Gift (and Generation-Skipping Transfer) Tax Return*, leading practitioners to conclude that the due date was not extended and remained April 15, 2021.

If a taxpayer's Form 1040 was already filed by May 17, 2021, Form 8892 should have been filed to extend only the due date for Form 709. If Form 1040 needed to be extended, then practitioners should have filed Form 4868, *Application for Automatic Extension of Time To File U.S. Individual Income Tax Return*, by April 15 to extend both returns to October 15, 2021. If a taxpayer failed to extend Form 709:

- If no tax is due (and the taxpayer is not close to using the full exemption), then no late filing penalties will be assessed.
- If tax is due or the taxpayer is close to using the full exemption, they should file and remit payment as soon as possible to avoid the further accrual of penalties and interest.

FBAR Filings Not Extended

The deadline for U.S. citizens, resident aliens, and any domestic legal entity required to file the annual Report of Foreign Bank and Financial Accounts (FBAR) remained April 15, 2021. The extension of the federal income tax filing due date and other tax deadlines for individuals to May 17, 2021, did not affect the FBAR requirement.

However, filers received an automatic extension until October 15, 2021, to file the FBAR even if they did not request an extension. Therefore, filers who failed to file their FBAR by the April 15, 2021, deadline will not face any penalties for their oversight.

¶ 605 CASE LAW OPINIONS

Recently, there have been several interesting case law opinions relating to the financial and estate planning world.

Warne v. Commissioner

In *Warne v. Commissioner*, TC Memo 2021-17, the taxpayer made gifts of limited liability company (LLC) interests to her children and grandchildren in 2012. The taxpayer then died in 2014. Among her bequests at death were transfers of additional LLC interests to charitable organizations. The key issues examined in the case were:

- Valuation of assets
- Discounting
- Charitable deductions

When the taxpayer died, the LLC ownership was split between the taxpayer's family trust and her children. The estate applied traditional discounting methods to the valuation of the LLC ownership interests owned by the taxpayer's trust to reduce the overall size of the taxpayer's gross estate. The commissioner contested the discounts claimed by the estate for lack of control and lack of marketability.

In relation to the lack of control discount claimed by the estate, the court ultimately determined that any discount for lack of control for the majority interests held by the family trust should be low. The operating agreements for the LLC granted significant power to the taxpayer, including the ability to (1) unilaterally dissolve the LLCs and (2) appoint and remove managers. The tax court commented that when LLC owners retain the types of control that existed in this case, the court has generally permitted no discount. However, the court granted a small discount in this case because the taxpayer and commissioner agreed to one which the court adopted in its opinion.

> **COMMENT:** When planning with LLCs and examining operating agreements, practitioners need to ensure that the powers of control retained by the taxpayer are not so great as to deny discounts that would otherwise be relied upon.

The court then examined the discount claimed by the estate for lack of marketability. The taxpayer and the commissioner both used experts to analyze the appropriate lack of marketability discount. Based on the data analyzed, the taxpayer's expert concluded the discount should be between 5 percent and 10 percent. The commissioner's expert concluded that mathematically, based on similar cases, the discount should be 14.25 percent. However, the expert then applied a 2 percent discount to the taxpayer's case without explanation. The court concluded that when an expert does not provide enough evidence to support his or her opinion, the opinion cannot be adopted. The court used the evidence from the taxpayer's expert to ultimately apply a 5 percent discount for marketability.

> **COMMENT:** Practitioners must review their expert's valuations, because if the experts come up with discount amounts that do not make sense based on the evidence, they could be attacked by the IRS.

The court then turned to the charitable deductions claimed by the estate in relation to a second LLC owned by the taxpayer. At the taxpayer's death, her trust included 100 percent ownership of Royal Gardens LLC. According to the terms of her estate plan, Charity 1 received a 75 percent interest in the LLC, and Charity 2 received the remaining 25 percent interest. In valuing the charitable deduction, Code Sec. 2055, Transfers for public, charitable, and religious uses, states:

> (a) In general—
>
> For purposes of the tax imposed by section 2001 [Estate Tax], the value of the taxable estate shall be determined by deducting from the value of the gross estate the amount of all bequests, legacies, devises, or transfers
>
> (1) To the United States
>
> (2) To Charitable Organizations
>
> (3) To Fraternal Societies and Organizations for Charitable Purposes
>
> (4) To Veterans Organizations Created by Congress
>
> (5) To Employee Stock Ownership Plan

The estate claimed that because 100 percent of Royal Gardens was 100 percent included in the estate, and the estate donated 100 percent of Royal Gardens to charity, the estate should be entitled to a deduction of 100 percent of Royal Gardens' value. The court pointed out that when property is split among multiple recipients, the estate may only claim a charitable deduction for estate tax purposes for what is actually received by the charity. Specifically, the court stated "[W]e do not value what an estate contributed; we value what the charitable organizations received."

In making its decision, the court relied on the case of *Ahmanson Foundation v. United States*, 674 F.2d 761 (9th Cir. 1981), in which the decedent owned (through a revocable trust) a corporation that had 100 shares. One of those shares was a voting share; the remaining 99 shares were nonvoting. The decedent bequeathed the one voting share to his son and the 99 nonvoting shares to a charitable foundation.

The Court of Appeals for the Ninth Circuit in *Ahmanson* determined that when valuing an asset for estate tax purposes, the entire interest held by the estate is valued, without regard to the later disposition of that asset. When property is split as part of a charitable contribution, the estate may only be allowed a deduction "for what is actually received by the charity—a principle required by the purpose of the charitable deduction." Again, the court does not value what an estate contributed—it values what the charitable organizations received.

The results in *Warne* were as follows:

- The estate must include 100 percent of the value of Royal Gardens in the value of the estate.
- The estate may deduct only the value of the 25 percent and the 75 percent interests received by the respective charities subject to traditional discounting principals.

- The taxpayer and commissioner stipulated that a 27.385 percent discount is appropriate for the 25 percent interest, and a 4 percent discount is appropriate for the 75 percent donation to the foundation.

The result of the *Warne* case can create situations of tax liability even when all assets are distributed among charities. Practitioners should be mindful of the result of this case when discussing distribution plans with clients since unanticipated results can be triggered by thoughtless planning.

> **EXAMPLE:** A gross estate includes an LLC valued at $21 million. The estate plan leaves the LLC equally to three charities ($7 million each). The lack of control discount of 15 percent is applied to each charitable deduction; therefore, the deduction equals $5.95 million for each charity. The net taxable estate = $21 million – $17.85 million = $3.42 million.

Schreier v. Drealan Kvilhaug Hoefker & Co. P.A.

The case of *Schreier v. Drealan Kvilhaug Hoefker & Co. P.A.*, 992 F.3d 674 (8th Cir. 2021), involved a malpractice claim against an accountant who failed to claim a deduction on the decedent's Minnesota estate tax return. At the time the estate tax return was due, a state-level deduction applicable to farm property was not applicable to the decedent's estate. After filing, Minnesota amended its tax code, which made the deduction retroactively applicable to the taxpayer's estate.

The decedent's family claimed the accountant committed malpractice by failing to claim the deduction on the originally filed estate tax return. However, the court found that the accountant was not negligent in failing to wait to file the return until the amendment was enacted because the "portion of the amendment that affected [taxpayer's] estate return was not added to the proposed amendment until . . . months after [the accountant] filed the return." The accountant was found not liable for failing to incorporate future legislation into the preparation of a return before the legislation was passed.

> **COMMENT:** Preparers should be cautious as legislation moves through Congress and new legislation is enacted. Changes could be brewing that will impact clients, possibly retroactively.

Hafen v. Famulary

In *Hafen v. Famulary*, 2021 WL 229356 (D. Utah 2021), a taxpayer invested $2,612,939.68 in a Ponzi scheme. At her death, the Ponzi scheme operators represented to her estate that her investment was worth $42 million. Because of the significant tax liability, the estate "liquidated" $16,479,500 of the estate's investment in the Ponzi scheme to pay its estate tax liability. The estate actually received these monies from the Ponzi scheme operators prior to the discovery of the fraud and paid the monies over to the IRS in satisfaction of the estate's estate tax liability.

Upon the discovery of the nature of the Ponzi scheme, the receiver took over to wind down the operations and return the monies to the victims. In the course of its investigation, the receiver determined that the estate received more than its original investment, which under state law was prohibited. The estate was ordered to return the excess it received over its initial investment, $13,866,560. As a result of this outcome at the state level, the estate is now faced with filing an amended Form 706, *United States Estate (and Generation-Skipping Transfer) Tax Return*, to obtain a refund of monies based on reporting an inflated value of the assets on the original return. If the statute of limitations has already passed to request a tax refund, the estate could be faced with the obligation of paying back a significant liability with no ability to obtain a refund for the inaccuracy of its original valuation of the estate assets.

¶605

STUDY QUESTIONS

1. Which statement about the advance premium tax credit is true?

    a. Under the American Rescue Plan Act, taxpayers with an excess advance premium tax credit for 2020 are not required to file Form 8962.

    b. Taxpayers who already paid back part of their advance premium tax credit before ARPA was enacted must file an amended tax return.

    c. The advance premium tax credit is only available to taxpayers who purchase their health insurance directly through an insurance company's sales representative.

    d. The advance premium tax credit is designed to offset unemployment compensation benefits.

2. Which of the following was *not* due on May 17, 2021?

    a. 2020 individual retirement account contributions

    b. 2020 contributions to a health savings account

    c. Form 1040

    d. Form 709

3. In which case was an accountant found not liable for failing to incorporate future legislation into the preparation of a return before the legislation was passed?

    a. *Warne*

    b. *Schreier*

    c. *Ahmanson Foundation*

    d. *Hafen*

¶ 606 TREASURY RELEASES

The following section summarizes various treasury releases that practitioners should be aware of in the coming months and years. Many of these changes are current proposals that may go into effect in the future and will impact clients' planning decisions.

Proposed Regulations Related to the American Indian Probate Process

When a member of an American Indian tribe passes away, assets they own as of the date of death are subject to an entirely different probate process than under the Uniform Probate Code or the state inheritance laws. Proposed rules have been released for the American Indian Probate Regulations (25 CFR 15; 43 CFR 30). The updated regulations allow the Office of Hearings and Appeals (OHA) to adjudicate probate cases more efficiently by:

- Establishing an expedited process for small, funds-only estates
- Reorganizing the purchase-at-probate process so that estates may be closed more quickly
- Streamlining notice to co-owners who are potential heirs while adding electronic notice to all by website posting

- Specifying which reasons justify reopening of closed probate estates
- Enhancing the OHA's processing by adding certainty as to how estates should be distributed when certain circumstances arise that are not addressed in the statute

In an effort to further streamline the post-death administrative process for families, a proposed change to 25 CFR 15.301 increases from $1,000 to $5,000 the amount that may be requested and approved for distribution from a decedent's Individual Indian Money (IIM) account to pay for funeral expenses. The proposed change also deletes the requirement for the IIM account to contain at least $2,500 and clarifies that funds, if approved, are taken from the balance of the account as of the date of death. Also included in the proposed regulations are the following changes:

- 43 CFR 30.200: Changes the qualification for summary probate proceedings from funds-only estates with a value of $5,000 or less to funds-only estates with a value of $300 or less.
- 43 CFR 30.501: Establishes that joint tenancy will be presumed where a testator devises the same interests to more than one person without specifying otherwise.

Solicitation of Comments Related to Form 8971

In "Solicitation of Comments on Form 8971 Related to Basis Consistency for Assets Reported on the Form 706 Series" (86 FR 9996), comments were invited on the following:

- Whether the collection of information on Form 8971 is necessary for the proper performance of the functions of the IRS
- The accuracy of the IRS's estimate of the burden of the collection of information
- Ways to enhance the quality, utility, and clarity of the information to be collected
- Ways to minimize the burden of the collection of information on respondents, including through the use of automated collection techniques or other forms of information technology; and
- Estimates of capital or start-up costs and costs of operation, maintenance, and purchase of services to provide information

Comments were due on April 19, 2021, so changes may arise in relation to Form 8971, *Information Regarding Beneficiaries Acquiring Property from a Decedent.* Form 8971 is intended to report information related to the decedent's taxable estate and the beneficiaries receiving assets as part of the administration process. The two-part filing provides the IRS with a list of all beneficiaries on the first page followed by a separate Schedule A for each beneficiary listing the assets received by that beneficiary and the date of death value of the assets reported on the decedent's Form 706. For example, if there are five beneficiaries, five Schedule As are attached to Form 8971. Each Schedule A lists the beneficiary's name, the asset they receive from the estate, and the corresponding value assigned to that asset by the estate. Preparers should send the first page and each Schedule A to the IRS. Then, they should send each beneficiary his or her individual Schedule A.

Basis Consistency and Form 8971

Since Form 8971 is relatively new and applies only to taxable estates, many practitioners may be unfamiliar with the form and its function, which relates primarily to Code Secs. 1014 and 6035. Code Sec. 1014 (and its predecessor, Code Sec. 1013) has been around for a long time. The main premise of Code Sec. 1014 is that the tax basis of assets belonging to a decedent is adjusted to the value of those assets as of the decedent's date of death. This is frequently referred to as the *step-up in basis.*

Recently, Code Sec. 1014 was modified to provide that even though the basis of assets owned by the decedent is adjusted at date of death, the adjustment will be limited, to the value reported on the decedent's estate tax return or the amount considered by the estate for evaluating estate tax liability.

In addition, Code Sec. 6035 provides that the executor of any estate that is required to file Form 706 must send a statement informing the beneficiary of the date of death value reported on Form 706 to ensure consistency. This process is similar to the cost basis rules implemented roughly 10 years ago that require brokerage houses to keep track of the taxpayer's cost basis.

Mandatory reporting to the beneficiary and the IRS of the cost basis in the property applies to any estate *required* to file Form 706 under Code Sec. 6018, meaning that estates filing Form 706 solely for portability are not required to file Form 8971. When lifetime gifting and the gross estate exceed the basic exclusion amount in the year of the taxpayer's death, Form 706 is required to be filed along with Form 8971. For 2020, the lifetime gift and estate basic exclusion amount is $11.58 million; for 2021, it is $11.7 million.

Form 8971 is *not* required in the following situations:

- The gross estate plus adjusted taxable gifts is less than the basic exclusion amount ($11.58 million in 2020; $11.7 million in 2021).
- The estate tax return is filed solely to elect portability of the deceased spousal exclusion amount (DSUE) or to make the qualified terminable interest property (QTIP) election.
- The estate tax return is filed solely to make an allocation or election respecting the generation-skipping transfer tax.
- Estate tax-related forms, other than those mentioned above, are filed (e.g., Forms 706-QDT, 706-CE, and 706-GS(D)).

Late QSST and ESBT Elections

IRS Private Letter Ruling 100223-20 addressed S corporation shares owned by several trusts. The owner of shares in an S corporation transferred shares to four different trusts. However, the trusts failed to make an electing small business trust election under Code Sec. 1361(e), which resulted in termination of the corporation's S election. The corporation submitted a private letter ruling request to reinstate its S election based on the inadvertent termination rules under Code Sec. 1362(f).

In order to be classified as an S corporation, an entity must meet the following requirements:

- Be domiciled in the United States
- Have only allowable shareholders, including individuals, certain trusts, and estates, and cannot include partnerships, corporations, or nonresident alien shareholders
- Have 100 or fewer shareholders
- Have just one class of stock
- Not be an ineligible corporation

Trusts may be shareholders of an S corporation if they comply with the requirements of Code Sec. 1361(e), including:

- Grantor trusts
- Trusts that were grantor trusts for the two years following the grantor's death

- Trusts to which stock is transferred by a will for the two years following the owner's death
- Trusts formed primarily to exercise voting power

If the trust does not fall under the preceding categories, it may still qualify as an S corporation shareholder by filing an election to be treated as a qualified subchapter S trust (QSST) or an electing small business trust (ESBT). A QSST election requires that all current income of the trust be distributed to the current income beneficiary and that during the term of the trust, no principal distributions can be made to anyone other than the income beneficiary. An ESBT election requires S corporation stock to be isolated and administered as a separate share of the trust. Income distribution deductions are not permitted from this separate share, and the trust pays tax on S corporation pass-through income at the trust level.

QSST election. The current income beneficiary of the trust makes the QSST election by signing and filing a statement that includes the following information (Code Sec. 1361(d)(3); Treas. Reg. § 1.1361-1(j)(6)):

- The name, address, and taxpayer identification number of the current income beneficiary, the trust, and the corporation
- Identifies the election as an election made under Code Sec. 1361(d)(2)
- Specifies the date on which the election is to become effective
- Specifies the date stock was transferred to the trust; and
- Provides all information and representations necessary to show that:
  - There will be only one income beneficiary of the trust
  - Corpus distributions will be made only to the current income beneficiary
  - The beneficiary's income interest in the trust will terminate on the earlier of the beneficiary's death or upon termination of the trust; and
  - Upon the termination of the trust during the life of such income beneficiary, the trust will distribute all its assets to such beneficiary

ESBT election. The current trustee of the trust makes the ESBT election by signing and filing a statement that includes the following information:

- The name, address, and taxpayer identification number of the trust, the potential current beneficiaries, and the S corporations in which the trust currently holds stock
- An identification of the election as an ESBT election made under Code Sec. 1361(e)(3)
- The first date on which the trust owned stock in each S corporation
- Representations signed by the trustee stating that the trust meets the definitional requirements of Code Sec. 1361(e)(1), including:
  - All of the trust's beneficiaries must be individuals or estates eligible to be S shareholders,
  - No interest in the trust may be acquired by purchase; and
  - The interests must be acquired by gift or bequest.

Due date for QSST and ESBT elections. The election cannot be made later than two months and 16 days after the desired effective date for the election (i.e., it must be made within two months and 15 days). If stock is held by a testamentary trust, then the due date is extended by two and a half months after the two-year anniversary of the grantor's death.

¶606

EXAMPLE: A decedent owned stock in his own name. His will directs the stock be transferred to an ongoing trust for the benefit of his beneficiary. The decedent dies on July 1. The trust beneficiary must file the election by September 15 of the second year after the date of the decedent's death.

Late election remedy. Rev. Proc. 2013-30 permits a late election when:

- The current income beneficiary or trustee intends to treat the trust as a QSST or ESBT, as of the intended effective date
- The beneficiary or trustee makes the request for relief within three years and 75 days after the intended effective date
- The failure to qualify as a QSST or ESBT must be solely because of the failure to timely file the proper election; and
- The failure was inadvertent, and the beneficiary or trustee has acted diligently to correct the mistake upon its discovery

Late Portability, Code Sec. 754, and Generation-Skipping Transfer (GST) Tax Credit Elections

The IRS has issued a series of private letter rulings for several other late election remedies that fall under Treas. Reg. § 301.9100-3. This regulation permits taxpayers to request late election remedies from the commissioner as long as the taxpayer acted reasonably and in good faith, and the relief will not prejudice the interests of the government. "Reasonable action and good faith" means:

- Relief is requested before the failure to make the regulatory election is discovered by the IRS
- The taxpayer's failure to make the election is due to intervening events beyond the taxpayer's control
- The taxpayer's failure to make the election is because, after exercising reasonable diligence, the taxpayer was unaware of the necessity for the election
- The taxpayer reasonably relied on the written advice of the IRS; or
- The taxpayer reasonably relied on a qualified tax professional, and the tax professional failed to make, or advise the taxpayer to make, the election

Remedy for late election under Code Sec. 754 (Private Letter Ruling 114132-20). Treas. Reg. § 1.754-1(b) sets forth the procedures for making an effective election under Code Sec. 754 to adjust the basis of partnership property under Code Secs. 734(b) and 743(b). This election is typically made after a distribution of property to a partner or a transfer of an interest in a partnership—most often as a result of the partner's death. The election must be made in a written statement filed with the partnership return for the taxable year during which the distribution or transfer occurs.

For the election to be valid, the return must be filed no later than the time prescribed by Treas. Reg. § 1.6031(a)-1(e) (including extensions) for filing the return for such taxable year. In Private Letter Ruling 114132-20, the taxpayer successfully requested relief for late filing of this election. Taxpayers in similar situations should consider the possible relief offered by requesting a similar ruling since the tax benefits of a favorable ruling could considerably outweigh the cost of the private letter ruling.

Remedy for late portability election under Code Sec. 2010(c)(5)(A) (Private Letter Rulings 202107003 and 202108007). Code Sec. 2010(c)(5)(A) provides that a deceased spouse's unused exclusion (portability) amount may not be used by a surviving spouse under Code Sec. 2010(c)(2) unless the executor of the deceased spouse's estate files an estate tax return which elects to transfer the deceased spouse's unused exclusion to the surviving spouse.

No election may be made if the estate tax return is filed after the time prescribed by law (including extensions) for filing such return. The due date for filing Form 706 is nine months after date of death plus the allowable six-month extension. However, if an estate is solely filing Form 706 to elect portability, Rev. Proc. 2017-34 permits timely filing any time before the two-year anniversary of the decedent's date of death. As illustrated by these private letter rulings, taxpayers are still unaware of this valuable benefit that can be claimed by timely filing Form 706. Practitioners should discuss the value of this filing early in the estate administration process, particularly in light of recent discussions concerning the reduction of the basic exclusion amount exempting client's assets from estate tax at death.

Remedy for late election under IRC 2632(c)(5) (Private Letter Ruling 202107001). A taxpayer requested a private letter ruling to reallocate the GST tax among the decedent's various trust entities. When the decedent passed away, his remaining GST tax exemption was automatically allocated to the taxpayer's transfer in trust. Code Sec. 2632(c)(1) provides that any unused portion of the GST exemption is treated as automatically proportionately allocated to an indirect skip transfer unless the taxpayer attaches an election out of the rules to a timely filed gift or estate tax return. Notice 2001-50 provides that taxpayers may seek an extension of time for electing out of the automatic allocation rules under the provisions of Treas. Reg. § 301.9100-3.

The taxpayer successfully obtained permission to reallocate the GST tax exemption to the taxpayer's transfers, which resulted in significant tax savings. Practitioners must be mindful that automatic allocations of tax exemptions may not always produce ideal tax results for taxpayers. If the taxpayer does not elect out of these automatic allocation rules, then tax efficiency may be lost.

Cost for Private Letter Rulings. Even though private letter rulings can provide relief for taxpayers who inadvertently miss tax saving opportunities, these requests are costly. Rev. Proc. 2021-1 provides a fee schedule for IRS Private Letter Ruling requests.

- The fee for a letter ruling request for general relief under Treas. Reg. § 301.9100-3 is $12,600.
- If the request involves a tax issue from a person whose gross income is less than $250,000, the fee is $3,000.
- If the request involves a tax issue from a person whose gross income is $250,000 to less than $1 million, the fee is $8,500.

These fees are in addition to the fees a professional tax adviser or attorney will charge to prepare the ruling request. Making the necessary elections in a timely manner will save the client thousands of dollars and the uncertainty regarding future tax savings.

Charitable Entity Application Determinations

IRS Determination Letter 202110044 responded to an exemption request from a foundation that was reportedly created for family support. The foundation's stated purpose was for receiving "Donations for the children of a deceased father. For general care and expenses to raise these two children into adulthood." The taxpayer submitted Form 1023, *Application for Recognition of Exemption Under Section 501(c)(3) of the Internal Revenue Code*, to request recognition of the foundation as a charitable entity under Code Sec. 501(c)(3).

The IRS denied the exemption request, citing among other authority Treas. Reg. § 1.501(c)(3)-1(d)(1)(ii), which states that an organization is not organized and operating exclusively for charitable purposes unless it serves a *public*, rather than a *private*, interest. Since the foundation was created solely to benefit the members of a single family rather than the public at large, charitable status was denied.

> **COMMENT:** In this age of GoFundMe and other crowdfunding platforms, many people believe that anytime they give money to a worthwhile cause, it constitutes a charitable contribution that can be claimed as a deduction for tax purposes. Determination Letter 202110044 reiterates that taxpayers must donate to organizations organized for the general benefit of the public, and not merely a singular fundraising effort for pre-identified individuals.

The IRS denied another application for charitable status submitted by a taxpayer to request recognition of a foundation as a charitable entity under Code Sec. 501(c)(3) that was created for the stated purpose of creating a lottery for borrowers of student loans to alleviate the debt burden. In Determination Letter 202109008, the IRS denied the exemption request, citing among other authority, Treas. Reg. § 1.501(c)(3)-1(d)(2), which requires that an organization be *exclusively* organized for a charitable purpose. Because all student loan borrowers (not just those who are poor and distressed) could apply for the lottery, the exclusivity test was not met, and charitable status was denied.

¶ 607 CLIENT PLANNING OPPORTUNITIES

In light of the foregoing legislative changes, treasury rulings, and case law decisions, the following planning opportunities may be useful for clients considering the creation of foundations, credit shelter trusts, and dynasty trusts protected from GST tax.

Foundations

With looming estate tax exemption reductions, tax practitioners may be looking to charitable deductions to minimize estate tax. Family foundations are a tool that enable clients to reduce their estates, minimize income taxes, and engage younger family members in the culture of giving. In tax year 2026, the basic exclusion amount returns to $5 million under Tax Cuts and Jobs Act (TCJA), and legislation introduced in Congress suggests that an earlier and/or lower basic exclusion amount may be implemented before 2026. The unlimited charitable deduction under Code Sec. 2522 could alleviate some of clients' tax stress.

A family foundation can be a good option for clients wishing to:

- Create a legacy focused on the client's philanthropic interests
- Control how charitable funds are invested over time
- Participate in the management of charitable projects
- Encourage others, such as family members, to appreciate the value of engaging in and supporting charitable projects
- Teach children and grandchildren how to manage wealth more efficiently and effectively
- Make lasting and impactful changes in areas of need, such as poverty, education, and health
- Contribute to organizations that helped shape the client's charitable interests, such as cultural, religious, and educational institutions

Basic requirements for a foundation. To qualify as a charitable entity eligible to claim a charitable deduction, a foundation must be organized and operated *exclusively* for exempt purposes set forth in Code Sec. 501(c)(3). Earnings may not be used for any private shareholder or individual. Also, the foundation may not be an action organization, that is, it may not attempt to influence legislation or participate in any campaign activities. A distribution for charitable purposes of 5 percent of assets annually is required by most private foundations to maintain their status.

Considerations during the estate planning phase. Taxpayers must consider whether to create and fund the foundation now or upon their death. If they are funding the foundation at death, discounting provisions could apply to reduce tax-saving opportunities. Taxpayers may consider funding partly during their life to obtain income tax deductions subject to 30 percent adjusted gross income limitations. Clients must also consider the board of directors' qualifications and succession rules. For example, some clients incorporate restrictions for their board of directors which might include any of the following:

- Must be a family member,
- Must contribute x amount of hours to the foundation, and
- Must participate in foundation activities to be eligible for distributions from a separate family trust.

The compensation for participating family members must be reasonable for the services rendered to the foundation, and self-dealing must be constantly analyzed. In addition to creating the governing structure of the foundation, clients must also consider which assets to contribute such as:

- Income in respect of a decedent (IRAs, annuities): No income tax is paid by the foundation when these are cashed in.
- Stocks/bonds: The foundation will pay an excise tax (1.39 percent) on any gains (net investment income) when sold, but this tax is lower than capital gains rates for beneficiaries.
- Rental properties: The foundation may continue renting out properties and receiving rental income. Usually, real estate cannot be debt financed. Unrelated business income taxes (UBIT) could apply in some instances.
- Personal property: Some clients have large collections of artwork and other valuable items they can contribute to charitable organizations or foundations that will use those items to further their charitable mission.

Reexamination of Credit Shelter Planning

As discussions relating to the reduction of the basic exclusion amount continue, clients have begun to reexamine whether credit shelter planning—the gold standard of planning in the 1990s and early 2000s—is advisable to reduce exposure to current and future estate tax laws. The allocation of a deceased taxpayer's GST tax exemption is also top of mind for clients since the GST tax exemption is not transferrable through portability to a surviving spouse.

Private Letter Ruling 202116006 highlighted these clients concerns when it addressed a request for an extension of time to allocate the GST tax exemption on Schedule R of Form 706 due to the accounting firm's failure to allocate. IRS Notice 2001-50 provides that, under Code Sec. 2642(g)(1)(B), taxpayers may seek an extension of time for allocating the GST exemption to lifetime transfers and transfers at death described in Code Sec. 2642(b)(1) or (b)(2) under the provisions of Treas. Reg. § 301.9100-3.

Estate tax and GST tax exemption planning used to be the norm. For example, if a decedent's estate totaled $15 million, the first $11.7 million of the assets (or whatever the individual had left of their lifetime exemption) would be allocated to a credit shelter trust, and the excess ($3.3 million) would pour over to the marital trust, taking advantage of the unlimited marital deduction. This strategy permits the estate to escape all tax upon the first spouse's death.

These tax concerns are highlighted in this private letter ruling, which is loosely based on the following scenario.

Note that these amounts are based on a 2017 death. Pursuant to the terms of husband's estate plan, the trustee allocated husband's assets to his Residual Trust. The Residual Trust was further divided into two separate trusts designated as the Credit Shelter Trust and the Marital Trust. Due to prior gifting, $1 million of husband's lifetime basic exclusion amount was already used, so the remaining $4.49 million (based on 2017's $5.49 million basic exclusion amount) was allocated to the Credit Shelter Trust. A QTIP election was made on the husband's Form 706 with respect to the Marital Trust, but no reverse QTIP election was made. Accordingly, husband's GST exemption was not allocated to the Marital Trust.

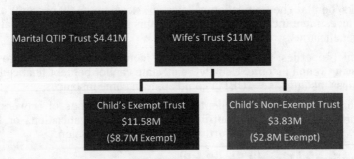

For purposes of this illustration, wife passes away in 2020. She is survived by her three children and three grandchildren. Her GST tax exemption based on her death in 2020 is $11.58 million. Since the total value of wife's assets exceeded her available GST tax exemption, wife's assets which totaled $15.41 million were divided into separate exempt and non-exempt trusts. The exempt trust held assets totaling wife's available GST tax exemption, and the non-exempt trust held the remaining assets.

The trustees instructed the accounting firm to prepare a Form 706 for the wife's estate. Form 706 was timely filed on extension. However, the accounting firm failed to prepare and include a Schedule R (Generation-Skipping Transfer Tax) with the Form 706. As a result, the automatic allocation rules applied, and wife's remaining GST tax exemption was proportionately allocated between the exempt and non-exempt trusts. The error was discovered when the attorney requested a copy of, and reviewed, the wife's Form 706. The forementioned private letter ruling requested permission to reallocate the GST tax exemption to comply with the exempt and non-exempt nature of the two trusts. Instead of relying on the automatic allocation rules, wife's GST tax exemption should have been affirmatively allocated wholly to Child's Exempt Trust on Form 706 as shown in the following illustration.

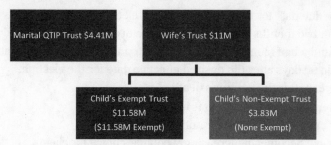

Ideally, modifications should have been made when husband passed away to maximize the couple's tax savings. The following chart shows how the exemptions should have been allocated at the husband's death so that the full GST tax exemption could be utilized. Doing so would have exempted an additional $1 million from future GST tax, resulting in a savings of at least $400,000.

Even though the estate and GST tax exemptions are large, practitioners should not become complacent with the automatic GST allocation, but instead need to carefully analyze these items. When analyzing the exemption allocation on the first spouse's death, it is always a good idea to proactively allocate the first spouse's GST tax exemption rather than relying on the surviving spouse's exemptions to cover the assets. Practitioners must also keep good track of generation-skipping transfers, particularly in the coming months, as changes to the transfer tax rules may require more vigilant reporting of taxable gifts.

STUDY QUESTIONS

4. Which of the following is included in the proposed rules for the American Indian Probate Regulations?

- **a.** Increasing the amount that may be requested and approved for distribution from a decedent's Individual Indian Money (IIM) account to pay for funeral expenses to $1,000.

- **b.** Eliminating the requirement for the IIM account to contain at least $2,500.

- **c.** Changing the qualification for summary probate proceedings from funds-only estates with a value of $5,000 or less to funds-only estates with a value of $1,000 or less.

- **d.** Establishing that tenancy in common will be presumed where a testator devises the same interests to more than one person without specifying otherwise.

5. What is the due date for the QSST and ESBT elections?
   a. Within two months and 15 days after the desired effective date for the election.
   b. Two and a half months after the two-year anniversary of the grantor's death
   c. Within 90 days after the desired effective date for the election.
   d. One year after the grantor's death.

6. Which statement about foundations is true?
   a. They can be established for non-exempt purposes.
   b. They will become an increasingly popular choice for clients.
   c. Their earnings can be used by private shareholders.
   d. They can be formed for political campaign activities.

MODULE 3: TAX DEVELOPMENTS AND UPDATES—Chapter 7: Mid-Year Tax Update

¶ 701 WELCOME

This chapter provides an update on the most recent tax changes to help practitioners navigate through the maze of tax legislation and case law.

¶ 702 LEARNING OBJECTIVES

Upon completion of this chapter, you will be able to:

- Identify employers who qualify for the employee retention credit (ERC)
- Recognize how to utilize strategies for maximizing Paycheck Protection Program (PPP) loan forgiveness
- Identify and apply tax rules from the Consolidated Appropriations Act (CAA) and the American Rescue Plan Act (ARPA)

¶ 703 ADMINISTRATIVE RELEASES AND CASE LAW

Electric Vehicle Credit

In June 2021, the IRS added more cars to the list of vehicles eligible for the Code Sec. plug-in electric drive motor vehicle credit. New plug-in vehicles on the list include the following:

- 2021 Ford Escape Plug-in Hybrid ($6,843 credit) and Mustang Mach-E ($7,500 credit)
- 2021 Porsche Taycan 4S EV, Turbo EV, and Turbo S EV ($7,500)
- 2021 Kia NIRO EV ($7,500 credit) and Plug-in Hybrid EV ($4,543 credit)
- 2021 Lincoln Corsair Reserve Grand Touring (PHEV) ($6,843 credit)
- 2021 Mitsubishi Outlander PHEV ($6,587 credit)
- 2021 Audi e-tron Sportback ($7,500), and certain e Quattros ($6,712 credit)

For more details and a full list of cars eligible for the credit, see: https://www.irs.gov/businesses/irc-30d-new-qualified-plug-in-electric-drive-motor-vehicle-credit. The credit begins to phase out after a manufacturer has sold more than 200,000 eligible cars. Tesla and GM are completely phased out now. If the car is for a taxpayer's personal use, the credit is nonrefundable (taxpayers must owe some income tax to get a benefit). The credit is claimed on Form 8936, *Qualified Plug-in Electric Drive Motor Vehicle Credit*.

Cryptocurrency

In FinCEN Notice 2020-2, the U.S. Treasury Department's Financial Crimes Enforcement Network (FinCEN) announced that it intends to amend Foreign Bank and Financial Accounts (FBAR) reporting rules so that cryptocurrency will be subject to filing on the FBAR form.

There are many indications that the IRS is intensifying its efforts in the cryptocurrency area. It has launched "Operation Hidden Treasure," a new initiative from the Office of Fraud Enforcement. The fraud enforcement initiative is dedicated to "finding, tracing, and attributing cryptocurrency to U.S. taxpayers." Two hundred employees throughout the IRS have been trained to "track, find, and work to seize cryptocurrency" in "both a civil and a criminal setting."

Additionally, the IRS recently issued summons to cryptocurrency exchanges to gather information on taxpayers who have engaged in cryptocurrency transactions.

Estate and Gift Taxes

The unified gift and estate tax exclusion for 2021 has increased to $11,700,000.

Unified Gift and Estate Tax Exclusion		
	2020	**2021**
Individuals	$11,580,000	$11,700,000

The Tax Cuts and Jobs Act doubled the exemptions under prior law. However, the double exemptions expire after 2025. High net worth taxpayers might wish to consider making gifts now because at least one legislative proposal would eliminate double exemption prior to its scheduled expiration in 2026.

The annual gift tax annual exclusion remains at $15,000 for 2021.

Pass-Through Income Taxes

Two states added pass-through entity taxes in 2021. Beginning in 2021, New York is adding an entity-level tax. Entities can "elect in" by October 15, 2021, and owners get a credit to avoid the double tax. Georgia is enacting an entity-level tax (beginning in 2022). An election must be made to be subject to the Georgia pass-through tax. Owners can exclude income to avoid the double tax.

In Notice 2020-75, the IRS announced rules that will be included in forthcoming proposed regulations regarding deductions for income taxes for partnerships and S corps. The proposed rules allow some partners and S corporation shareholders to avoid the $10,000 state and local tax (SALT) limit. They clarify that partnerships and S corporations can deduct income taxes if all the following requirements are met:

- Taxes are paid by a partnership or S corporation,
- To a state or political subdivision of a state,
- Directly imposed on income of the entity (even if the result of the entity making an election to be taxed).

The entity-level deduction is allowed even if the owners receive a credit or other benefit for the entity's payment. States that tax the entity-level income of partnerships and S corporations typically offer shareholders an offset for the taxes paid by the entity. Some provide the shareholders or partners a tax credit for taxes paid by the entities. Other jurisdictions provide a state-level exclusion of the K-1 income for taxes paid by the entity. This is essential to avoid double taxation.

Partnerships and S corporations qualifying for this deduction will reduce non-separately stated income. This will reduce the partnership's or S corporation's income reported on Schedule K-1, line 1.

Many states had previously adopted entity-level taxes to reduce the impact of the $10,000 limit for taxes claimed as itemized tax deductions. Connecticut levies mandatory income taxes for partnerships and S corporations. Other states with elective entity-level taxes include Wisconsin, Oklahoma, Louisiana, Rhode Island, and New Jersey. States that are considering taxes on pass-through entities include California, Minnesota, Arkansas, Virginia, and North Carolina; many more states are expected to be added to this list.

Charitable Contributions

A lawyer ran afoul of the IRS in a recent Tax Court case. In *Chiarelli v. Commissioner*, TC Memo 2021-27, the Tax Court denied a deduction for the taxpayer's alleged contributions to Goodwill and the Salvation Army of almost $100,000 of household items, ruling that the taxpayer did not properly document them under the strict documentation rules that apply to charitable contributions. He failed to meet the documentation standards for "qualified appraisals" and to obtain a contemporaneous written acknowledgement from the charities. Either of these shortcomings, by itself, would have resulted in disallowance.

Qualified appraisals are generally required for property contributions with a fair market value greater than $5,000. For tax purposes, when determining whether a qualified appraisal is required, similar items of property are grouped, such as the following:

- Coin collections
- Paintings
- Books
- Jewelry
- Clothing
- Furniture
- Electronic equipment
- Toys
- China
- Crystal
- Everyday kitchenware
- Jewelry, non-publicly traded stock, land, or buildings (Treas. Reg. § 1.170A-13(c)(7)(iii))

Mr. Chiarelli had made many separate gifts of used clothing during the year (including many separate contributions totaling $54,000 for a "large bags of clothes"), furniture, and antiques. These contributions were "grouped" to determine whether the total was greater than $5,000. After grouping, the categories of grouped contributions exceeded $5,000, and therefore a qualified appraisal was required. Such an appraisal must provide a list of each item contributed and must also list the age of each item of property contributed.

Mr. Chiarelli had obtained an appraisal from an auctioneer. However, the appraisal failed to meet the strict requirements of a "qualified appraisal" (e.g., it failed to describe the physical condition and age of individual items of property donated, the qualifications of the appraiser, the fair market value of individual items donated, and a statement that the appraisal was prepared for tax purposes), so the deduction was disallowed. Although taxpayers can qualify for a reasonable cause exception to the "qualified appraisal" requirements, the Tax Court held that Mr. Chiarelli wasn't eligible for relief;

¶703

since he was an attorney admitted to practice before the Tax Court (and presumably should have known better), he didn't qualify for the reasonable cause exception.

In addition to lacking a qualified appraisal, Mr. Chiarelli also failed to get contemporaneous written acknowledgements (CWAs) from the charities (Code Sec. 170(f)(8)). CWAs are required when the value of a single charitable contribution is $250 or more. Note that CWAs are required for both cash and noncash contributions. CWAs must include the charity's name and EIN and, in the case of noncash contributions, a list of the items donated. They are also required to include a statement that indicates whether any goods or services were received in exchange for the contribution. There is no "reasonable cause" or "substantial compliance" exception for failure to obtain a CWA.

The Tax Court found that the taxpayer failed to get CWAs from the charities to which he donated the property. He didn't have CWAs from Goodwill or the Salvation Army for most of the contributions. He also failed to provide a statement from each charity that he didn't receive goods or services in return (which is required as part of the CWA). The failure to obtain CWAs automatically precluded a tax deduction.

Tax practitioners should be wary of very large noncash charitable contributions to charities such as Goodwill, especially if any category of property (after grouping) is over $5,000. They should also be alert to cash or noncash contributions of $250 or more, and check whether clients have a CWA. For large contributions, both of these are required.

Hobby Losses

The tax issue surrounding hobby losses is whether the taxpayer had an "actual and honest objective of making a profit" from the hobby. The objective is not required to be reasonable but must be "genuine." The IRS has noticed that almost all taxpayers say they have an actual and honest objective to make a profit from "hobby" activities. Consequently, the Treasury issued regulations that include a nine-factor test to check whether an activity is considered a hobby for tax purposes.

Hobby losses are relevant today; a quick review of tax cases indicates that this is a common area for preparer penalties.

The IRS recently announced that it will focus more audit activity on Schedule Cs with expenses greater than $100,000 and no income reported. Hobby losses are among the most frequently litigated issues each year. It's a complex area, with inconsistent cases.

Consider the case of *Stephen Whatley v. Commissioner*, TC Memo 2021-11. Stephen Whatley, a savvy businessperson, started his own successful bank. His family had been involved in farming for 11 generations, although Mr. Whatley had no personal experience on farms. He had, however, been involved briefly in a timber operation 35 years before. Whatley bought a cattle farm with timber, but the "catch" was that there were no cattle on the farm for the years at issue. The court applied the nine-factor test provided by Treas. Reg. § 1.183-2. Its findings are summarized in the following chart:

Nine-Factor Test for Hobby Losses—*Whatley*		
Factor	**Whatley**	**Outcome**
Conducts activity in business-like manner	No separate bank account, no financials, etc. Didn't use financial information to make changes. No business plan, no changes to *be* profitable.	Taxpayer loses
Taxpayer/adviser expertise	No experience; consulted some experts.	Taxpayer loses

Nine-Factor Test for Hobby Losses—*Whatley*		
Time/effort spent on the activity	Full-time banker, no experienced workers.	Taxpayer loses
Expectation that assets used in the activity may increase in value	Timber might have appreciated (but not enough to offset farm losses).	Neutral
Taxpayer's success in *other* activities	Owned timber 35 years before. No cattle experience. *But* he was an entrepreneur.	Tie
Taxpayer's history of losses from *this* activity	Big losses every year.	Taxpayer loses
Occasional profits earned	No profits ever (big losses for 10 years).	Taxpayer loses
Taxpayer's financial status	Lots of other income.	Taxpayer loses
Whether the activity is for personal pleasure	Mr. Whatley enjoyed it.	Taxpayer loses

Ultimately, the Tax Court had little difficulty denying Mr. Whatley's losses.

Although the IRS wins many hobby losses cases, taxpayers prevail on occasion. This was the case in *Shane Robison v. Commissioner*, TC Memo 2018-88. Shane Robison, a successful tech executive with wages over $10 million in one year, bought a Utah ranch in 1999. He had a family background in ranching and farming. The ranch was initially a horse-breeding business, but he shifted the focus to cattle in 2000. Robison never made a profit, typically losing $500,000 per year. He hired a ranch manager who had formal agricultural training, and a ranch hand, and they had weekly meetings. The Tax Court applied the same nine factors as it applied the Whatley case.

Nine-Factor Test for Hobby Losses—*Robison*		
Factor	**Robison**	**Outcome**
Conducts activity in business-like manner	Used records to reduce loss, had separate bank account, changed operations (bought water rights, produced hay).	Taxpayer wins
Taxpayer/adviser expertise	Consulted ranch attorney, trainers, breeders, vet.	Taxpayer wins
Time/effort spent on the activity	Hired experienced manager, had weekly meetings.	Taxpayer wins
Expectation that assets used in the activity may increase in value	(Appreciation + sales) > "intervening loss" *until* year of "hoped for" future profits. Didn't show fair market value.	Tie
Taxpayer's success in *other* activities	Not discussed.	N/A
Taxpayer's history of losses from *this* activity	16 straight years of losses.	IRS wins
Occasional profits earned	Not discussed.	N/A
Taxpayer's financial status	Lots of other income.	IRS wins
Whether the activity is for personal pleasure	Not discussed.	N/A

Although Mr. Robinson's case was a close call, his losses were allowed.

Paycheck Protection Program (PPP) Loans

In May 2021, the SBA reported that PPP funds were exhausted, and it stopped accepting new applications for the program.

¶ 704 CONSOLIDATED APPROPRIATIONS ACT (CAA)

PPP Loans

Income on PPP relief is excluded from tax (CARES Act Sec. 1106(i)). Controversy had arisen about whether tax-free debt relief precluded taxpayers from deducting associated expenses used to provide forgiveness of PPP loans. The CAA resolved any controversy. Expenses are fully deductible. Related provisions include the following:

- Debt relief increases the basis of S corporation shareholders and partners.
- Other tax attributes are *not* reduced as a result of the tax-free discharge.

> **EXAMPLE:** Ronnie's Pizzeria, Inc., received an $85,000 PPP loan. All of the loan is forgiven due to payment of wages and rents of $85,000; all $85,000 in expenses are fully deductible. Ronnie's tax basis in stock is increased by the $85,000 of tax-free debt relief.

The remaining issue involves the *timing* of basis increases for S corporation shareholders. When does the basis increase occur? Some clients will be limited unless debt relief is recognized in 2020. Support for a 2020 basis increase (even if actual formal forgiveness occurs in 2021) comes from *Friedman v. Commissioner* (216 F.3d 537) and *Milenbach v. Commissioner* (318 F.3d 924 [CA9]). These cases noted there is a discharge when "it becomes clear that the debt will never have to be paid." A "[p]ractical assessment of the facts and circumstances" needs to be conducted to assess the likelihood of payment. The IRS has not yet issued guidance in this area.

The CAA also greatly simplified the filing of the PPP loan forgiveness forms. Taxpayers whose PPP loans were $150,000 or less can file Form 3508-S, which consists of a single page and requires no documentation of expenses.

Restaurant Meals

The CAA, which was enacted in December 2020, amended Code Sec. 274(n) to make restaurant meals 100 percent deductible; previously, they were 50 percent deductible. The 100 percent deduction applies only for 2021 and 2022 (for calendar-year taxpayers) but does *not* apply to meals in 2020, which are still 50 percent deductible.

The IRS has provided guidance on the definition of restaurant meals. IRS Notice 2021-25 defines a *restaurant* as "a business that prepares and sells food or beverages to retail customers for immediate consumption, regardless of whether the food or beverages are consumed on the business's premises." According to the guidance, the following are *not* considered restaurants:

- Businesses that primarily sell prepackaged food or beverages *not* for immediate consumption, such as grocery stores; specialty food stores; beer, wine, or liquor stores; drugstores; convenience stores; newsstands; vending machines; and kiosks;
- Eating facilities located on the business premises of the employer used in furnishing meals excluded from an employee's gross income under the "convenience of the employer" rule of Code Sec. 119; or
- Any employer-operated eating facility treated as a *de minimis* fringe under Code Sec. 132(e)(2) (e.g., a company cafeteria).

Other CAA Changes

Among the many changes in the CAA affecting individual taxpayers are the following:

- The tuition deduction is eliminated beginning in the 2021 tax year.

- The lifetime learning credit phaseout is increased beginning with the 2021 tax year, so more people will qualify for it. The beginning of the phaseout range is raised from $116,000 to $160,000 for married taxpayers filing a joint return.

- The work opportunity tax credit is extended through the end of 2025.

- Mortgage insurance premiums will continue to be treated as mortgage interest through 2021.

- The above-the line charitable deduction for cash contributions is extended through 2021; it is $300 for single taxpayers and $600 for married taxpayers filing jointly.

- Taxpayers can qualify for tax-free discharge qualified principal residence indebtedness through 2025, but the maximum of $2 million has been reduced to $750,000.

- Student loans: Employers can provide a tax-free benefit up to $5,250 per employee per year in student loan repayment assistance through an educational assistance program under Code Sec. 127. This was extended through 2025.

- The Code Sec. 179D tax deduction for energy-efficient commercial building property has been made permanent.

- Other energy provisions include the extension of the nonbusiness energy credit (through 2021) for building envelope improvements and certain other energy-efficient improvements to a principal residence.

¶705 AMERICAN RESCUE PLAN ACT

The American Rescue Plan Act of 2021 (ARPA), signed into law on March 11, 2021, is a $1.9 trillion package designed to combat the COVID-19 pandemic by delivering direct relief to families and workers and spurring economic recovery. Its anticipated effects on revenue are outlined in the following table:

ARPA: Estimated Revenue Effects	
ARPA Provision	**Revenue Impact**
Economic income payment (EIP) recovery rebates	$410 billion
Child tax credit	$110 billion
Premium tax credit	$45 billion
Paid sick and family leave (COVID-19 related)	$35 billion
Earned income tax credit	$26 billion
Employee retention credit	$10 billion
Source: Joint Committee on Taxation, JCX-14-21	

Economic Impact Payments

ARPA adds a "third round" of recovery rebates for the 2021 tax year. This supplements two prior rounds of recovery rebates. To provide stimulus to the economy during the pandemic, Congress made *advance* payment of the recovery rebate to taxpayers based upon their prior income. These advance payments are referred to as *economic impact payments*, also known as EIPs.

The maximum EIP is $1,400 per qualified individual ($2,800 for married couples filing jointly; both spouses must have a Social Security number). In addition, a $1,400 EIP is available for each qualifying dependent under Code Sec. 152. EIPs and the recovery rebate are phased out based on adjusted gross income (AGI):

Filing Status	Full EIP if AGI Is *Below*:	No EIP if AGI Is *Above*:
Single	$75,000	$80,000
Head of household (HOH)	$112,500	$120,000
Married filing jointly (MFJ)	$150,000	$160,000

Taxpayers who don't qualify for the maximum EIP advance payment may qualify for a recovery rebate on their 2021 Forms 1040. Qualification for the recovery rebate will be based upon 2021 taxable income and the phaseout covered above. The recovery rebate will be reduced by any EIP the taxpayer received.

If a taxpayer's income is too high in 2020 (or 2019 if the 2020 return had not yet been filed at the time advance payments were made) for a full third-round EIP, the taxpayer should claim the recovery rebate credit on 2021 Form 1040. This will typically apply if their income drops, or if they have an additional child in 2021.

> **EXAMPLE:** Felicia, a single taxpayer, received less than the maximum EIP, $1,200 (based on her 2020 income), because her income resulted in a partial phaseout of her EIP. In 2021, her income drops to $73,000, so she's below the phaseout threshold. She should claim the additional $200 as a recovery rebate on her 2021 Form 1040.

The third-round EIPs (largely issued in March and April 2021) are technically an advance payment of the recovery rebate credit that would otherwise be claimed on the taxpayer's 2021 tax return.

The IRS will mail taxpayers who receive a third-round EIP a Notice 1444-C, "Your 2021 Economic Impact Payment." Taxpayers should keep this letter with their tax year 2021 records since it will reduce the amount of recovery rebate they are entitled to on their 2021 tax returns.

The 2021 recovery rebate credit will be reduced by any previous EIP, but not below zero. Taxpayers who are married should consider the effect of filing separately on their recovery rebates (especially in separate property states).

Taxpayers can check the status of their EIP at https://www.irs.gov/coronavirus/get-my-payment. If a stimulus check is returned to the IRS as undeliverable, the taxpayer can switch to direct deposit at the same site. If the EIP was issued to a closed bank account, the IRS will mail a check to the taxpayer.

Deceased taxpayers (i.e., those who died before January 1, 2021) are not supposed to receive an EIP, unless they were a member of the armed forces in 2020. Note that some EIPs will undoubtedly be sent to taxpayers who were deceased before January 1, as the IRS isn't always aware that taxpayers have passed away.

Some taxpayers who received a reduced third-round EIP will receive a "plus-up payment" during 2021 without having to take any action. If the original EIP was based on the taxpayer's 2019 tax return, and the taxpayer later filed a 2020 return showing reduced income (or additional dependents) that would have resulted in larger EIP, the IRS will automatically issue a plus-up check (Rev. Proc. 2021-24).

EXAMPLE: Cory received a third-round EIP in February 2021 of $700 (it was reduced due to partial phaseout based on his 2019 income, since his 2020 tax return had not yet been filed). In April 2021, he files his 2020 return, and his income supports a full $1,400 payment. The IRS will send Cory an additional $700 "plus-up payment." This will be automatically mailed, separate from any 2020 refund. The "plus-up" payment will reduce any recovery rebate that Cory would otherwise be eligible to receive on his 2021 tax return.

Economic Injury Disaster Loan (EIDL)

The Small Business Administration (SBA) offered COVID-19 EIDL grants of up to $15,000 that do not need to be repaid. EIDL grants are similar to other federal grants but do not include the requirements that come with federal government grants. Note that the SBA has indicated that 2021 EIDL grants are no longer available.

The EIDL grants are not required to be repaid and are tax-free. Additionally, any otherwise deductible expenses paid for by the grant are deductible. If the EIDL is received by an S corporation or partnership, the owner's basis is increased by the grant.

Unemployment Exclusion

New Code Sec. 85(c) provides for per-taxpayer exclusion from income of up to $10,200 of unemployment compensation paid in 2020. To qualify, a taxpayer's modified AGI must be less than $150,000. Note that the threshold amount is the same no matter what the taxpayer's filing status is. To determine if his or her AGI is $150,000 or more, the taxpayer should calculate modified AGI and then reduce it by the amount of unemployment compensation.

EXAMPLE: Taxpayer A's modified AGI is $155,000 (including unemployment compensation). The taxpayer received $6,000 in unemployment compensation. Because the $6,000 in unemployment income is subtracted from modified AGI, Taxpayer A is eligible for the unemployment exclusion.

This is a "cliff." For example, AGI of $150,000 means the taxpayer must pay tax on all unemployment compensation. At an AGI of $149,999, the taxpayer can exclude up to $10,200. Therefore, if a taxpayer's AGI is just a little above $150,000, planning may be important. Perhaps the taxpayer should make a SEP-IRA contribution, or take bonus depreciation, if eligible. Filing a separate tax return may be advisable in some instances.

According to its FAQs on unemployment compensation, the IRS appears to believe that in a community property state, each spouse reports half of the other spouse's unemployment. This can provide a benefit in community property states where one spouse received unemployment benefits greater than $10,200 and the other spouse did not. For more information, see the IRS website at https://www.irs.gov/newsroom/2020-unemployment-compensation-exclusion-faqs

Student Loan Forgiveness

Under the ARPA, for 2021 through 2025, a broad exclusion is provided in the case of forgiveness of indebtedness on any eligible student loans. Discharge can be excluded from income, regardless of whether the loan is from an educational institution or is made directly to the borrower. To qualify, the loan must be provided expressly for postsecondary educational expenses. The forgiveness applies to loans made, insured, or guaranteed by U.S. states or colleges, or private education loans made by certain educational organizations (Code Sec. 108(f)(5)). The provision covers almost all discharge of student loans for this period.

COBRA Credit

The ARPA includes a provision that allows many taxpayers who lost their job or had their hours reduced and elected COBRA insurance to receive COBRA continuation coverage premiums for health coverage periods on or after April 1, 2021, through September 30, 2021 (IR-2021-115). An employer or plan to whom COBRA premiums are payable is entitled to a tax credit for the amount of the premium assistance. Note that taxpayers who can receive health insurance under their spouse's plan, a new employer's plan, or Medicare are not eligible.

Eligible individuals do not pay the health insurance premium; instead, the "person to whom COBRA premiums are payable" (usually the employer, but sometimes the insurer, or plan) pays the premiums. Then the employer will receive a tax credit. The employee is relieved from the obligation of paying COBRA premiums (IRS Notice 2021-31). The employer receives a refundable credit for paying the balance.

COBRA applies to companies with more than 20 employees, and health plans will notify eligible taxpayers. The IRS issued detailed guidance on this provision in May 2021 (IRS Notice 2021-31).

Paid COVID-Related Sick Leave and Family Leave Credits

The ARPA extended the emergency paid sick and family leave credits through September 30, 2021 (Code Secs. 3131(h) and 3132(h)), even though the legal requirement to pay has lapsed. In essence, employers who voluntarily pay for eligible leave will qualify for the credit.

Qualified days are expanded to include time spent getting a COVID-19 vaccination or recovering from issues arising from such vaccination. Also, qualified paid family leave is expanded to include time spent caring for a family member with COVID-19 (not just for children who cannot attend school/daycare due to the pandemic). The credit was increased for employer FICA tax (both Social Security and Medicare). The IRS has five years to assess extra taxes if a taxpayer took too large of a credit. Employers must comply with the Family Medical Leave Act of 1993 to qualify (this, among other rules, prohibits employer retaliation and other interference).

The self-employed paid sick leave and family medical leave credits are also extended through September 30, 2021. Self-employed taxpayers can take the credit in 2021 even if they also took it in 2020 (ARPA Sec. 9642(b)(c)(B)).

Child Tax Credit

The ARPA made significant changes to the child tax credit. All of these changes apply to the 2021 tax year only.

For all taxpayers, the maximum age of qualifying children has been raised from 16 to 17. The ARPA also increased the child tax credit for lower income and moderate-income taxpayers and expanded its coverage with the goal to reduce child poverty and help families. For higher income taxpayers, there is no change in the amount of the credit.

For lower and moderate-income taxpayers, the tax credit for qualifying children aged five or younger has been increased from $2,000 to $3,600/child; for qualifying children aged six to 17, the credit has been increased to $3,000/child. There is no change in the credit for other dependents (those over age 17); that tax credit is still $500 (Rev. Proc. 2021-24).

¶705

For the 2021 tax year only, the child tax credit is fully refundable if the taxpayer's principal place of abode is in the United States, even if the taxpayer has $0 earned income. The $3,000 credit applies to children who are six years old or older by the end of 2021. To be eligible for the $3,600 child tax credit, the child must be younger than age six on December 31, 2021.

There will be two separate phaseouts for 2021. The first phase-out applies only to the *increased* portion of the credit. The increased credit is $1,600 for children under six years old (from $2,000 to $3,600), and $1,000 for children ages six through 17 (from $2,000 to $3,000). The phaseout for the increased portion of credit is 5 percent of income over the threshold. The full phaseout depends on the number of children the taxpayer has.

To summarize, the child tax credit will have two phaseouts for 2021 based upon modified adjusted gross income:

- The first phaseout (at lower income amounts) that affects just the "increased portion" of the credit only.

- The second phaseout for the $2,000 original child tax credit. This is the same phaseout that applied under prior law.

	First Phaseout ("Increased Portion" of Credit Amount Only) Begins at MAGI of:
Single	$75,000
Head of household	$112,500
Married filing jointly	$150,000

In an effort to provide more regular cash flows for families, ARPA provides for advance payments of the child tax credit (Code Sec. 7527A). According to IR-2021-113, 88 percent of children in the United States will automatically receive monthly child tax credit checks.

Advance payments began to be issued in July 2021. The Department of the Treasury is advancing 50 percent of the expected 2021 child tax credit monthly. The advance payment will ultimately reduce the credits that taxpayers will receive on their 2021 tax returns. Taxpayers can claim the remaining credit (if any) when they file their 2021 tax returns in 2022. If the advance payment is greater than the actual child tax credit (e.g., if the taxpayer's 2021 income was much higher), the taxpayer generally will need to pay back the advance.

Advances reduce the taxpayer's amount of refund (or increase taxes due) on the 2021 Form 1040. For example, if a taxpayer receives an advance payment of $1,800 and the final credit received is $3,600, the net credit on the tax return is $1,800.

New Code Sec. 7527A provides that the advance payment of the child tax credit equals the "annual advance amount" for the last six months of 2021 (July through December). This is 50 percent of the amount the IRS estimates the taxpayer will receive as a credit for the 2021 tax year, up to $250 per month for children aged six though 17, and $300 per month for children under age six. The remaining credit, if any (net of advances), will be refunded with the taxpayer's tax return.

Advances are based on income reported on taxpayers' 2020 tax returns, or 2019 income if the 2020 return has not yet been filed (Code Sec. 7527A).

Lower/moderate-income taxpayers are protected from any possible repayment requirement by a safe harbor, but *only* if the overpayment (through advance payments) was caused by a drop in the number of qualifying children (Code Sec. 24(j)(2)). There is no safe harbor protection for unexpected increases in income. The safe harbor phases out at the following income levels:

	Full Waiver *No* Repayment	No Waiver *Full* Repayment
Single	$40,000	$80,000
Head of household	$50,000	$100,000
Married filing jointly	$60,000	$120,000

The IRS has established an online portal through which taxpayers can express their wish not to receive advance payments, or to report a birth or adoption of a child, a change in marital status, or other factors that would usually increase the amount of advance payment. Some taxpayers may wish to opt out of the advance payment system if they are concerned about the possibility of having to repay the advances. The IRS portal is at https://www.irs.gov/credits-deductions/child-tax-credit-update-portal.

By January 31, 2022, the IRS is to send an annual notice to taxpayers who received advance payments of the total paid in 2021 (Code Sec. 7527A(d)). Tax practitioners should ask their clients for the amount of advance payments that were received, since these will reduce the credit. Some may want to contact their clients about "opting" out of advance child tax credit payments, to avoid the possibility of having to repay the advances if income has increased or the number of dependents has decreased.

Dependent Care Benefits Credit and Employer-Provided Assistance

There were significant changes to the dependent care credit for the 2021 tax year only. Although, as under prior law, only children under age 13 (at the time the payment for care is made) will qualify, the credit has been changed significantly in other respects. The credit is refundable (even if there is no tax liability), and the maximum credit is $8,000 for taxpayers with two qualifying children. The credit can phase out if a taxpayer's income is too high.

Qualifying expenditures for 2021 are increased as shown in the following table:

	One Child	Two or More Children
2020	$3,000	$6,000
2021	**$8,000**	**$16,000**
2022	$3,000	$6,000

The credit percentage has been increased significantly for lower and moderate-income taxpayers.

Credit Rates (2021 only)	
Income	**Credit Percentage**
<$125,000	50%
$125,001–$183,000	21%–50%
$183,001–$400,000	20%
$400,001–$438,000	1%–20%
>$438,001	0%

For the 2021 tax year only, the complete phaseout (for higher income taxpayers only) begins at $400,000. The credit is fully phased out at AGI in excess of $438,000 (the taxpayer will receive no credit at all). Taxpayers over this amount will receive a smaller dependent care credit for 2021 than for the 2020 tax year. The credit percentage is decreased in 2021 (for higher income taxpayers only).

¶705

	Credit Percentage for High-Income Taxpayers
2020	20%
2021	0%
2022	20%

EXAMPLE: Parmjit and Sue have a 12-year-old daughter and daycare expenses. Their AGI is $450,000. They will receive a dependent care credit in 2020, but not in 2021 (since the credit will be fully phased out for high-income taxpayers).

Also, for 2021 only, the ARPA raises the excludible benefit for employer-provided dependent care assistance from $5,000 to $10,500 (Code Sec. 129(a)(2)(D)). Employers can retroactively amend their plans.

The IRS also extended the period to spend unused amounts (Notice 2021-26). This is important, as many daycare providers were shut down due to the COVID-19 pandemic.

Earned Income Tax Credit (EITC)

Under the ARPA, several changes are made to the EITC for *childless* taxpayers (i.e., taxpayers with no qualifying children). The maximum childless EITC has increased from $543 to $1,502 for 2021. The changes for childless taxpayers apply to the 2021 tax year only. The changes include the following:

- Age eligibility restrictions were adjusted for the 2021 tax year only: The minimum age for eligibility generally dropped from age 25 to age 19. However, a special higher minimum age for eligibility applies in two instances: The minimum age for eligibility is decreased to 18 if the child is a qualified former foster youth/homeless youth. The minimum age is increased to 24 if the child is a specified student (eligible student for at least five months). The maximum age for eligibility is removed (taxpayers will qualify even if older than 65).
- Increased amount of earned income that qualifies to receive the maximum credit and increased the income limit on eligibility.
- Increased the credit rate (for childless taxpayers) to 15.3 percent (basically FICA tax) from 7.65 percent.

In addition, for all taxpayers claiming the credit for the 2021 tax year only, when computing the EITC, taxpayers can choose to substitute their 2019 income instead of using actual 2021 income. This is available only if the taxpayer's earned income was less in 2021 than in 2019. This should help taxpayers who had significantly reduced income due to the pandemic, or for other reasons (ARPA Act section 9626).

EXAMPLE: Ross's earned income is less in 2021 than it was in 2019. For 2021 only, Ross can elect to substitute his 2019 earned income for his 2021 earned income when calculating the EITC.

ARPA also allows some spouses who utilize the married filing separate status to claim the EITC (Code Sec. 32(d)(2)). This rule applies for 2021 *and* later years. The credit is now allowed for separated spouses who:

- Do not file a joint return,
- Live with the qualifying child for more than 6 months, *and*

- Either
  - Didn't live together in last six months, or
  - Have a separation, support decree, etc., at year end (other than a decree of divorce).

For 2021 and later years, the disqualified investment income test increased to $10,000 (adjusted for inflation).

Premium Tax Credit

The Marketplace Exchanges will advance payments for health insurance of eligible individuals. However, these payments are based on prior income. If income increases in the current year, the taxpayer might be required to repay the advance. For the 2020 tax year *only*, taxpayers are not required to repay excess advance premium assistance tax payments (and no Form 8962 is required). See Code Sec. 36B(f)(2)(B)(iii). If they have a credit (as opposed to having received excess advances), they can file Form 8962 to claim the additional credit (IR-2021-84).

Taxpayers who receive unemployment compensation (or who have been approved to receive unemployment compensation) during 2021 will have their 2021 contribution percentage dropped to 133 percent (and taxpayers are deemed to meet 100 percent to 400 percent of the federal poverty level requirement) even if their income is actually higher (Code Sec. 36B(g)). This will generally decrease the taxpayer's "contribution amount" and thereby increase the amount of the premium tax credit.

For 2021 and 2022, the ARPA temporarily expands eligibility so that even taxpayers with incomes greater than 400 percent of the federal poverty level can get the premium tax credit. However, higher income also increases the taxpayer's required contribution toward insurance, and therefore reduces the credit.

> **EXAMPLE:** John's household income is greater than 400 percent of the federal poverty level for 2021 and 2022. He will be able to qualify for the Code sec. 36B credit if he meets the other requirements (buying Marketplace insurance, etc.). In prior years, he would not be eligible for the premium tax credit under these circumstances. John will be able to claim a premium tax credit for 2021 and 2022. However, it will not be a large credit (since the taxpayer's contribution amount increases).

Taxpayers who are eligible for this credit are required to pay a portion of their health insurance premium for Marketplace insurance. This was not changed by the ARPA. However, the *amount* of the taxpayer's contribution has been reduced for the tax years 2021 and 2022. Special lower "contribution percentages" are provided for 2021 and 2022. For 2020, the contribution percentage for household income of 300 percent of the federal poverty level is 9.78 percent of household income. It drops to 6.0 percent for 2021 and 2022.

Fixing Mistakes Due to Retroactive Effect of ARPA

Some of the ARPA provisions were effective retroactively. More than 10 million 2020 tax returns had already been filed before the ARPA was passed. The IRS will be correcting mistakes made in tax returns filed before the ARPA became law on March 11, 2021. The IRS has stated that in most cases, there is no need for taxpayers to file amended tax returns; the IRS will fix the returns automatically (IR-2021-111).

For example, the IRS will correct returns in connection with the unemployment exclusion. The IRS has indicated it will send refunds to taxpayers who qualified for the unemployment exclusion but failed to claim the exclusion on their tax returns. The refunds will be mailed in two phases:

- First phase: Single taxpayers with simple returns, including taxpayers who failed to claim children or any refundable credits. Refunds were to start being sent the week of May 10, 2021.
- Second phase: For more complex returns, the IRS will send refunds through the end of summer 2021.

The refunds will be direct deposits if the IRS has the taxpayer's bank information. Taxpayers will receive a notice explaining the correction within 30 days (IR-2021-111).

The IRS will also automatically correct issues related to certain other ARPA provisions. These include taxpayers who erroneously paid the 2020 excess advance premium tax credit (IR-2021-111) and taxpayers without children whose EITC increased under ARPA. However, taxpayers who have children and whose EITC *increased* due to ARPA changes should file Form 1040-X.

Credit Card Merchant Reporting

You can expect clients to begin receiving more Forms 1099-K for the 2022 tax year. Under prior law, third-party settlement organizations (e.g., Ebay, Airbnb, etc.) were only required to report credit card transactions to merchants if they had more than 200 transactions totaling more than $20,000 per year. Under the ARPA, however, third-party organizations must report such transactions if they total $600 per year. The new rule is effective beginning with payment transactions settled *after* December 31, 2021.

Excess Business Losses

The Code Sec. 461(l) business loss limit was originally scheduled to expire at the end of 2025 but was extended by ARPA through 2026. The CARES Act suspended the limit for 2018–2020, but the limit returns for the 2021 tax year. Net business losses are limited to $250,000 for single taxpayers and $500,000 for MFJ taxpayers. Excess net business losses are not lost, but rather are converted to net operating losses in the succeeding year.

Restaurant Revitalization Fund Tax Treatment

The Restaurant Revitalization Fund was a significant program designed to provide assistance to eligible restaurants, bars, and other qualifying businesses affected by the COVID-19 crisis. However, as of this writing, the program has been closed because all allocated funds have been extended. Businesses eligible for the program included the following:

- Restaurants
- Food stands, food trucks, food carts
- Caterers
- Bars, saloons, lounges, taverns
- Licensed facilities or premises of a beverage alcohol producer where the public may taste, sample, or purchase products
- Other similar places
- Snack and nonalcoholic beverage bars
- Bakeries (whose on-site sales to the public are at least 33 percent of gross receipts)
- Brewpubs, tasting rooms, taprooms, wineries, distilleries, etc. (whose on-site sales to the public are at least 33 percent of gross receipts)
- Inns (whose on-site sales of food and beverages to the public were at least 33 percent of gross receipts in 2019).

¶705

The amounts received under this program are tax-free. Full deductibility is allowed for the funds received, and if the funds have been received by a partnership or S corporation, the owners receive an increase in basis (ARPA Sec. 9673).

STUDY QUESTIONS

1. Which legislation made restaurant meals 100 percent deductible for 2021 and 2022?

    a. American Rescue Plan Act (ARPA)

    b. Consolidated Appropriations Act (CAA)

    c. Tax Cuts and Jobs Act (TCJA)

    d. CARES Act

2. In *Chiarelli v. Commissioner*, what did Mr. Chiarelli do that resulted in an automatic disallowance of his large noncash charitable contribution?

    a. He concealed from the court the fact that he was an attorney.

    b. He did not provide a qualified appraisal of the property donated, nor did he receive a contemporaneous written acknowledgement.

    c. He donated the property to Goodwill.

    d. He had donated the property in a previous tax year.

3. In which case did the taxpayer meet the nine-factor test for a hobby loss?

    a. *Stephen Whatley v. Commissioner*

    b. *Shane Robison v. Commissioner*

    c. *Chiarelli v. Commissioner*

    d. *Friedman v. Commissioner*

4. What is the goal of Operation Hidden Treasure?

    a. To help taxpayers pay back student loans

    b. To uncover fraudulent charitable contributions

    c. To send stimulus payments to American taxpayers

    d. To identify taxpayers who have unreported cryptocurrency transactions

5. In the third round of ARPA economic impact payments, what is the maximum EIP per qualified individual?

    a. $600

    b. $1,200

    c. $1,400

    d. $2,800

6. Which agency provided economic injury disaster loans (EIDLs) in 2021?

    a. SBA

    b. IRS

    c. FBAR

    d. COBRA

¶706 2021 EMPLOYEE RETENTION CREDIT (ERC)

Coverage Period

The ERC was changed both by the CAA and the ARPA. The discussion that follows applies only to the ERC for 2021.

Under new Code Sec. 3134, the ERC is extended through December 31, 2021. However, at the time of this writing, proposed legislation, HR 3684, if enacted, would terminate the ERC after September 30, 2021, except for "recovery startup businesses."

Credit Calculation

For 2021, businesses can claim a credit against 70 percent of "qualified wages." Qualified wages include not only wages, but also health insurance paid for the employees (provided the employee is able to exclude the insurance cost under Sec. 106).

Qualified wages are limited to $10,000 per employee, per quarter. Therefore, the maximum credit is $7,000 per employee, per quarter ($10,000 limit × 70 percent credit rate).

The ERC can provide substantial tax credits.

> **EXAMPLE:** Ronnie's Pizzeria, Inc., has 10 employees who make at least $10,000 in each quarter in 2021. Assume the business meets the "significant decline in gross receipts test" for each quarter in 2021.
>
> The maximum credit for Ronnie's for 2021 is $280,000 (10 employees × $10,000/quarter limit × 70 percent credit rate × 4 quarters).

The ERC is fully refundable; although the credit may appear to be limited to the employer-paid FICA taxes, any excess over these taxes is fully refundable (Code Sec. 3134(b)(3) and CARES Act Sec. 2301(b)(3)).

General Eligibility for the ERC (Three Independent Ways to Qualify)

Note that employers may qualify for the ERC for 2021 under any one of three qualification methods:

- Qualification method #1: "Partial suspension" of operations: For the period of time the business had both:

  — Operations partially or fully suspended, and

  — This was caused by a pandemic governmental order in effect.

- Qualification method #2: "Significant decline in gross receipts": Businesses that have significant decline in gross receipts also qualify for each quarter they meet the test.

- Qualification method #3: Recovery start-up businesses qualify for an ERC of up to $50,000 per quarter, provided they don't meet *either* of the above qualification methods in a quarter (partial suspension or significant decline tests). Please note this method for recovery startup businesses is available only for the third and fourth quarters of 2021.

Eligibility Under Partial or Full Suspension Test

For employers who qualify under the full or partial suspension rule, the credit may be claimed for eligible wages paid during the specific period for which a COVID government order was in effect and this caused the employer to experience a partial or full suspension of operations. This rule differs from the "significant decline" test (discussed below) in that it applies only during the specific period that both conditions are satisfied (as opposed to the "significant decline" test, which applies on a quarter-by-quarter basis, for all qualified wages paid during that quarter).

> **EXAMPLE:** Ronnie's Pizzeria, Inc., does not meet the significant decline test. However, it experiences a partial suspension of operations due to a governmental COVID-19 order. The partial suspension caused by the governmental order lasts from June 3, 2021, through June 24, 2021. Only wages paid during this three-week period are eligible for the credit.

In addition to full or partial suspensions, taxpayers can also qualify under the "significant decline" test or the recovery startup business qualification methods (see following discussions). If there is no partial suspension, a taxpayer can still get an ERC if it qualifies under either of the other two methods.

Notice 2021-20 provides examples of circumstances that qualify as partial suspensions.

Facts	Partial Suspension?
Grocery store – No salad bar allowed, but this is nominal part of business.	No
Retail store – customer density in store limited, but only short wait outside for customers.	No
Essential business, but customers not coming in.	No
Workplace closed, but business continues at comparable level as before COVID-19 (remote work by employees).	No
Taxpayer has both essential and nonessential businesses.	Yes, if nonessential is more than 10 percent of gross receipts or hours
Essential business, but suppliers can't provide enough materials (e.g., auto parts store).	Yes
Restaurant, takeout only.	Yes
Hospital, elective surgeries put off.	Yes, if more than nominal (10 percent)
Restaurant, dining-in limited to 25 percent capacity.	Yes

Eligibility Under Significant Decline in Gross Receipts Test

Employers who experience a "significant decline in gross receipts" during a quarter in 2021 can also qualify for the ERC. The significant gross receipts method is based upon gross receipts in the current quarter being less than 80 percent of the gross receipts compared to the same quarter in 2019 (i.e., the same quarter *two years* prior). Taxpayers who weren't in business at the beginning of the same quarter in 2019 can use quarters in 2020 in lieu of using 2019 as the comparison quarter (Code Sec. 3134(c)(2)(A), flush language).

> **EXAMPLE:** An employer had the following gross receipts in the following quarters in 2021 (this employer will qualify for both quarters):

	2021	2019	Percentage	Qualify?
Q1	$79,000	$100,000	79%	Yes
Q2	$75,000	$100,000	75%	Yes

For 2021, employers have two options. They can determine whether there is a "significant decline" in the current quarter in 2021 compared to the same quarter in 2019. *Or,* as an alternative, they can elect to use the *prior* quarter to measure whether a significant decline has occurred (and the comparable quarter in 2019). The election to use the prior quarter can provide two advantages:

- Certainty that the employer will qualify: This is important if the employer wants to recover through reduced payroll tax deposits.

- Two-for-one benefit: In essence, the employer can qualify for the ERC in two quarters under the 80 percent rule, even if the taxpayer only meets the test for one quarter.

  EXAMPLE: Alisha's Salon, Inc., has the following gross receipts:
  - 2021 Q1 versus 2019 Q1 = 79 percent.
  - 2021 Q2 versus 2019 Q2 = 81 percent.

  Alisha's Salon can qualify for both quarters: Q1 based on the actual Q1 percentage, and Q2 based on the election to use the Q1 percentage (79 percent).

Eligibility for Recovery Start-up Businesses

Recovery start-up businesses qualify for the ERC *only* for the third and fourth quarters of 2021 (provided they don't also meet either the partial suspension or the "significant decline in gross receipts" tests). This credit also utilizes the same $10,000 per quarter limit for each employee and the 70 percent credit rate. However, total credits claimed under this provision can't exceed $50,000 per quarter. The requirements to qualify as a recovery start-up business are as follows:

- The entity began carrying on any trade or business after February 15, 2020. Note that it's possible to be formed on or before February 15, but not yet in business. Entities that have not begun to function as a going concern in a particular quarter are not eligible to be treated as recovery start-up businesses for that quarter (Notice 2021-49, Sec. III.D).

- Average annual gross receipts for the three-taxable-year period preceding the calendar quarter that credit is claimed do not exceed $1 million. Gross receipts are determined under Code Sec. 448(c)(3) (including the requirement that gross receipts for short taxable years must be annualized and that if an entity was only in existence for part of the preceding three-year period, only the periods it was in existence are counted). Gross receipts include gross receipts of related businesses under common control.

- The entity is not otherwise eligible to claim the ERC under the partial suspension or significant decline in gross receipts tests.

No Double-Counting Rules

Double counting the same wages for the ERC and PPP loans is not permitted. In addition, employers may *not* count the same wages for the ERC and for any of the following credits claimed under the following Code Sections:

- Code Sec. 41 (the research credit)
- Code Sec. 45A (the Indian employment credit)
- Code Sec. 45P (credit for active-duty members of uniformed services)

- Code Sec. 51 (the work opportunity credit)

- Code Sec. 1396 (the empowerment zone employment credit)

- Code Secs. 3131 and 3132 (the COVID-19 paid sick leave and emergency paid family leave credits)

However, employers may claim the Code Sec. 45B credit for "excess employer social security tax" paid on tips and also claim the ERC for tips that are included in wages (Notice 2021-49, Sec. IV.B). See the discussion of tips later in this chapter.

Taxpayers are also prevented for the third and fourth quarters of 2021 from counting the same wages for the ERC as are utilized for the shuttered venue program or the restaurant revitalization grants under the ARPA (Code Sec. 3134(h)).

Large Employers

A special restriction applies to large employers. Large employers are limited in the type of wages that qualify for the ERC. For 2021, large employers are defined as employers that had more than 500 full-time employees in 2019.

Generally, wages for large employers qualify for the ERC only if they were paid during times the employee was *not* providing services (e.g., furloughed periods). Wages to workers for services performed are not eligible. However, "severely financially distressed" large employers may claim the ERC for all wages (see discussion later in this chapter).

"Severely financially distressed employers" are tested under rules similar to the "significant decline" test discussed earlier; however, the rules substitute 10 percent for 80 percent.

> **EXAMPLE:** ABC, Inc., had 600 full-time employees in 2019, so it is treated as a large employer for 2021. Generally, it would only be able to count as qualified wages amounts paid to workers who were not providing services. However, it meets the requirements of a "severely financially distressed employer" for 2021 Q2 (its gross receipts were less than 10 percent compared to the same quarter in 2019). Therefore, qualified wages paid by ABC during Q2 will include both wages paid for services and wages paid for employees who were not providing services (e.g., furloughed workers).

Reducing Tax Deductions by the ERC

Taxpayers must reduce their deductions by the amount of the ERC (Code Secs. 280C and 2301(g)), even if they file a 2020 Form 941-X in 2021. However, the ERC credit is received tax-free, so ultimately the income and deduction will net to zero (Notice 2021-20, Question 61). There can be timing differences, however, as illustrated by the following examples:

> **EXAMPLE:** Ronnie's Pizzeria, Inc., files its 2020 Q2 Form 941-X in February 2021. The business receives a $5,000 ERC credit on its Form 941 in March 2021. Ronnie's Pizzeria must reduce its 2020 deductions (wages) by $5,000. In the case of business taxpayers, this will create a M-1 difference (increase taxable income). In 2021, Ronnie's receives a $5,000 credit and reports it as $5,000 in tax-free income. The M-1 for the tax-free credit offsets the M-1 adjustment for wages in 2020; however, a timing difference is created.

EXAMPLE: Ronnie's Pizzeria, Inc., files its 2021 Q1 Form 941 in April 2021. In May 2021, it receives a $7,000 ERC. Ronnie's Pizzeria must reduce its 2021 deductions (wages) by $7,000. It will create a M-1 difference (increase taxable income). Ronnie's reports a credit of $7,000 in tax-free income (M-1 adjustment; Notice 2021-20, FAQ 61). The M-1 difference ($7,000) reduces its taxable income. This offsets the wage decrease, so the net difference is $0.

How to Claim the ERC If Not Claimed on Original Form 941

If a taxpayer neglected to claim the ERC on an originally filed Form 941, it can file Form 941-X, *Adjusted Employer's Quarterly Federal Tax Return or Claim for Refund.*

Extended Statute of Limitations

For the third and fourth quarters of 2021 only, the statute of limitations is extended to five years after the due date of the Form 941 (or the date actually filed, if later). For example, Q4 2021 can be audited up until April 15, 2027.

New Development: Eligibility of Wages Paid to Majority Shareholders and Certain Relatives

The IRS issued new guidance on the ERC eligibility of wages paid to majority shareholders on August 4, 2021 (Notice 2021-49). This guidance stakes out a new position on wages paid to majority shareholders, their spouses, and certain other relatives, compared to prior guidance. The new provision is retroactively effective for ERCs claimed in both 2020 and 2021.The change will *not* affect eligibility for wages paid to shareholders who own 50 percent or less of the stock (after taking attribution into account). Wages paid to such shareholders will be eligible for the ERC (see the example later in this chapter).

The ERC rules incorporate by reference the rules of Code Sec. 51(i). This provision renders wages paid to certain persons related to the majority shareholders ineligible for the ERC. The new interpretation in Notice 2021-49 takes a circuitous route to also remove from eligibility not only wages paid to *relatives* of majority shareholders, but also wages paid to the majority shareholders and their spouses, if they have any living relatives (see list below). The position is based on the following:

- The rules of attribution of stock under Code Sec. 267(c) are incorporated into the majority shareholder provision (including attribution of the majority shareholders' stock to their relatives).

- These attribution rules of Code Sec. 267(c) attribute stock owned by majority shareholders to certain of their relatives (see list below). Therefore, the stock owned by majority shareholders is deemed to be owned by the relatives under the attribution rules.

- The relatives of a majority shareholder thereby (according to the IRS) become majority shareholders themselves.

  — And the actual shareholder is now a relative of a deemed majority shareholder (through application of Code Sec. 267(c)).

Notice 2021-49 provides that the relatives covered by attribution are the following (Code Sec. 152(A)–(H)):

- A child or a descendant of a child

- A brother, sister, stepbrother, or stepsister

- The father or mother, or an ancestor of either
- A stepfather or stepmother
- A niece or nephew
- An aunt or uncle
- A son-in-law, daughter-in-law, father-in-law, mother-in-law, brother-in-law, or sister-in-law
- An individual (other than a spouse) who for the taxable year has the same principal place of abode as the taxpayers.

NOTE: Spouses are not relatives for purposes of this rule. However, Notice 2021-49 provides that wages paid to spouses of majority shareholders are generally ineligible for the credit. See the following examples.

The following examples of the majority shareholder rule are provided in Notice 2021-49:

EXAMPLE: Corporation B is owned 100 percent by Individual G. Individual H is the child of Individual G. Corporation B is an eligible employer with respect to the first calendar quarter of 2021. Individual G is an employee of Corporation B, but Individual H is not. Pursuant to the attribution rules of section 267(c) of the Code, Individual H is attributed 100 percent ownership of Corporation B, and both Individual G and Individual H are treated as 100 percent owners. Individual G has the relationship to Individual H described in section 152(d)(2)(C) of the Code. Accordingly, Corporation B may not treat as qualified wages any wages paid to Individual G because Individual G is a related individual for purposes of the employee retention credit.

OBSERVATION: This example illustrates the IRS's argument underlying what some call the "any living relative" rule. If a majority shareholder has a relative who qualifies under the relationship rules, the majority shareholder's stock is then attributed to the relative (other than a spouse). After this attribution, the relative is now, himself or herself, deemed to be a majority shareholder (i.e., the relative who is deemed to be a majority shareholder through the rules of attribution). Since the actual majority shareholder is now related to a *deemed* majority shareholder (the relative), wages paid to the actual majority shareholder are now ineligible for the credit (since the *actual* majority shareholder is treated as related to the *deemed* majority shareholder).

EXAMPLE: Corporation C is owned 100 percent by Individual J. Corporation C is an eligible employer with respect to the first calendar quarter of 2021. Individual J is married to Individual K, and they have no other family members as defined in section 267(c)(4) [note: see the list of relatives above] of the Code. Individual J and Individual K are both employees of Corporation C. Pursuant to the attribution rules of section 267(c), Individual K is attributed 100 percent ownership of Corporation A, and both Individual J and Individual K are treated as 100 percent owners. However, Individuals J and K do **not** have any of the relationships to each other described in section 152(d)(2)(A)-(H) of the Code. Accordingly, wages paid by Corporation C to Individual J and Individual K in the first calendar quarter of 2021 may be treated as qualified wages if the amounts satisfy the other requirements to be treated as qualified wages.

EXAMPLE: Corporation D is owned 34 percent by Individual L, 33 percent by Individual M, and 33 percent by Individual N. Individual L, Individual M, and Individual N are siblings. Corporation D is an eligible employer with respect to the first calendar quarter of 2021. Individual L, Individual M, and Individual N are employees of Corporation D. Pursuant to the attribution rules of section 267(c) of the Code, Individual L, Individual M, and Individual N are treated as 100 percent owners. Individual L, Individual M, and Individual N have the relationship to each other described in section 152(d)(2)(B) of the Code. Accordingly, Corporation D may not treat as qualified wages any wages paid to Individual L, Individual M, or Individual N.

Notice 2021-49 will not affect the eligibility of shareholders who own 50 percent or less of the stock (after taking into account stock attributed under Code Sec. 267(c)). The following example illustrates this principle:

> **EXAMPLE:** AB, Inc., is owned by Al and Bob (each owns 50 percent). Al and Bob are not related. Wages paid to Al and Bob (as well as wages paid to their family members) are eligible for the credit. Neither is a "majority shareholder" since neither owns more than 50 percent.

Aggregation

All persons under common control are treated as a single employer under Code Sec. 52(a) or (b). See Notice 2021-20, footnote 13 for information on common control under Code Sec. 52. In addition, aggregation is required for entities described in Code Sec. 414(m) or (o). They are treated as a single employer for all purposes related to the ERC (see Code Sec. 3134(d)), including measuring whether a significant decline in gross receipts has occurred, a partial suspension exists, and counting the number of employees in a business to determine whether it's a large employer or whether it has experienced a partial suspension of operations due to a governmental order.

> **EXAMPLE:** Bob's Roofing, Inc. (81 percent decline in gross receipts in 2021 Q3) and Bob's Concrete Services, Inc. (50 percent decline in gross receipts in 2021 Q3) are under common control (Bob owns 100 percent of both). They will be measured under the "significant decline in gross receipts" test as if they were a single employer. If, after aggregating their gross receipts (for both Q3 2021 and Q3 2019) as if they were a single company, they have a combined decline of 67 percent, both corporations will be eligible for the ERC.

> **EXAMPLE:** ABC, Inc., and DEF, LLC, are under common control. Neither business meets the "substantial decline" in gross receipts text. ABC has a partial suspension due to a government order; DEF does not have a partial suspension. However, because they are treated as one company, they are treated as *both* having partial suspensions (IRS FAQ number 37).

Tips

Notice 2021-49 also provides guidance on tips. Although tips are not actually paid by an employer, they are treated as qualified wages and eligible for the credit (Notice 2021-49, Sec. IV. B).

Record Retention

According to IRS Notice 2021-20, taxpayers must retain, for at least four years, the following records for the ERC:

- Governmental order (if partial suspension)
- Records to show a significant decline in gross receipts
- Which employees received qualified wages

- How the taxpayer computed allocable health expenses
- Copies of the taxpayer's Forms 941

Since the statute of limitations is longer (five years) for ERCs claimed for the third and fourth quarters of 2021 (see earlier discussion), records should be retained longer for these quarters.

¶ 707 RELATIONSHIP BETWEEN PPP FORGIVENESS AND ERC

Taxpayers cannot double-count same wages for both PPP loan forgiveness and the ERC. Wages used to provide for PPP loan forgiveness provide a greater benefit than the ERC (since there is a dollar-for-dollar benefit in the PPP area, as opposed to a 70 percent credit under the ERC), so taxpayers will generally choose *first* to use sufficient wages to receive full PPP loan forgiveness, and then apply excess wages to obtain the ERC if they are eligible. This requires electing not to claim the ERC for an amount necessary to receive full PPP forgiveness. IRS Notice 2021-20 provides that a taxpayer is deemed to elect out of the ERC if it uses the payroll costs for PPP loan forgiveness (so no formal election is required).

> **EXAMPLE:** Ronnie's Pizzeria, Inc., has three employees, and the business received a PPP loan. Ronnie's will first want to allocate enough wages to get full PPP loan forgiveness. This requires election out of the ERC. (Ronnie's will simply not claim the ERC for the wages needed to get full PPP forgiveness, thereby making a "deemed" election.) Then, Ronnie's can allocate any remaining wages to the ERC. There are wage allocation planning opportunities, discussed later, that allow Ronnie's Pizzeria to allocate wages between the PPP and the ERC in a manner that provides full forgiveness and maximizes the ERC.

PPP Forgiveness and the ERC

Taxpayers cannot double-count the same payroll costs for the ERC and PPP loan forgiveness. The objective for taxpayers is to use the minimum amount of wages and health insurance necessary to get the full PPP forgiveness but also try to maximize the ERC.

Maximizing PPP loan forgiveness and the ERC is like "walking the tightrope." Taxpayers want to receive full discharge from the PPP loan while preserving as much qualified wages as possible for the ERC. Taxpayers may consider doing the following:

- Use up "40 percent" nonpayroll costs to the full extent possible (this includes covered rents, utilities, etc.). These costs are not eligible for the ERC and therefore should be used to the full extent possible for PPP forgiveness. However, these costs are limited to 40 percent of total PPP forgiveness.
  - Maximizing nonpayroll costs may require waiting until a full 24 weeks in a covered period have passed to file a forgiveness application.
- Use "payroll costs" that are eligible for PPP forgiveness (pension contributions, state unemployment tax) but are not eligible for the ERC.
- Report forgivable expenses in the best manner on the PPP forgiveness application (see later discussion).
  - Report all eligible nonpayroll costs as forgivable costs on Form 3508 or 350S up to the 40 percent of forgiveness limit.
- Allocate employee wages to optimize the ERC (see later discussion).

- Pay eligible shareholders wages evenly each quarter (see earlier discussion for wages paid to *majority* shareholders and their relatives that the IRS says aren't eligible for the ERC in Notice 2021-49).

  — Note that wages paid to majority shareholders should be allocated to PPP loan forgiveness to the full extent possible ($20,833) since they will not be eligible for the ERC.

- Use wages for PPP purposes in quarters for which the employer doesn't qualify for the ERC.

IRS Notice 2021-20 opens up planning opportunities. Employers are given a great deal of latitude to allocate specific wages to PPP forgiveness (and preserve other wages for the ERC). However, the employer must be able to *demonstrate* which wages were used on the PPP loan and should keep a spreadsheet to support the PPP loan forgiveness application.

It is possible to significantly increase the ERC by careful PPP forgiveness reporting. A taxpayer can report the smallest possible "payroll costs" on the PPP forgiveness application—just enough to get full forgiveness. Note that at least 60 percent of the amount forgiven must be "payroll costs." That means that if the PPP loan was for $100,000, the taxpayer must have at least $60,000 in payroll costs to get full forgiveness. If the taxpayer has $70,000 in payroll costs, it might consider only reporting $60,000 on the PPP loan forgiveness application (Form 3508S). The remaining $40,000 can be eligible nonpayroll costs (provided the taxpayer has that much in nonpayroll costs).

Some payroll costs do not qualify for the ERC, such as SUTA tax and pension contributions. The taxpayer should use these up to the full extent (since they satisfy the requirement of being "payroll costs" for purposes of the PPP 60 percent payroll cost forgiveness requirement). If the taxpayer shows $0 *nonpayroll* costs on the PPP loan forgiveness application, all forgiveness will be allocated to payroll costs, and this will reduce the ERC (Notice 2021-20, FAQ 49).

EXAMPLE: Ronnie's Pizzeria, Inc., received a PPP loan for $100,000. Its payroll costs were $100,000, but only $60,000 is needed for full loan forgiveness (60 percent of forgiveness). The business's nonpayroll costs are $50,000. These will be limited to $40,000 toward loan forgiveness (they cannot be more than 40 percent of forgiveness). On Form 3508S, Ronnie's enters only $60,000 in payroll costs and enters $100,000 in forgiveness. This implies at least $40,000 in eligible nonpayroll costs (although there is nowhere to disclose this on the form). Ronnie's has preserved $40,000 of wages for the ERC (which could provide up to $28,000 in credits).

In ERC planning, taxpayers can choose a covered period for PPP up to a full 24 weeks if necessary to "fill-up" 40 percent of nonpayroll costs. If necessary, employers should use the *full* 24-week period to accumulate additional nonpayroll costs (covered utilities, covered rent, etc.)

EXAMPLE: AZ Corp.'s PPP loan equals $100,000. After 16 weeks, its payroll costs are $80,000 and its nonpayroll costs are $20,000. AZ should wait until the end of the full 24-week period so it can get its nonpayroll costs up to $40,000. Doing so would "preserve" more wages for the ERC.

Another method to maximize the ERC is to allocate more wages for PPP purposes in quarters it isn't eligible for the ERC.

EXAMPLE: SN, Inc., is eligible for the ERC in the first quarter and second quarter of 2021. However, it is not eligible for the third quarter. SN's PPP covered period runs from March 3 to August 7, 2021. It should allocate as much wage expense to the PPP forgiveness to the third quarter as possible (since it isn't eligible for the PPP in the third quarter). Taxpayers should retain documentation (e.g., a spreadsheet) to show how they made this allocation.

Employers can also choose which wages are "used" on the PPP loan. Remember that not all wages qualify for the ERC; qualified wages are limited to $10,000 per quarter per employee.

EXAMPLE: Ronnie's Pizzeria, Inc.'s covered period is from April 1 to September 16, 2021. It received a PPP loan of $100,000 (and needs $60,000 payroll costs for full loan forgiveness). The pizzeria's payroll costs are $120,000, and nonpayroll costs are $40,000. Its objective is to get as many employees as possible $10,000 per quarter in ERC wages. Wages by employee (evenly paid over 24 weeks) are as shown in the following table. By using up Iris's wages (she is not a shareholder) to the full extent possible, Stu's wages can be saved for the ERC.

	Wages 24 Weeks	Used for PPP	PPP Q2	PPP Q3	ERC Q2	ERC Q3
Ronnie	$40,000	$20,000	$10,000	$10,000	$10,000	$10,000
Stu	$20,000	$0	$0	$0	$10,000	$10,000
Iris	$60,000	$40,000	$20,000	$20,000	$10,000	$10,000
TOTAL	$120,000	$60,000	$30,000	$30,000	$30,000	$30,000
ERC credit (70%)					$21,000	$21,000

Many industries were hit hard by the pandemic (including restaurants and hospitality businesses). They may need all their payroll costs to get full forgiveness of the PPP loan. However, they should still have some eligible wages since the PPP "covered period" is at most 24 weeks.

EXAMPLE: Jack's Bistro, Inc., gets a $100,000 PPP loan. Its payroll costs over a 24-week period are $60,000. Jack's will need to use all the payroll costs to get the full relief. The 60 percent payroll requirement means all wages must be used. But if the covered period runs from February 5, 2021, to July 23, 2021, Jack's Bistro can still count wages in the "wedge periods" from January 1 to February 4, and wages after July 23, 2021, to qualify for the ERC.

¶ 708 IRS PRACTICE AND PROCEDURE

There recently has been a sea change in IRS procedure. Some of the actual enforcement efforts will depend on the IRS obtaining more funds. Most moderate-income taxpayers have their income reported to the IRS (very low unreported income), and higher income taxpayers often have significant income *not* reported to the IRS (higher unreported income). Therefore, practitioners should take care to explain tax changes to their high-income clients.

Tax noncompliance is concentrated at the top of the distribution. A recent study indicated that the "top 1 percent" failed to report 20 percent of their income, neglecting to pay nearly $175 billion owed in taxes annually. This tax gap is estimated to cost $7 trillion over 10 years. Consequently, the IRS needs more resources to conduct investigations into unreported income. Twenty-first-century technology data analytics tools are needed to unpack complex tax returns and track income across various opaque sources. Better information is also needed.

High-Income Audits

A report from the National Bureau of Economic Research on high-income audits revealed that 98 percent of millionaires are not audited. It estimated that unreported income (as a fraction of actual income) for the bottom 50 percent income taxpayers (mainly wages) is 7 percent, whereas for the top 1 percent income taxpayers, it was 21 percent—in other words, triple the amount of underreporting. This points to a need for better trained auditors for high-income audits, not just more auditors.

Peer-to-Peer Payments

The IRS's watchdog, the U.S. Treasury Inspector General for Tax Administration (TIGTA), investigated the agency's ability to detect unreported income in peer-to-peer (PTP) payment applications. People use PTP applications, such as Venmo, to transfer money directly to another person using their smartphone. The money is taken from a person's bank account or card. Currently, many PTP payors are not reporting the transaction information to the IRS. TIGTA estimates that taxpayers "potentially" failed to report up to $29 billion of payments. .

Tax Gap

The IRS is increasingly focusing on the tax gap—the difference between the taxes people properly owe and how much tax they actually pay. According to recent IRS studies, the tax gap could be as much as $441 billion to $750 billion per year. IRS commissioner Rettig told a Senate panel that the tax gap "could approach and possibly exceed $1 trillion." Based on this broad range of estimates, it is safe to say that there is some uncertainty regarding the size of the tax gap.

A recent Treasury publication noted that there are approximately 8,600 virtual currencies in use now (not just bitcoin). These are not included in the IRS estimate of the tax gap but are a substantial contributing factor.

Major sources of underpayment, according to the IRS, include sole proprietors, farmers, royalties, rentals, S corporations, and partnerships. About 60 percent comes from underreporting.

The IRS believes the answer to the tax gap problem is more information reporting. If information reporting (Forms 1099, W-2) is in place, taxpayer compliance is as high as 95 percent. If there is no information reporting, compliance is as low as 45 percent. The IRS also believes underreporting is more significant at higher income levels; for example, the IRS estimates that the high-income taxpayers in the "top 1 percent" underreport more than 20 percent of their income.

IRS efforts at reducing the tax gap focus on the following:

- More information reporting
- More regulation of return preparers (including requiring a minimum level of tax knowledge)
- More electronic filing
- Required withholding on Form 1099 income

¶ 709 INCREASED LLC AUDITS

In other developments, the IRS has increased limited liability company (LLC) audits for self-employment income. The application of self-employment tax to LLC members has long been unclear. For example, LLC members treated as limited partners have no self-employment tax on Form K-1, Box 1 income, whereas LLC members treated as general partners do have self-employment tax on Form K-1, Box 1 income.

The IRS issued proposed regulations on this issue 24 years ago, but they were never finalized. However, there is some case law. In *Renkemeyer, Campbell & Weaver, LLP* (136 TC No. 7 (2011)), the court ruled that the tax attorney working full-time was a general partner and reported self-employment tax on Box 1 income. However, in *Stephen Hardy v. Commissioner* (TC Memo. 2017-16), a doctor who owned interest in a surgical center was found to be a limited partner (a mere investor), with no self-employment tax on Box 1 income.

¶ 710 RECOVERING EIPs FROM DECEASED TAXPAYERS

The IRS sent EIPs to many deceased taxpayers who did not qualify for them. The IRS has attempted to recover these payments, but about half have not yet been recovered. As of July 2011, it appears the IRS is giving up on getting these payments back. The U.S. Government Accountability Office (GAO) reported that "IRS officials have determined that further actions . . . Could be burdensome to taxpayers, the federal court system and IRS."

STUDY QUESTIONS

7. Which statement about the child tax credit is correct?

    a. The ARPA decreased the child tax credit.

    b. The child tax credit will have no phaseout for 2021.

    c. For the 2021 tax year, the child tax credit is fully refundable if the taxpayer's principal residence is in the United States.

    d. The ARPA increased the child tax credit for high-income taxpayers.

8. Which tax credit maximum did the ARPA increase from $543 to $1,502 for 2021?

    a. Child tax credit

    b. Dependent care credit

    c. Earned income tax credit for childless taxpayers

    d. Employee retention credit

9. For 2021, businesses can claim an employee retention credit (ERC) against 70 percent of qualified wages paid for each employee, up to how much in qualified wages per quarter?

    a. $7,000

    b. $10,000

    c. $28,000

    d. $50,000

10. For which of the following has the IRS increased audits for self-employment income?

    a. C corporations

    b. Limited liability companies (LLCs)

    c. S corporations

    d. Nonprofit entities

11. Which statement about erroneously issued economic impact payments to the deceased is correct?

    a. Ninety percent of the erroneous EIPs have been recovered.

    b. No EIPs were sent in error to taxpayers.

    c. The IRS does not have authority to recover such payments.

    d. The IRS has essentially given up on recovering these EIPs.

12. Which statement about peer-to-peer payments (PTPs) is true?

    a. Many PTP transactions are not reported to the IRS.

    b. Because PTPs are direct transfers, they are not subject to tax.

    c. Venmo is the only IRS-approved PTP application.

    d. The IRS can easily identify all cases of tax noncompliance with regard to PTPs.

CPE NOTE: When you have completed your study and review of chapters 5-7, which comprise Module 3, you may wish to take the Final Exam for this Module. Go to **cchcpelink.com/printcpe** to take this Final Exam online.

¶ 10,100 Answers to Study Questions

¶ 10,101 MODULE 1—CHAPTER 1

1. a. *Incorrect.* Although during the audit appointment, the tax professional will file a power of attorney for the client and begin interacting with the auditor to determine the scope of the examination, this is not the longest phase of the audit.

b. *Incorrect.* This stage of the audit, which entails evaluating the client's records and systems, preparing responses, and other pre-audit steps, can be lengthy, but it is not the longest of the audit phases.

c. *Correct.* **The issue development phase is the longest of the four phases of a field audit. It is where the tax professional responds to the document requests from the IRS, reviews and analyzes any issues, and negotiates with the IRS auditor, especially when the facts are unclear.**

d. *Incorrect.* In this audit phase, the tax professional receives the RAR and consults with the taxpayer to decide whether to agree with the report findings or appeal. However, another phase of the audit process is likely longer.

2. a. *Correct.* **This type of income contributes the substantial majority to misreporting by income category. This includes income such as nonfarm proprietor income, rents, and royalties.**

b. *Incorrect.* Income subject to information reporting and withholding does not contribute the most to the small business tax gap. This type of income includes wages and salaries.

c. *Incorrect.* This type of income includes pensions and annuities, unemployment compensation, dividend income, interest income, and taxable Social Security benefits. It does not constitute the largest contribution to the tax gap.

d. *Incorrect.* This type of income includes partnership/S corporation income, capital gains, and alimony income. It is not the largest contributor to the tax gap.

3. a. *Incorrect.* Form 1040 is used by U.S. taxpayers to file an annual income tax return. For tax year 2018, taxpayers will no longer use Form 1040A or Form 1040EZ, but instead will use the redesigned Form 1040. Many people will only need to file Form 1040 and no schedules.

b. *Incorrect.* Form 1120 (officially the *U.S. Corporate Income Tax Return*) is one of the IRS tax forms used by corporations (specifically, C corporations) in the United States to report their income, gains, losses, deductions, credits and to figure out their tax liability.

c. *Incorrect.* Form 1065 is used for partnerships. Regarding the percentage of small businesses, 2.7 million are LLCs and 20 percent are domestic general partnerships.

d. *Correct.* **Form 1120S, called the *U.S. Income Tax Return for an S Corporation*, is a tax document that is used to report the income, losses, and dividends of S corporation shareholders.**

4. a. *Incorrect.* Responding on time is one of the best practices regarding mail audits. Another best practice is to fax your response if you're within a week of the deadline.

b. *Correct.* **You should not respond to a mail audit by filing a Form 1040X. You must respond directly with documentation to the IRS Correspondence Examination Unit.**

c. *Incorrect.* Following up by phone for status is a best practice with respect to mail audits. Another best practice is that you should include one complete response.

d. *Incorrect.* You should always request an appeal if the IRS disagrees. Furthermore, if you miss the 30-day or 90-day letters, you should request a reconsideration from the IRS.

5. a. *Incorrect.* This is the error rate found in IRS construction audits related to gross receipts for Form 1120S, not depreciation.

b. *Incorrect.* This is the error rate found in IRS construction audits related to gross receipts for Form 1065. This is not the rate related to depreciation.

c. *Incorrect.* This is the error rate found in IRS construction audits related to cost of sales for Schedule C, not depreciation.

d. *Correct.* This is the error rate found in construction audits with respect to depreciation on Form 1065. The error rate for other deductions on Form 1065 was 86 percent.

6. a. *Correct.* This is not one of the identified fraud red flags. Instead, one of the red flags is transfers of assets for purpose of concealment.

b. *Incorrect.* This is one of the fraud red flags. Another fraud red flag is attempts to hinder the investigation by failing or refusing to answer questions, canceling appointments, or refusing to supply records.

c. *Incorrect.* This is one of the fraud red flags. Another fraud red flag is destruction of books and records.

d. *Incorrect.* If the issues and IDRs are related to unreported income, and multiple years are under examination, this may be a sign that the IRS agent is looking for fraud.

7. a. *Incorrect.* The GAO study did not find understatement of rental income and expenses to be the most prevalent problem.

b. *Correct.* According to the GAO's data, the most prevalent misreporting issue is the overstatement of such expenses. The study also found that the most likely noncompliant profiles are self-managed properties.

c. *Incorrect.* The GAO study did not suggest that the use of a tax preparer is a prevalent issue in the misreporting of rental income and expenses.

d. *Incorrect.* The failure to substantiate such expenses was not mentioned as a prevalent issue in the GAO study.

¶ 10,102 MODULE 1—CHAPTER 2

1. a. *Correct.* The EPSLA is part of the Families First Coronavirus Response Act (FFCRA), which was signed into law on March 18, 2020.

b. *Incorrect.* The CAA includes $900 billion in stimulus relief for the COVID-19 pandemic as well as $1.4 trillion in spending for the 2021 federal fiscal year. However, the EPSLA is not among its provisions.

c. *Incorrect.* The ARPA provides direct relief to families and workers impacted by the COVID-19 pandemic. It does not include the EPSLA.

d. *Incorrect.* The EPSLA is not part of COBRA. COBRA allows employees who lose their employer health benefits to choose to continue the benefits for a limited amount of time.

2. a. *Incorrect.* Form 1065 is an information return used to report the income, gains, losses, deductions, credits, etc., from the operation of a partnership. A partnership does not pay tax on its income but "passes through" any profits or losses to its partners on a Schedule K-1.

b. *Incorrect.* This form is the application for recognition of exemption under Section 501(c)(3) of the Internal Revenue Code.

c. *Incorrect.* Form 1120 (officially the *U.S. Corporate Income Tax Return*) is one of the IRS tax forms used by corporations (specifically, C corporations) in the United States to report their income, gains, losses, deductions, and credits, and to figure out their tax liability. This form is not used to change accounting methods.

d. *Correct.* The IRS has issued Form 7200 to allow qualifying employers to file in advance to receive the refundable tax credits for qualified sick and family leave and the employee retention tax credit.

3. a. *Incorrect.* The CARES Act and the Coronavirus Response and Relief Supplemental Appropriations Act of 2021 provided fast and direct economic assistance for American workers, families, and small businesses, and to preserve jobs for American industries.

b. *Correct.* Covered employers are those with fewer than 500 employees. Small businesses with fewer than 50 employees may qualify for an exemption if the leave requirements would jeopardize the viability of the business as a going concern.

c. *Incorrect.* The Paycheck Protection Program (PPP) provided loans to help businesses keep their workforce employed during the Coronavirus crisis.

d. *Incorrect.* The Health and Economic Recovery Omnibus Emergency Solutions Act, or HEROES Act, was proposed legislation acting as a $3 trillion stimulus package in response to the COVID-19 pandemic and was intended to supplement the earlier CARES Act stimulus package.

4. a. *Incorrect.* This is not the maximum employee retention credit for 2021. Instead, the maximum credit is significantly higher than $2,000.

b. *Incorrect.* This is not the maximum employee retention credit for 2021. Instead, this represents the maximum for 2020.

c. *Incorrect.* This is not the maximum employee retention credit for 2021. Instead, this is the maximum amount per quarter for each employee in 2021. There is a limit on the number of quarters that can be claimed, though.

d. *Correct.* The employee retention credit (ERC) can be substantial for 2021. It can be up to $28,000 per employee per year (i.e., $7,000 per quarter for up to four quarters).

5. a. *Correct.* Total sales (net of returns and allowances) are included within the gross receipts. All amounts received for services are also included within gross receipts.

b. *Incorrect.* The employee retention credit is not included when determining the gross receipts. Note that any income from investments, and from incidental or outside sources, should be included when calculating gross receipts.

c. *Incorrect.* Sales tax should be excluded if legally imposed on the purchaser, and the taxpayer merely collects and remits.

d. *Incorrect.* Repayment of a loan is excluded from the gross receipts calculation. This is analogous to PPP loan proceeds.

6. a. *Incorrect.* Employers use Form 941 to report income taxes, Social Security tax, or Medicare tax withheld from employees' paychecks.

b. *Correct.* **Form 7200 should not be used for a quarter in the past. If Form 941 is already filed, it's too late.**

c. *Incorrect.* Employers who paid wages to agricultural employees who are subject to income tax, Social Security, or Medicare withholding must file Form 943, *Employer's Annual Federal Tax Return for Agricultural Employees*, to report those wages.

d. *Incorrect.* Form 944 is an IRS tax form that reports the taxes—including federal income tax, Social Security tax, and Medicare tax—that the taxpayer has withheld from its employees' paychecks.

7. a. *Incorrect.* According to Code Sec. 52, corporate taxpayers may be required to aggregate as a parent-subsidiary controlled group, a brother-sister controlled group, or a combined group of corporations.

b. *Incorrect.* The aggregation rules are applicable to trusts, partnerships, estates, or sole proprietorships in businesses under common control.

c. *Incorrect.* Entities are aggregated for the ERC for several purposes, including this determination.

d. *Correct.* **According to IRS FAQ number 25, all members of an aggregated group are treated as a single employer for ERC purposes.**

¶ 10,103 MODULE 1—CHAPTER 3

1. a. *Correct.* **This is one of the new loss limitation hurdles post-TCJA. Another loss limitation hurdle post-TCJA is the excess loss limitation.**

b. *Incorrect.* This is not a new loss limitation post-TCJA. Instead, the basis loss limitation was around before the TCJA.

c. *Incorrect.* The at-risk loss limitation is not a new loss limitation post-TCJA. Instead, it has been around prior to the passage of the TCJA.

d. *Incorrect.* The passive loss limitation is not a new loss limitation post-TCJA. The requirements related to this limitation are prescribed by Code Sec. 469.

2. a. *Incorrect.* This is not the threshold amount in 2020 for single taxpayers. Instead, this is the threshold amount for single filers in 2019. It was increased for 2020.

b. *Correct.* **This is the threshold amount in 2020 for single taxpayers. Excess business losses are equal to excess of aggregate deductions attributable to trades or businesses, over the sum of aggregate gross business income or gain, plus a threshold amount.**

c. *Incorrect.* This is not the threshold amount in 2020 for single taxpayers. Instead, this is the threshold amount for married filing jointly filers in 2019.

d. *Incorrect.* This is the threshold amount for married filing jointly filers in 2020. It is not the threshold amount in 2020 for single taxpayers.

3. a. *Incorrect.* This is an incorrect statement. Instead, the CARES Act reinstated Code Sec. 461(l) for after 2020. Prior to the CARES Act, the TCJA deleted it for years 2018 through 2020.

b. *Incorrect.* This is an incorrect statement. Instead, the CARES Act put these disclosures back on the table in 2021. It also put Form 1120S K-1 disclosures back on the table.

c. *Correct.* **For tax years beginning after December 31, 2017, and before January 1, 2026, excess business losses of a taxpayer (other than a corporation) are not allowed.**

d. *Incorrect.* This is an incorrect statement. Based on the CARES Act, as well as the TCJA, capital gain income does equal business income.

4. a. *Incorrect.* While the majority of carrybacks are no longer allowed, carrybacks continue to be allowed for certain farming losses. These were not eliminated as a result of the TCJA.

b. *Incorrect.* The carryover of NOLs is indefinite as a result of the TCJA. Prior to this change, the carryover was limited to 20 years.

c. *Incorrect.* Under the TCJA, the NOL deduction was limited to 80 percent of taxable income (determined without regard to the deduction). Additionally, carryovers to other years are adjusted to take account of this limitation.

d. *Correct.* **Prior to TCJA, an NOL may generally be carried back two years and carried over 20 years to offset taxable income in such years. However, different carryback periods apply with respect to NOLs arising in different circumstance**

5. a. *Incorrect.* The deduction allows for a larger percentage deduction on qualifying business income. The deduction is available to any taxpayer other than a corporation.

b. *Incorrect.* The deduction allows for a larger percentage deduction on qualifying business income. The deduction is limited to the greater of (1) 50 percent of the W-2 wages with respect to the trade or business, or (2) the sum of 25 percent of the W-2 wages, plus 2.5 percent of the unadjusted basis immediately after acquisition of all qualified property (generally, tangible property subject to depreciation under Code Sec. 167).

c. *Correct.* **The Code Sec. 199A deduction allows taxpayers other than corporations a deduction of 20 percent of qualified business income earned in a qualified trade or business, subject to certain limitations. It may be phased out if taxable income exceeds a threshold amount.**

d. *Incorrect.* The deduction allows for a smaller percentage deduction on qualifying business income. Furthermore, qualified business income is the net amount of qualified items of income, gain, deduction, and loss with respect to a qualified trade or business that are effectively connected with the conduct of a business in the United States.

6. a. *Incorrect.* The deduction for business interest expense cannot exceed the sum of three specific figures. One of these figures is business interest income.

b. *Incorrect.* The deduction for business interest expense cannot exceed the sum of three figures. However, it's important to note that small business (<$30 million in gross receipts) are not subject to the limit.

c. *Correct.* **This is not one of the figures that are summed up to assess the business interest expense limit. Instead, the three figures are business interest income, 30 percent of adjusted taxable income, and floor financing interest expense.**

d. *Incorrect.* The deduction for business interest expense cannot exceed the sum of three figures. One of these three figures are floor financing interest expenses.

7. a. *Correct.* CARES Act Section 2307, retroactive to property placed in service after December 31, 2017, renders QIP as 15-year property.

b. *Incorrect.* QIP inadvertently became 39-year property under the TCJA, not the CARES Act.

c. *Incorrect.* QIP does not include residential, exterior, expansion, or structural improvements, nor elevators and escalators.

d. *Incorrect.* According to a CARES Act technical correction, bonus depreciation applies only to improvements made by the taxpayer.

¶ 10,104 MODULE 2—CHAPTER 4

1. a. *Correct.* This is the correct amount. Key provisions include allocation of funds for vaccine distribution, schools, small businesses, and anti-poverty programs.

b. *Incorrect.* The new law extends certain features of the CARES Act and Consolidated Appropriations Act, including PPP loans, supplemental unemployment benefits and employee retention tax credits, as well as adds important new tax provisions such as an expanded child tax credit.

c. *Incorrect.* This is the incorrect amount. The law also provides an immediate direct payment to taxpayers at and below certain income levels.

d. *Incorrect.* This is the incorrect amount. The total package amount is less than $4.9 trillion. Note that one of the key provisions is the allocation of funds for vaccine distribution.

2. a. *Incorrect.* Eligibility levels are one of the factors controlled by state programs. Another factor controlled by state programs is whether benefits are charged to employer accounts.

b. *Correct.* This is not something that state programs determine. Note that states generally follow federal guidelines.

c. *Incorrect.* Benefit amounts are one of the factors controlled by state programs. Another factor controlled by state programs is whether UI is available for individuals who are self-employed.

d. *Incorrect.* Duration of benefits is one of the factors controlled by state programs. Another factor controlled by state programs is whether UI is available for individuals who are unable to work, quit, were fired for misconduct, etc.

3. a. *Correct.* Note that the CAA also creates a new program for Mixed Earners Unemployment Compensation (MEUC).

b. *Incorrect.* Instead, the CARES Act provided an increase of a flat payment of $600 (not $200) per week to the amount regularly available for unemployment under state law that lasted through July 31, 2020.

c. *Incorrect.* The CAA provided an increase of a flat payment of $300 (not $600) per week to the amount regularly available for unemployment under state law.

d. *Incorrect.* This is the incorrect date. Instead, the ARPA extends the flat payment of $300 per week to September 6, 2021.

4. a. *Incorrect.* This is the incorrect number of weeks. Instead, the CAA increased the maximum total benefits to more than 42 weeks.

b. *Incorrect.* Note that applicants for PUA must provide self-certification that they are (1) partially or fully unemployed or (2) unable and unavailable to work for specified reasons.

c. *Correct.* **Also note that the ARPA provides up to 79 weeks of unemployment benefits (and up to 86 weeks for individuals in states with high levels of unemployment).**

d. *Incorrect.* This is the incorrect number of weeks. Instead, the CAA increased the maximum total benefits to less than 75 weeks.

5. a. *Incorrect.* This is the incorrect amount that can be claimed as an above-the-line deduction. Instead, the amount that is allowed is more than $150.

b. *Correct.* **This is the correct amount. This above-the-line charitable contribution is allowed for 2020 tax returns as well as for 2021 returns. The amount has been increased for 2021 tax returns.**

c. *Incorrect.* This is the incorrect amount that can be claimed as an above-the-line deduction. Instead, the amount that is allowed is less than $750.

d. *Incorrect.* This is the incorrect amount that can be claimed as an above-the-line deduction. The amount that is allowed is less than $999 and applies equally to single and married filing joint taxpayers.

6. a. *Correct.* **Eligible employees may withdraw $100,000 from their IRA or 401(k) without penalty. The distribution will be subject to normal taxation rules regarding distributions.**

b. *Incorrect.* The CARES Act adds a new exception to the 10 percent early withdrawal penalty tax under Code Sec. 72(t) for those who take retirement distributions prior to age 59½.

c. *Incorrect.* While eligible employees may withdraw a certain amount from their IRA or 401(k) without penalty, they cannot withdraw up to $250,000.

d. *Incorrect.* While eligible employees may withdraw a certain amount from their IRA or 401(k) without penalty, they cannot withdraw up to $500,000. One type of individual that is eligible is an individual diagnosed with COVID-19.

7. a. *Incorrect.* The ability to deduct qualified mortgage insurance premiums as qualified residence interest has been extended through 2021, not made permanent.

b. *Incorrect.* The credit for energy-efficient improvements to personal residences has been extended to December 31, 2021, although there is a lifetime limit on this credit of $500.

c. *Incorrect.* The CAA extends the Qualified Fuel Cell Motor Vehicle Credit through 2021; it did not make it permanent. The credit ranges from $4,000 to $40,000 depending on the vehicle purchased.

d. *Correct.* **The CAA permanently reduces the threshold for the medical expense deduction to 7.5 percent of AGI. Without this provision, the 7.5 percent threshold was set to revert to 10 percent in 2021.**

8. a. *Correct.* **Claimants must also provide a self-certification that their unemployment, partial unemployment, or inability to work are attributable to a qualifying reason under the CARES Act and identify the specific reason for each week that PUA is claimed.**

b. *Incorrect.* To combat fraud, the CAA requires a claimant to substantiate certain factors (as opposed to providing only a self-certification) and directs states to implement a process to verify the claimant's identity.

c. *Incorrect.* This is not something that is required to be substantiated by the CAA. In addition to these claimant-based obligations, states must prepare and implement procedures for identity verification to validate PUA claims.

d. *Incorrect.* This is not something that is required to be substantiated by the CAA. For individuals filing claims on or after January 31, 2021, the claimant must provide documentation substantiating the factor in question.

9. a. *Incorrect.* The ARPA repeals Code Sec. 864(f) in its entirety. Code Sec. 864(f), which first went into effect in the 2021 tax year, would have allowed multinational taxpayers to allocate interest expense on a worldwide basis.

b. *Incorrect.* The ARPA amends Code Sec. 6050W to provide that increased reporting will be required (with a reporting trigger point of $600 instead of the prior law's $20,000 threshold) on IRS Form 1099-K, *Payment Card and Third-Party Network Transactions*, starting for payments in 2022.

c. *Incorrect.* Applicable to tax years beginning after December 31, 2026, the ARPA provides a change in the law whereby publicly traded companies are denied deductions for compensation in excess of $1 million for the eight highest-paid employees, plus the chief executive officer and chief financial officer.

d. *Correct.* Code Sec. 461(l) was amended to provide that the limitation on the deduction for excess business losses will continue to apply to noncorporate taxpayers for taxable years beginning after December 31, 2017, and before January 1, 2027 (previously January 1, 2026).

10. a. *Correct.* Also note that the IRS announced that it scheduled over $90 million in stimulus payments to be sent out by March 17, 2021.

b. *Incorrect.* These payments are treated as tax credits and therefore will not be includible in the recipient's 2021 taxable income.

c. *Incorrect.* This is the incorrect amount. Instead, the ARPA authorizes a third round of COVID-19 stimulus payments, up to $1,400 per eligible individual.

d. *Incorrect.* The stimulus begins to phase out for single taxpayers with AGI between $75,000 and $80,000.

11. a. *Incorrect.* The maximum amount of EITC for childless households will increase from $540 to $1,500.

b. *Correct.* Pursuant to the ARPA, individual taxpayers (with no qualifying children) will see changes to the computation of their EIC, including increases in (1) the phaseout percentage, (2) the earned income amount, and (3) the phaseout amount.

c. *Incorrect.* For taxpayers with no qualifying children in the 2021 taxable year, the provision increases both the credit percentage and phaseout percentage from 7.65 percent to 15.3 percent.

d. *Incorrect.* For purposes of calculating the 2021 EITC, individual taxpayers may choose to use their 2019 (not 2018) income if it was higher than their 2021 income.

12. a. *Correct.* This is an important expansion of PPP eligibility that creates a new class of potential beneficiaries.

b. *Incorrect.* The eligibility requirements for small business and nonprofit PPP loans under the ARPA are essentially the same as they were under the CARES Act.

c. *Incorrect.* Under the ARPA (and the CARES Act), most small businesses or nonprofit organizations are potentially eligible to receive a PPP loan if the organization employs 500 employees or fewer.

d. *Incorrect.* Under the CAA and ARPA, businesses are now eligible to take the employee retention credit even if they previously received PPP funding and loan forgiveness.

13. a. *Incorrect.* States cannot use the funds to offset revenue losses resulting from any tax cut, tax delay, or tax rebate enacted after March 3, 2021.

b. *Correct.* **Funds allocated from each of the State Fiscal Recovery Funds and Local Fiscal Recovery Funds may be used to respond to the COVID-19 emergency and address its economic effects.**

c. *Incorrect.* Funds allocated from each of the State Fiscal Recovery Funds and Local Fiscal Recovery Funds may be used to provide premium pay to essential employees of state or local governments or make grants to the employers of essential employees.

d. *Incorrect.* Funds allocated from each of the State Fiscal Recovery Funds and Local Fiscal Recovery Funds may be used to provide government services to the extent of any revenue reduction resulting from COVID-19.

14. a. *Incorrect.* Also note that it does not include a state or local government operated business, or a company that as of March 13, 2020, operates in more than 20 locations.

b. *Correct.* **Eligible entities include restaurants or other specified food businesses, and businesses operating in an airport terminal.**

c. *Incorrect.* The amount appropriate to struggling restaurants is less than $34.6 billion. The assistance does not apply to a business that has a pending application for, or has received, a grant under the Economic Aid to Hard-Hit Small Businesses, Non-Profits and Venues Act.

d. *Incorrect.* The amount appropriate to struggling restaurants is less than $34.6 billion. Also note that the calculated amount of the grant will be reduced by unrepaid PPP loans.

15. a. *Incorrect.* The SVOG program includes over $16 billion in grants to shuttered venues, such as live venue operators or promoters, theatrical producers, live performing arts organization operations, museum operators, motion picture theater operators, and talent representatives.

b. *Incorrect.* This is the incorrect percentage. To be eligible, applicants generally must have experienced not less than a 25 percent reduction in gross earned revenue.

c. *Correct.* **The proposed regulations state that the SBA will review complete applications in the order in which it receives them, based on the availability of funds and priorities related to the extent of the applicant's revenue loss.**

d. *Incorrect.* Eligible applicants may qualify for SVOGs equal to 45 percent of their 2019 gross earned revenue, with the maximum amount available for a single grant award of $10 million.

¶ 10,105 MODULE 3—CHAPTER 5

1. a. *Incorrect.* Closed virtual currencies have value in online games but not in the real world.

b. *Correct.* **Airline frequent flyer programs are examples of a single flow virtual currency.**

c. *Incorrect.* Convertible virtual currencies can be purchased and sold on the open market.

d. *Incorrect.* There is no such thing as a public virtual currency.

2. a. *Correct.* **Bitcoins were used for online betting at PrimeDice.com on May 18, 2013.**

b. *Incorrect.* The Financial Action Task Force issued warnings of money laundering using virtual currencies in 2010.

c. *Incorrect.* Silk Road was established in 2011, and Bitcoins were used to purchase illegal drugs.

d. *Incorrect.* The government warned of terrorists using virtual currencies to fund operations in 2010.

3. a. *Incorrect.* A Texas judge ruled that Bitcoin was a currency on August 6, 2013.

b. *Incorrect.* Bitcoin transaction volume surpassed Western Union's transaction volume on November 19, 2013.

c. *Incorrect.* The FBI seized Silk Road on October 2, 2013.

d. *Correct.* **Mt. Gox filed for bankruptcy in February of 2014.**

4. a. *Incorrect.* The IRS has ruled that virtual currency transactions create taxable events.

b. *Correct.* **The IRS considers virtual currencies to be property.**

c. *Incorrect.* Even though a Texas judge ruled Bitcoins to be a currency, the IRS considers them to be property.

d. *Incorrect.* Virtual currencies are not considered to be securities by the IRS even though the SEC considers them to be securities.

5. a. *Incorrect.* Closed virtual currencies have no value outside of a gaming environment and are not taxable.

b. *Correct.* **Even though the IRS considers this to be taxable income if received for business purposes, it does not enforce compliance because of issues with mixing personal and business awards in one account.**

c. *Incorrect.* Convertible virtual currencies are taxable.

d. *Incorrect.* Cryptocurrencies are a subset of convertible virtual currencies that are taxed.

6. a. *Incorrect.* LIFO is legal even though the IRS prefers that taxpayers use specific identification.

b. *Incorrect.* The IRS prefers the specific identification method but will allow the use of FIFO.

¶10,105

c. *Correct.* The IRS prefers that taxpayers use the specific identification method, which entails tracking every cryptocurrency or partial cryptocurrency, and specifically identifying what they are buying or selling and what they still own.

d. *Incorrect.* Even though the IRS will accept the average cost method, it would prefer that taxpayers use the specific identification method.

¶ 10,106 MODULE 3—CHAPTER 6

1. a. *Correct.* For tax year 2020, taxpayers do not have to file Form 8962; nor do they have to report or pay any excess advance premium tax credit repayment on their 2020 Form 1040 or Form 1040-SR, Schedule 2, Line 2.

b. *Incorrect.* Taxpayers who already paid back part of their advance premium tax credit do not need to file an amended return. The IRS will process the refunds automatically.

c. *Incorrect.* The credit is available only to taxpayers who purchase their health insurance through a Health Insurance Marketplace.

d. *Incorrect.* The credit is designed to offset anticipated health insurance costs, not unemployment compensation.

2. a. *Incorrect.* The due date for 2020 IRA contributions was extended from April 15, 2021, to May 17, 2021.

b. *Incorrect.* The due date for taxpayers to make 2020 contributions to their health savings accounts was extended from April 15, 2021, to May 17, 2021.

c. *Incorrect.* The due date for Form 1040 was extended from April 15, 2021, to May 17, 2021.

d. *Correct.* No official guidance was issued concerning the due date for Form 709, so the due date was presumed to not be extended to May 17, 2021.

3. a. *Incorrect.* The *Warne v. Commissioner* case did not involve such allegations about an accountant. The court in *Warne* stated that when property is split as part of a charitable contribution, the estate may only claim a charitable deduction for estate tax purposes for what is actually received by the charity.

b. *Correct.* In *Schreier v. Drealan Kvilhaug Hoefker & Co. P.A.*, the court found that the accountant was not negligent in failing to wait to file a tax return until an amendment to the state tax code was enacted because the part of the amendment that affected the return was not added until months after the return was filed.

c. *Incorrect.* The issue in *Ahmanson Foundation v. United States* was the valuing of an asset for estate tax purposes, not the actions of an accountant with regard to amended legislation.

d. *Incorrect.* In *Hafen v. Famulary*, the court ruled that an estate had to return the excess over its initial investment in a Ponzi scheme. It did not involve a malpractice claim against an accountant.

4. a. *Incorrect.* The amount is currently $1,000. The proposed rules would increase it to $5,000.

b. *Correct.* The proposed rules delete the minimum requirement of $2,500 and clarify that funds, if approved, are taken from the balance of the account as of the date of death.

c. *Incorrect.* The change in the proposed rules is from funds-only estates with a value of $5,000 or less to funds-only estates with a value of $300 (not $1,000) or less.

d. *Incorrect.* The proposed rules would establish that joint tenancy, not tenancy in common will be presumed in this situation.

5. a. *Correct.* **The election cannot be made later than two months and 16 days after the desired effective date for the election.**

b. *Incorrect.* This represents the due date extension if stock is held by a testamentary trust.

c. *Incorrect.* Ninety days is not the correct time period in regard to the due date for the election.

d. *Incorrect.* The due date for QSST and ESBT elections does not hinge on the date of the grantor's death even though the death does trigger the two-year transfer grace period.

6. a. *Incorrect.* Foundations must be organized and operated exclusively for exempt purposes.

b. *Correct.* Due to looming estate tax exemption reductions and possible increases in income tax rates, foundations will be more attractive for estate planning and taking advantage of annual charitable giving opportunities.

c. *Incorrect.* Foundation earnings may not be used for any private shareholder or individual.

d. *Incorrect.* Foundations cannot be action organizations; they may not try to influence legislation or participate in any campaign activities.

¶ 10,107 MODULE 3—CHAPTER 7

1. a. *Incorrect.* The ARPA does not contain a provision regarding deductibility of restaurant meals.

b. *Correct.* **The CAA amended Code Sec. 274 to make restaurant meals 100 percent deductible for 2021 and 2022; previously, they were 50 percent deductible.**

c. *Incorrect.* For 2018 and beyond, the TCJA did not increase the deductible amount for business-related meals.

d. *Incorrect.* The Coronavirus Aid, Recovery, and Economic Security (CARES) act did not include this deduction.

2. a. *Incorrect.* Mr. Chiarelli did not hide his profession from the U.S. Tax Court.

b. *Incorrect.* Mr. Chiarelli did provide an appraisal of the property, but it lacked the required statement that it was for tax purposes and did not include other required information. However, these facts did not result in the automatic disallowance.

c. *Incorrect.* The fact that he donated the property he had inherited from his mother to Goodwill and the Salvation Army was not the reason the contribution was disallowed.

d. *Correct.* **Failing to get a CWA from the charity automatically precluded a tax deduction in this case.**

3. a. *Incorrect.* In *Whatley,* the court found that the taxpayer did not meet the nine-factor test. He did not conduct the activity in a businesslike manner, did not spend sufficient time or effort on the activity, suffered big losses, made no profits from the activity, and so on.

b. *Correct.* **The court found that although Robison had 16 straight years of losses from his cattle ranch, he met enough of the other factors of the test.**

c. *Incorrect.* The *Chiarelli* case involved the deductibility of charitable contributions, not hobby losses.

d. *Incorrect.* This case involved arguments for a 2020 basis increase; it was not related to hobby losses.

4. a. *Incorrect.* Student loan payment assistance is provided by legislation such as the CAA; it is not the focus of Operation Hidden Treasure.

b. *Incorrect.* Operation Hidden Treasure is an initiative from the IRS Office of Fraud Enforcement that focuses on a different goal than one involving charitable contributions.

c. *Incorrect.* Stimulus payments are provided by legislation such as the ARPA; they are not the focus of a special operation.

d. *Correct.* **Operation Hidden Treasure is an initiative from the Office of Fraud Enforcement dedicated to "finding, tracing, and attributing cryptocurrency to U.S. taxpayers."**

5. a. *Incorrect.* An additional EIP of $600 was issued to qualified individuals in an earlier round of stimulus payments in 2020.

b. *Incorrect.* This was the amount of the EIP for eligible individuals under the CARES Act in 2020.

c. *Correct.* **In addition, a $1,400 EIP is available for each qualifying dependent under Code Sec. 152.**

d. *Incorrect.* This is the maximum EIP for married couples filing jointly under the ARPA.

6. a. *Correct.* **In 2021, the Small Business Administration (SBA) offered COVID-19 EIDLs of up to $15,000 that do not need to be repaid.**

b. *Incorrect.* The IRS did not issue these types of loans in 2021.

c. *Incorrect.* The Foreign Bank and Financial Accounts (FBAR) is a report of certain foreign financial accounts, such as bank accounts, to the Treasury Department. It is not an agency that provides EIDLs.

d. *Incorrect.* COBRA is an act that gives workers and their families who lose their health benefits the right to choose to continue them. It does not issue loans.

7. a. *Incorrect.* The ARPA increased the child tax credit for lower and moderate-income taxpayers and expanded its coverage.

b. *Incorrect.* On the contrary, the child tax credit will have two phaseouts for 2021.

c. *Correct.* **This is true even if the taxpayer has $0 earned income.**

d. *Incorrect.* The ARPA made no change to the child tax credit for higher income taxpayers.

8. a. *Incorrect.* These amounts do not reflect the ARPA changes to the child tax credit for 2021.

b. *Incorrect.* The dependent care credit amounts are different than the ones given.

c. *Correct.* **Under the ARPA, the maximum childless EITC was raised from $543 to $1,502 for 2021.**

d. *Incorrect.* The ERC has not been increased by this amount. The ARPA extended the ERC.

9. a. *Incorrect.* The ERC qualified wages limit is higher than $7,000.

b. *Correct.* **The limit for the ERC is $10,000 in qualified wages per quarter.**

c. *Incorrect.* For 2021, businesses can receive up to $28,000 per employee per year, not per quarter.

d. *Incorrect.* The limit is up to $50,000 per quarter for "recovery startup businesses" formed on or after February 15, 2020.

10. a. *Incorrect.* The IRS is not increasing its auditing efforts for C corporations with regard to self-employment income.

b. *Correct.* **The IRS has increased audits for limited liability companies (LLCs) claiming self-employment income. Note that the application of self-employment tax to LLC members has long been unclear, and the proposed regulations on this issue were never finalized.**

c. *Incorrect.* S corporations are not the focus of an increasing number of IRS audits for self-employment income.

d. *Incorrect.* The IRS has not increased the number of audits of nonprofits with regard to the self-employment tax exemption.

11. a. *Incorrect.* The IRS has recovered only about half of these EIPs.

b. *Incorrect.* The IRS sent many erroneous EIPs to taxpayers.

c. *Incorrect.* The IRS has the authority to recover these EIPs and has recovered some.

d. *Correct.* **The IRS seems to have given up on recovery. According to the GAO, "IRS officials have determined that further actions . . . Could be burdensome to taxpayers, the federal court system and IRS."**

12. a. *Correct.* **The U.S. Treasury Inspector General for Tax Administration (TIGTA) has estimated that taxpayers have potentially failed to report up to $29 billion of PTPs.**

b. *Incorrect.* PTPs are direct transfers of money that result in income that is subject to taxation.

c. *Incorrect.* The IRS does not "approve" specific PTP applications, and many such apps are currently in use, including Venmo, Zelle, Google Pay, and others.

d. *Incorrect.* Tax noncompliance with regard to PTPs is difficult for the IRS to detect, although the agency is working to improve its efforts in this area.

Index

References are to paragraph (¶) numbers.

U

V

W

¶ 10,200 Glossary

Affiliated business: For purposes of the Restaurant Revitalization Program, a business in which an eligible entity has an equity or right to profit distributions of not less than 50 percent, or in which an eligible entity has the contractual authority to control the direction of the business, provided that such affiliation shall be determined as of any arrangements or agreements in existence as of March 13, 2020.

American Families Plan: A plan proposed in 2021 by the Biden administration to expand access to education and reduce the cost of childcare, financed by additional taxes on the wealthy and pass-through businesses. The proposal includes $1 trillion in new spending and $800 billion in tax credits.

American Jobs Plan: A $2.65 trillion plan proposed in 2021 by the Biden administration that includes upgrading and repairing the United States' physical infrastructure; investing in manufacturing, research, and development; and expanding long-term healthcare services.

American Rescue Plan Act of 2021: A $1.9 trillion stimulus package designed to help America recover from the coronavirus pandemic.

Bitcoin: A type of virtual currency.

Blockchains: Lists of records held on diverse computers (nodes) that are used to record and verify data.

Business interest expense: The cost of interest that is charged on business loans used to maintain operations.

CARES Act: The Coronavirus Aid, Relief, and Economic Security (CARES) Act, which provides fast and direct economic assistance for American workers and families, small businesses, and preserves jobs for American industries.

C corporation: Any corporation that is taxed separately from its owners.

Child tax credit: A tax credit granted to parents for each qualifying dependent child. The child tax credit in the American Rescue Plan Act is the largest child tax credit to date.

Closed virtual currencies: Virtual currencies used in a closed community, most commonly multi-player online games. The currency is fictional and has no value outside the game.

COBRA: Consolidated Omnibus Budget Reconciliation Act, which gives workers and their families who lose their health benefits the right to choose to continue group health benefits provided by their group health plan for limited periods of time under certain circumstances, such as voluntary or involuntary job loss.

Consolidated Appropriations Act (CAA): A massive tax, funding, and spending bill that contains a nearly $900 billion coronavirus aid package. Its aim was to bolster the economy, provide relief to small businesses and the unemployed, deliver checks to individuals, and provide funding for COVID-19 testing and the administration of vaccines. The bill was signed by President Trump on December 27, 2020.

Contemporaneous written acknowledgement (CWA): A receipt that a charitable organization provides to a donor when the value of a donor's single charitable contribution is $250 or greater.

COVID-19: An infectious disease caused by a newly discovered strain of coronavirus which is a type of virus known to cause respiratory infections in humans.

Credit shelter trust: A trust that is designed to allow a taxpayer to shelter assets equal to his or her remaining basic exclusion amount from future estate tax.

Cryptocurrency: A digital currency using cryptography to secure transactions and to control the creation of new currency units.

Data breach: The release or taking of data from a secure source to an unsecured third-party location (computer).

Dependent care credit: A tax credit for a percentage of the work-related expenses a taxpayer incurs for the care of a qualifying dependent so that the taxpayer can work or look for employment.

Earned income tax credit (EITC): A refundable tax credit for low- to moderate-income working individuals and couples, particularly those with children.

Economic impact payment (EIP): A payment made by the U.S. government to provide financial relief to individuals and families during the COVID-19 pandemic. EIPs are also known as *stimulus checks* or *recovery rebates*.

Economic injury disaster loan (EIDL): Provides economic relief to small businesses and nonprofit organizations that are currently experiencing a temporary loss of revenue.

Electing small business trust (ESBT) election: Requires S corporation stock to be isolated and administered as a separate share of the trust so that the corporation maintains its status as an S corporation and does not revert to C corporation status.

Employee retention credit: A refundable tax credit against certain employment taxes that businesses can claim on qualified wages paid to employees. It encourages businesses to keep employees on their payroll. The refundable tax credit is 50 percent of up to $10,000 in wages paid by an eligible employer whose business has been financially impacted by COVID-19.

Excess business loss: Under Code Section 461(l)(3)(A), the excess of (1) the taxpayer's aggregate trade or business deductions for the tax year over (2) the sum of the taxpayer's aggregate trade or business gross income or gain plus $250,000 (as adjusted for inflation).

Families First Act: An Act of Congress meant to respond to the economic impacts of the ongoing coronavirus pandemic. The act provides funding for free coronavirus testing, 14-day paid leave for American workers affected by the pandemic, and increased funding for food stamps.

FinCEN: The U.S. Treasury Department's Financial Crimes Enforcement Network, whose mission is to "safeguard the financial system from illicit use, combat money laundering and its related crimes including terrorism, and promote national security through the strategic use of financial authorities and the collection, analysis, and dissemination of financial intelligence."

Floor plan financing: A revolving line of credit that allows the borrower to obtain financing for retail goods.

GAAP: Generally Accepted Accounting Principles; the accounting principles and standards accepted by consensus among professional accountants.

Generation-skipping transfer (GST) tax trust: A trust in which the taxpayer's lifetime GST tax exemption is allocated to protect assets from GST tax when they are passed on to the grantor's grandchild, great-niece, or great-nephew, or anyone who is at least 37.5 years younger than the grantor.

Gross receipts: Total sales (net of returns and allowances), all amounts received for services, as well as income from investments and from incidental or outside sources.

Hobby losses: Nondeductible losses a taxpayer incurs in connection with an activity that the taxpayer engages in for enjoyment and not for profit.

I-9: A form used to document an employee's legal right to work in the United States.

Mixed Earners Unemployment Compensation (MEUC): A temporary, federal program that provides an extra $100 to self-employed individuals who have earned at least $5,000 in net earnings in the tax year prior to when the applicant filed for regular unemployment benefits.

Money laundering: Taking funds from an illegal source, hiding the source of funds, and making the funds available for use without legal restrictions or penalties.

Net operating loss (NOL): A loss taken in a period where a company's allowable tax deductions are greater than its taxable income.

Pandemic: A disease prevalent over a whole country or the world.

Paycheck Protection Program: A $669 billion business loan program established by the Coronavirus Aid, Relief, and Economic Security Act to help certain businesses, self-employed workers, sole proprietors, certain nonprofit organizations, and tribal businesses continue paying their workers.

Ponzi scheme: A fraudulent scheme in which victims are tricked into investing in a nonexistent enterprise. Profits are paid to earlier investors with money from more recent investors.

Premium tax credit: A refundable tax credit designed to help eligible individuals and families cover the premiums for their health insurance purchased through the Health Insurance Marketplace.

Qualified business income deduction (QBID): Provides for a deduction of up to 20 percent of qualified business income, applied at the individual level, and subject to certain limitations.

Qualified disaster: For purposes of the Consolidated Appropriations Act (CAA), any area with respect to which a major disaster was declared, during the period beginning on January 1, 2020, and ending on the date that is 60 days after the date of the enactment of the CAA.

Qualified disaster distribution: For purposes of the Consolidated Appropriations Act (CAA), any distribution from an eligible retirement plan made on or after the first day of the incident period of a qualified disaster and before the date that is 180 days after the date of the enactment of the CAA, and to an individual whose principal place of abode at any time during the incident period of such qualified disaster is located in the qualified disaster area with respect to such qualified disaster and who has sustained an economic loss by reason of such qualified disaster.

Qualified subchapter S trust (QSST) election: Requires that all current income of the trust be distributed to the current income beneficiary and that during the term of the trust, no principal distributions can be made to anyone other than the income beneficiary.

Restaurant: As defined in IRS Notice 2021-25, a business that prepares and sells food or beverages to retail customers for immediate consumption, regardless of whether the food or beverages are consumed on the business's premises.

Restaurant Revitalization Fund: A program established by the American Rescue Plan Act and administered by the Small Business Administration to provide emergency assistance for eligible restaurants, bars, and other qualifying businesses impacted by the COVID-19 pandemic.

S corporation: A closely held corporation (or, in some cases, a limited liability company or a partnership) that makes a valid election to be taxed under Subchapter S of Chapter 1 of the Internal Revenue Code.

Shuttered Venue Operators Grant (SVOG): A program established by the Economic Aid to Hard-Hit Small Businesses, Nonprofits, and Venues Act, and amended by the American Rescue Plan Act. It program includes over $16 billion in grants to eligible venues that were shuttered as a result of the COVID-19 pandemic.

Social Security: A federal insurance scheme providing benefits for pensioners and those who are unemployed or disabled.

Step-up in basis: Under Code Sec. 1014, any asset owned by a decedent has its tax basis adjusted to the value as of the decedent's date of death. Since assets often appreciate, the tax basis of assets typically is adjusted upward at date of death; hence the term, step-up in basis.

Tax Cuts and Jobs Act: A congressional revenue act originally introduced in Congress that amended the Internal Revenue Code of 1986. Major elements of the changes include reducing tax rates for businesses and individuals, and a personal tax simplification by increasing the standard deduction and family tax credits but eliminating personal exemptions and making it less beneficial to itemize deductions.

Tax gap: The difference between the amount of taxes taxpayers owe and the amount of taxes they pay.

Virtual currency: A currency that only exists in cyber space. There is no physical or tangible item to represent the currency.

¶ 10,300 Final Exam Instructions

To complete your Final Exam go to **cchcpelink.com/printcpe,** click on the title of the exam you wish to complete and add it to your shopping cart (you will need to register with CCH CPELink if you have not already). Click **Proceed to Checkout** and enter your credit card information. Click **Place Order** to complete your purchase of the final exam. The final exam will be available in **My Dashboard** under **My Account**.

This Final Exam is divided into three Modules. There is a grading fee for each Final Exam submission.

Online Processing Fee:	Recommended CPE:
$164.00 for Module 1	7 hours for Module 1
$94.00 for Module 2	4 hours for Module 2
$188.00 for Module 3	8 hours for Module 3
$446.00 for all Modules	19 hours for all Modules
IRS Program Number:	**Federal Tax Law Hours:**
Module 1: 4VRWB-T-04273-21-S	7 hours for Module 1
Module 2: 4VRWB-T-04274-21-S	4 hours for Module 2
Module 3: 4VRWB-T-04275-21-S	8 hours for Module 3
	19 hours for all Modules
CTEC Program Numbers:	
Module 1: 1075-CE-2475	
Module 2: 1075-CE-2476	
Module 3: 1075-CE-2477	

Instructions for purchasing your CPE Tests and accessing them after purchase are provided on the **cchcpelink.com/printcpe** website. **Please note, manual grading is no longer available for Top Federal Tax Issues. All answer sheets must be submitted online for grading and processing.**

Recommended CPE credit is based on a 50-minute hour. Because CPE requirements vary from state to state and among different licensing agencies, please contact your CPE governing body for information on your CPE requirements and the applicability of a particular course for your requirements.

Expiration Date: December 31, 2022

Evaluation: To help us provide you with the best possible products, please take a moment to fill out the course Evaluation located after your Final Exam.

Wolters Kluwer, CCH is registered with the National Association of State Boards of Accountancy (NASBA) as a sponsor of continuing professional education on the National Registry of CPE Sponsors. State boards of accountancy have final authority on the acceptance of individual courses for CPE credit. Complaints regarding registered sponsors may be submitted to the National Registry of CPE Sponsors through its website: www.learningmarket.org.

Additional copies of this course may be downloaded from **cchcpelink.com/printcpe.** Printed copies of the course are available for $6.50 by calling 1-800-344-3734 (ask for product 10024491-0009).

¶ 10,301 Final Exam Questions: Module 1

1. Approximately how much annually does the U.S. Treasury lose due to noncompliance?

    a. $321 million

    b. $540 million

    c. $200 billion

    d. $630 billion

2. Approximately what percentage of the tax gap is accounted for by individuals?

    a. 24 percent

    b. 33 percent

    c. 68 percent

    d. 81 percent

3. Each of the following is one of the verifications the IRS conducts routinely at the start of a small business audit, *except:*

    a. AR confirmation

    b. Return to trial balance

    c. Cash-T

    d. Bank deposit analysis

4. Determining whether the activity is a personal pleasure activity is one of the six litmus test questions to ask with respect to which of the following considerations?

    a. Unreported income

    b. Business versus hobby

    c. Losses in excess of basis

    d. Worker status

5. Misreported losses exceeded basis limitations by _____ per taxpayer in audits of Forms 1040 with pass-through losses from Form 1120S between 2006 and 2008.

    a. $10,400

    b. $15,600

    c. $21,600

    d. $34,900

6. The old IRS Audit Technique Guide (ATG) for the construction industry noted that residential construction is of particular interest because this group of taxpayer's accounts for _____ of the return filings but reports only 10 percent of the gross receipts.

    a. 41 percent

    b. 55 percent

    c. 68 percent

    d. 73 percent

7. Regarding worker status, the IRS uses how many factors to determine control?

   a. 1

   b. 2

   c. 3

   d. 4

8. In what year did the IRS institute mandatory audit techniques for businesses that have e-commerce activity?

   a. 2012

   b. 2016

   c. 2017

   d. 2018

9. Which of the following identifies the maximum failure to file penalty with respect to Form 1099s and misclassification of workers?

   a. 10 percent

   b. 25 percent

   c. 35 percent

   d. 50 percent

10. In small businesses, most fraud cases stem from which of the following?

   a. Unreported income

   b. Depreciation overstatement

   c. Phantom equity

   d. PP&E

11. Based on Notice 2020-22, no Code Sec. 6656 failure to deposit penalty is applied for failure to deposit employment taxes if Families First Coronavirus Response Act (FFCRA) qualified leave (or ERC eligible) wages were paid, the amount of payroll tax deposits not made equals or exceeds anticipated FFCRA (and/or ERC) credit(s), and there is no advance requested on which of the following forms?

   a. Form 1040

   b. Form 7200

   c. Form 941

   d. Form 941-X

12. To receive the employee retention credit (ERC), an employer _____ offset against employment tax deposits otherwise due.

   a. Can

   b. Must

   c. Should

   d. Cannot

13. Which of the following is *not* one of the second quarter 2021 Form 941 changes?

   a. FFCRA emergency sick pay and family leave credits extended by ARPA

   b. COBRA employment tax credits created by ARPA

   c. New start-up business ERC eliminated

   d. Seasonal employer ERC qualification changes

14. Which of the following identifies the minimum credit provided on Form 7200?

    a. $25

    b. $100

    c. $500

    d. $1,000

15. Who is authorized to sign a corporation's Form 7200?

    a. Any employee of the corporation

    b. The CEO's administrative assistant

    c. The corporation's president or vice president

    d. A fiduciary

16. The Families First Coronavirus Response Act (FFCRA) applies to government agencies as well as private employers with fewer than how many employees?

    a. 500

    b. 650

    c. 800

    d. 999

17. Based on the American Rescue Plan Act (ARPA), the family leave maximum was expanded to what amount?

    a. $10,000

    b. $11,500

    c. $12,000

    d. $15,500

18. Regarding the Families First Coronavirus Response Act (FFCRA), which of the following is a reason an employee is unable to work that falls within the scope of family and medical leave?

    a. Federal, state, or local quarantine or isolation order

    b. Caring for a child if school closed

    c. Obtaining a diagnosis due to COVID-19 symptoms

    d. Self-quarantining under the advice of healthcare provider

19. After an employee loses his/her job, the employee may continue to maintain coverage under the prior employer's health plan through COBRA coverage by paying up to _____ of the prior employer's cost of such coverage.

    a. 102 percent

    b. 105 percent

    c. 117 percent

    d. 126 percent

20. For purposes of gross receipts with respect to the employee retention credit (ERC), gross receipts _____ include the repayment of a loan.

    a. Do

    b. Always

    c. Sometimes

    d. Do not

21. Based on the Tax Cuts and Jobs Act, for tax years beginning after December 31, 2017, and before January 1, 2026, excess business losses of a taxpayer (other than a corporation) _____ allowed for the tax year.

    a. Are

    b. Are not

    c. May be

    d. Are always

22. When calculating excess business losses, which of the following identifies the threshold amount in 2020 for taxpayers who are married filing jointly?

    a. $255,000

    b. $259,000

    c. $510,000

    d. $518,000

23. Each of the following statements regarding the new Code Sec. 461(l) is correct, *except:*

    a. It is vague, with sparse legislative history.

    b. It does not appear to be high on the Treasury Department guidance list.

    c. It raises $250 billion over five years.

    d. Practitioners must make up their own stories.

24. Based on the CARES Act and the elimination of W-2 wages as Code Sec. 461(l) business income, this change applies retroactive to 2018, 2019, and 2020 and applies to:

    a. All future years

    b. Only 2021

    c. Years 2023–2025 only

    d. Only years past 2027

25. Code Sec. 461(l) excess business loss limits apply to partners and S corporation shareholders at the _____ level.

    a. Member

    b. Owner

    c. Partner

    d. Entity

26. Under the Tax Cuts and Jobs Act, net operating losses (NOLs) generated in years beginning after 2017 may only offset _____ of taxable income.

    a. 60 percent

    b. 70 percent

    c. 80 percent

    d. 90 percent

27. Which of the following entities are ineligible for the qualified business income deduction (QBID)?

    a. Individuals

    b. Trusts

    c. Estates

    d. C corporations

28. Which of the following statements regarding the qualified business income deduction (QBID) is correct?

   a. QBID reduces self-employment income.

   b. QBID reduces the income tax effective rate.

   c. QBID reduces investment income.

   d. QBID reduces basis in a partnership interest.

29. Regarding Code Sec. 163(j), for years beginning in 2019 and 2020, the CARES Act increased the 30 percent adjusted taxable income (ATI) limit to what percentage?

   a. 50 percent

   b. 60 percent

   c. 70 percent

   d. 80 percent

30. In Revenue Procedure 2020-23, the IRS allows Bipartisan Budget Act (BBA) partnerships (those who did not elect out of the Centralized Partnership Audit Regime) to file amended _____ Forms 1065 to retroactively benefit.

   a. 2017 and 2018

   b. 2018 and 2019

   c. 2019 and 2020

   d. 2020 and 2021

31. Which of the following is a final audit assessment from the IRS?

   a. Letter 2205

   b. Letter 525

   c. Letter 3219

   d. Notice CP22E

32. On average, approximately how long does it take the IRS to conduct an audit of each tax year for a small business?

   a. 24 hours

   b. 46 hours

   c. One week

   d. 30 days

33. Which of the following requires employers to pay sick leave and medical leave to workers afflicted by COVID-19 who are unable to work?

   a. American Rescue Plan Act (ARPA)

   b. Coronavirus Aid, Relief, and Economic Security (CARES) Act

   c. Families First Coronavirus Response Act (FFCRA)

   d. Consolidated Appropriations Act of 2021 (CAA)

34. According to Code Sec. 461(l), an excess business loss equals:

    a. The excess of aggregate deductions attributable to the business, over the aggregate gross business income or gain

    b. The excess of aggregate deductions attributable to the business, over the sum of aggregate gross business income or gain, minus a threshold amount

    c. The excess of aggregate deductions attributable to the trade or business, over the sum of aggregate gross business income or gain, plus a threshold amount

    d. The excess of aggregate deductions attributable to the business, multiplied by the aggregate gross business income or gain

35. The Tax Cuts and Jobs Act (TCJA) repealed the alternative minimum tax for which of the following?

    a. Inidividuals

    b. C corporations

    c. Estates

    d. Trusts

¶ 10,302 Final Exam Questions: Module 2

1. The CARES Act provided an increase of a flat payment of _____ per week to the amount regularly available for unemployment under state law.

    a. $400

    b. $500

    c. $600

    d. $750

2. The American Rescue Plan Act (ARPA) extends the flat payment with respect to federal pandemic unemployment of $300 per week to what date?

    a. September 6, 2021

    b. October 31, 2021

    c. November 30, 2021

    d. December 15, 2021

3. The _____ program is an optional $100 per week supplement to Federal Pandemic Unemployment Compensation (FPUC) for individuals who: (1) have received at least $5,000 of self-employment income in the most recent taxable year; (2) are receiving a form of unemployment compensation other than Pandemic Unemployment Assistance; and (3) submit documentation substantiating the claimed self-employment income.

    a. EITL

    b. ABC

    c. MEUC

    d. SVOG

4. Regarding pandemic unemployment assistance, the Consolidated Appropriations Act (CAA) increased the maximum total benefits from _____ weeks to 50 weeks.

    a. 24

    b. 31

    c. 39

    d. 42

5. The Pandemic Emergency Unemployment Compensation (PEUC) program provides additional assistance to those individuals who have exhausted their:

    a. State law unemployment benefits

    b. 401(k) plans

    c. IRAs

    d. Savings accounts

6. Regarding Pandemic Emergency Unemployment Compensation (PEUC), the Consolidated Appropriations Act (CAA) extended benefits to up to 24 weeks and through March 14, 2021. However, the American Rescue Plan Act (ARPA) extends benefits up to _____ weeks and through September 6, 2021.

    a. 46

    b. 48

    c. 51

    d. 53

7. The American Rescue Plan Act amended which of the following to provide that increased reporting will be required on IRS Form 1099-K, *Payment Card and Third-Party Network Transactions*, starting for payments in 2022?

    a. Code Sec. 6050W

    b. Code Sec. 461(l)

    c. Code Sec. 864(f)

    d. Code Sec. 162(m)

8. The American Rescue Plan Act authorizes a third round of COVID-19 stimulus payments up to what amount per eligible individual?

    a. $1,000

    b. $1,200

    c. $1,400

    d. $2,400

9. The American Rescue Plan Act direct payment stimulus begins to phase out for single taxpayers with adjusted gross income starting at _____.

    a. $45,000

    b. $65,000

    c. $75,000

    d. $95,000

10. The American Rescue Plan Act expands the child tax credit and increases the credit amount for each qualifying child for the 2021 taxable year to _____.

    a. $1,000

    b. $2,000

    c. $3,000

    d. $5,000

11. The American Rescue Plan Act requires employers to provide, on a tax-free basis, a subsidy to employees and their qualified beneficiaries to pay what percent of the COBRA continuation premium for group health plan coverage?

    a. 50 percent

    b. 75 percent

    c. 80 percent

    d. 100 percent

12. The original deadline to apply for Paycheck Protection Program (PPP) loans under the American Rescue Plan Act was March 31, 2021. However, the PPP Extension Act was passed by Congress and the president signed it into law on March 30, 2021, extending the deadline to apply for PPP loans to _____.

    a. May 31, 2021

    b. June 15, 2021

    c. August 31, 2021

    d. September 15, 2021

13. Regarding the employee retention credit, the American Rescue Plan Act (ARPA) maintained the credit percentage at _____ as previously increased from the Consolidated Appropriations Act (CAA)?

   a. 50 percent

   b. 60 percent

   c. 70 percent

   d. 80 percent

14. Regarding the direct aid to states from the American Rescue Plan Act (ARPA), all funds must be spent on costs incurred on or before _____.

   a. December 31, 2023

   b. December 31, 2024

   c. December 31, 2025

   d. December 31, 2026

15. Individual taxpayers can postpone federal income tax payments for the 2020 tax year due on April 15, 2021, to what date, without penalties and interest, regardless of the amount owed?

   a. May 17, 2021

   b. June 17, 2021

   c. July 17, 2021

   d. August 17, 2021

16. The American Rescue Plan Act (ARPA) provides small businesses in low-income communities with EIDL grants up to how much?

   a. $10,000

   b. $20,000

   c. $50,000

   d. $75,000

17. Regarding the Restaurant Revitalization Program, as of March 13, 2020, the applicant (together with any affiliated businesses) must own or operate no more than how many locations?

   a. 5

   b. 10

   c. 15

   d. 20

18. Grants provided from the Restaurant Revitalization Fund will equal the pandemic-related revenue loss of the eligible entity with a cap of _____ million for each eligible entity.

   a. $1

   b. $5

   c. $10

   d. $15

19. The Shuttered Venues Operations Grant (SVOG) program includes over _____ billion in grants to shuttered venues, such as live venue operators or promoters, theatrical producers, live performing arts organization operations, museum operators, motion picture theater operators, and talent representatives.

   a. $16

   b. $34

   c. $49

   d. $88

20. If a business is approved for a Shuttered Venues Operations Grant (SVOG) before it received a Paycheck Protection Program (PPP) loan number, it is _____ for/to the PPP loan.

    a. Ineligible

    b. Eligible

    c. Qualified

    d. Entitled

21. The Consolidated Appropriations Act (CAA) allows farmers who elected a two-year net operating loss carryback prior to the CARES Act to elect to retain that two-year carryback rather than claim the _____ carryback provided in the CARES Act.

    a. 3-year

    b. 4-year

    c. 5-year

    d. 6-year

22. The Tax Cuts and Jobs Act limited the deductibility of business meal expenses to 50 percent of the cost for food and beverages provided by a restaurant. However, the Consolidated Appropriations Act (CAA) permits businesses to deduct _____ of these business meals expenses during 2021 and 2022.

    a. 60 percent

    b. 75 percent

    c. 85 percent

    d. 100 percent

23. The Consolidated Appropriations Act (CAA) retroactively corrected an error in the Tax Cuts and Jobs Act so that the _____ cost recovery period is available for all residential rental property regardless of when it was placed into service.

    a. 15-year

    b. 20-year

    c. 30-year

    d. 40-year

24. Which of the following allows a qualified disaster distribution of up to $100,000 to be made from most defined contribution retirement plans even if the participant does not satisfy the usual hardship distribution rules?

    a. Tax Cuts and Jobs Act

    b. Consolidated Appropriations Act

    c. CARES Act

    d. American Rescue Plan Act

25. A business is ineligible for the Restaurant Revitalization Fund Grant (RRFG) program if as of March 13, 2020, it operates in more than how many locations?

    a. 5

    b. 7

    c. 10

    d. 20

¶ 10,303 Final Exam Questions: Module 3

1. Which of the following is *not* true of blockchain technology?

    a. Data is stored on computer nodes.

    b. Public blockchains are "open source" and can be used by anyone.

    c. Private blockchains are maintained on closed or private networks.

    d. Blockchains cannot be hacked or compromised.

2. Where was the first Bitcoin ATM located?

    a. San Diego, CA

    b. New York, NY

    c. Toyoko, Japan

    d. London, England

3. Mt. Gox would best be defined as which of the following?

    a. The inventor of Bitcoin

    b. A Bitcoin exchange

    c. A money laundering operation

    d. A terrorist organization

4. When the FBI shut down Silk Road in October of 2013, it seized _____ in Bitcoin.

    a. $2.6 million

    b. $3 million

    c. $3.6 million

    d. $4 million

5. A University of Texas study released in June of 2018 claims the 2017 price increases for Bitcoin were driven by _____.

    a. Consumer acceptance

    b. Investors

    c. Government acceptance

    d. Price manipulation

6. Which of the following federal agencies wants to regulate initial coin offerings (ICOs)?

    a. IRS

    b. SEC

    c. FBI

    d. CIA

7. Which type of virtual currency wallet is the safest from online hacking?

    a. Paper

    b. Desktop

    c. Mobile

    d. Web

8. The IRS requires virtual currencies to be reported at _____ value.

    a. Market

    b. Fair

    c. Exchange

    d. Fair market

9. Taxpayers who receive virtual currencies for "mining" must report the fair market value of the coins received as _____.

    a. Passive income

    b. Gross income

    c. Capital gains

    d. A gift

10. When using virtual currencies to pay wages, employers must also pay _____ tax to the IRS

    a. FICA

    b. Worker's compensation

    c. Self-employment

    d. Excise

11. In which court case did both the taxpayer and the commissioner use experts to analyze the appropriate lack of a marketability discount?

    a. *Schreier v. Drealan Kvilhaug Hoefker & Co.*

    b. *Hafen v. Famulary*

    c. *Warne v. Commissioner*

    d. *Ahmanson Foundation v. United States*

12. When was the American Rescue Plan Act (ARPA) enacted?

    a. March 11, 2021

    b. March 10, 2020

    c. March 6, 2021

    d. February 24, 2021

13. In tax year 2026, the basic exclusion amount for individual taxpayers will return to which amount?

    a. $1 million

    b. $2 million

    c. $5 million

    d. $10 million

14. Which tax form can taxpayers use to compare their advance premium credit and eligible credit to determine if a refund or additional tax is due?

    a. Form 709

    b. Form 4868

    c. Form 8892

    d. Form 8962

15. Under the American Rescue Plan Act (ARPA), for taxpayers whose income is $150,000 or less, up to _____ of unemployment compensation is **not** taxable at the federal level.

   a. $5,200

   b. $10,000

   c. $10,200

   d. $12,000

16. The adjustment of the tax basis of assets belonging to a decedent to the value of those assets as of the decedent's date of death is called a _____.

   a. Consistent basis

   b. Step-up in basis

   c. Basic exclusion

   d. Step-down in basis

17. Which type of election requires S corporation stock to be isolated and administered as a separate share of the trust?

   a. QSST

   b. ESBT

   c. Grantor trust

   d. Qualified revocable trust

18. According to the Internal Revenue Code and recent IRS Private Letter Rulings, which of the following would be recognized as a charitable entity?

   a. An organization operating exclusively for charitable purposes that serves the general public

   b. A foundation organized to help an individual pay his medical bills

   c. An organization that set up a lottery to help people pay their late rent payments

   d. A GoFundMe account raising money for a family whose primary breadwinner died

19. In 2021, the deadline for filing the annual Report of Foreign Bank and Financial Accounts (FBAR) was:

   a. April 15, 2021

   b. May 17, 2021

   c. October 1, 2021

   d. October 15, 2021

20. What is the lifetime gift and estate tax exemption amount in 2021?

   a. $11.4 million

   b. $11.58 million

   c. $11.7 million

   d. $12.1 million

21. Restaurant meals are _____ deductible in 2020. They are ____ deductible in 2021 and 2022.

   a. 100 percent; 50 percent

   b. 50 percent; 100 percent

   c. 50 percent; 50 percent

   d. 100 percent; 100 percent

22. Which statement about economic injury disaster loan (EIDLs) is true?

    a. EIDL advance grants are taxable.

    b. Any expenses paid with EIDLs are not tax deductible.

    c. EIDL advance grants are not taxable, and any expenses paid with the funds are fully deductible.

    d. Many EIDLs were still available as of July 2021.

23. The exclusion for unemployment under the American Rescue Plan Act (ARPA) can be described as a(n) _____. If income is exactly $150,000, there is no exclusion at all.

    a. "Anomaly"

    b. "Obstacle"

    c. "Valley"

    d. "Cliff"

24. Which of the following statements is true regarding payroll costs for the employee retention credit (ERC) and Paycheck Protection Program (PPP) loan forgiveness?

    a. The same payroll costs can be counted for PPP loan forgiveness and for the ERC.

    b. Taxpayers cannot double-count the same payroll costs for the ERC and PPP loan forgiveness.

    c. All payroll costs qualify for the ERC.

    d. Taxpayers cannot choose which wages are "used up" on a PPP loan.

25. According to recent reports, which type of taxpayer has the largest amount of unreported income?

    a. Low-income taxpayers

    b. Moderate-income taxpayers

    c. High-income taxpayers

    d. Taxpayers who make peer-to-peer payments

26. Which statement is true about funds under the Restaurant Revitalization program?

    a. As of July 2021, most of the funds had already been allocated.

    b. Funds received from the program are fully taxable.

    c. Funds received from the program are not deductible.

    d. Receipt of the funds is tax-free, and expenses are deductible.

27. There are many indications that the IRS is focusing its audit activity on which type of taxpayers?

    a. Low-income

    b. Median-income

    c. High-income

    d. Late filing

28. What is the maximum employee retention credit (ERC) an employer with 10 employees could claim for 2021?

    a. $10,000

    b. $28,000

    c. $100,000

    d. $280,000

29. According to IRS Notice 2021-20, how long must taxpayers retain records for the employee retention credit (ERC)?

    a. At least two years

    b. At least three years

    c. At least four years

    d. At least seven years

30. For individual taxpayers, what is the unified gift and estate tax exclusion for 2021?

    a. $11,500,000

    b. $11,580,000

    c. $11,700,000

    d. $12,000,000

31. Which of the following was signed into law on March 11, 2021?

    a. American Rescue Plan Act

    b. American Families Act

    c. American Jobs Act

    d. CARES Act

32. In the third round of ARPA economic impact payments, what is the maximum EIP for married couples filing jointly?

    a. $1,000

    b. $1,400

    c. $2,800

    d. $3,500

33. The third round of economic impact payments (issued in March and April 2021) are technically a credit claimed on which tax return?

    a. 2019

    b. 2020

    c. 2021

    d. Both 2020 and 2021

34. What is the threshold adjusted gross income (AGI) amount for purposes of the unemployment compensation exclusion?

    a. $100,000

    b. $120,000

    c. $150,000

    d. $180,000

35. Under the American Rescue Plan Act, for which period can student loans be excluded from income?

    a. 2021–2025

    b. 2020–2024

    c. 2019–2022

    d. 2018–2023

36. Which statement about the emergency paid sick leave credit under the American Rescue Plan Act is true?

    a. It has been extended through September 30, 2022.

    b. It is not refundable.

    c. It does not cover self-employed individuals.

    d. It applies to 100 percent of qualified sick leave wages and cannot exceed $200 per day.

37. The American Rescue Plan Act increased the tax credit for qualifying children who are five years old or younger to _____ per child.

    a. $500

    b. $2,000

    c. $3,000

    d. $3,600

38. Which statement about advance child tax credit payments is *not* correct?

    a. Advance payments are based on the taxpayer's 2021 income.

    b. The advance payment will reduce credits the taxpayer receives on the 2021 tax return.

    c. Taxpayers can claim the remaining credit (if any) when they file their 2021 tax returns in 2022.

    d. If the advance payment is greater than the actual child tax credit, the taxpayer generally will need to pay back the advance.

39. For the 2021 tax year, what is the maximum dependent care credit for taxpayers who have two qualifying children?

    a. $6,000

    b. $8,000

    c. $10,000

    d. $16,000

40. A taxpayer is deemed to elect out of the employee retention credit (ERC) for specific wages if it does which of the following?

    a. Elects out of the ERC to provide sufficient wages for a Paycheck Protection Program (PPP) loan

    b. Uses payroll costs for PPP loan forgiveness

    c. Has less than $1 million in annual gross receipts

    d. Experiences full or partial suspension of operations due to a government order restricting commerce

¶ 10,400 Answer Sheets

¶ 10,401 Top Federal Tax Issues for 2022 CPE Course: MODULE 1

Go to **cchcpelink.com/printcpe** to complete your Final Exam online for instant results.

A $164.00 processing fee will be charged for each user submitting Module 1 to **cchcpelink.com/printcpe** for online grading.

Module 1: Answer Sheet

Please answer the questions by indicating the appropriate letter next to the corresponding number.

1. _____	9. _____	17. _____	25. _____	33. _____
2. _____	10. _____	18. _____	26. _____	34. _____
3. _____	11. _____	19. _____	27. _____	35. _____
4. _____	12. _____	20. _____	28. _____	
5. _____	13. _____	21. _____	29. _____	
6. _____	14. _____	22. _____	30. _____	
7. _____	15. _____	23. _____	31. _____	
8. _____	16. _____	24. _____	32. _____	

Please complete the Evaluation Form (located after the Module 3 Answer Sheet). Thank you.

¶ 10,402 Top Federal Tax Issues for 2022 CPE Course: MODULE 2

Go to **cchcpelink.com/printcpe** to complete your Final Exam online for instant results.

A $94.00 processing fee will be charged for each user submitting Module 2 to **cchcpelink.com/printcpe** for online grading.

Module 2: Answer Sheet

Please answer the questions by indicating the appropriate letter next to the corresponding number.

1. ___	13. ___	25. ___
2. ___	14. ___	
3. ___	15. ___	
4. ___	16. ___	
5. ___	17. ___	
6. ___	18. ___	
7. ___	19. ___	
8. ___	20. ___	
9. ___	21. ___	
10. ___	22. ___	
11. ___	23. ___	
12. ___	24. ___	

Please complete the Evaluation Form (located after the Module 3 Answer Sheet). Thank you.

¶ 10,403 Top Federal Tax Issues for 2022 CPE Course: MODULE 3

Go to **cchcpelink.com/printcpe** to complete your Final Exam online for instant results.

A $188.00 processing fee will be charged for each user submitting Module 3 to **cchcpelink.com/printcpe** for online grading.

Module 3: Answer Sheet

Please answer the questions by indicating the appropriate letter next to the corresponding number.

1. ____	11. ____	21. ____	31. ____
2. ____	12. ____	22. ____	32. ____
3. ____	13. ____	23. ____	33. ____
4. ____	14. ____	24. ____	34. ____
5. ____	15. ____	25. ____	35. ____
6. ____	16. ____	26. ____	36. ____
7. ____	17. ____	27. ____	37. ____
8. ____	18. ____	28. ____	38. ____
9. ____	19. ____	29. ____	39. ____
10. ____	20. ____	30. ____	40. ____

Please complete the Evaluation Form (located after the Module 3 Answer Sheet). Thank you.

¶ 10,500 Top Federal Tax Issues for 2022 CPE Course: Evaluation Form

(10024491-0009)

Please take a few moments to fill out and submit this evaluation to Wolters Kluwer so that we can better provide you with the type of self-study programs you want and need. Thank you.

About This Program

1. Please circle the number that best reflects the extent of your agreement with the following statements:

		Strongly Agree				Strongly Disagree
a.	The Course objectives were met.	5	4	3	2	1
b.	This Course was comprehensive and organized.	5	4	3	2	1
c.	The content was current and technically accurate.	5	4	3	2	1
d.	This Course content was relevant and contributed to achievement of the learning objectives.	5	4	3	2	1
e.	The prerequisite requirements were appropriate.	5	4	3	2	1
f.	This Course was a valuable learning experience.	5	4	3	2	1
g.	The Course completion time was appropriate.	5	4	3	2	1

2. What do you consider to be the strong points of this Course?

3. What improvements can we make to this Course?

THANK YOU FOR TAKING THE TIME TO COMPLETE THIS SURVEY!